SOCRATES DISSATISFIED

SOCRATES DISSATISFIED

An Analysis of Plato's *Crito*

ROSLYN WEISS

ROWMAN & LITTLEFIELD PUBLISHERS, INC.
Lanham • Boulder • New York • Oxford

ROWMAN & LITTLEFIELD PUBLISHERS, INC.

Published in the United States of America
by Rowman & Littlefield Publishers, Inc.
4720 Boston Way, Lanham, Maryland 20706
www.rowmanlittlefield.com

12 Hid's Copse Road
Cumnor Hill, Oxford OX2 9JJ, England

British Library Cataloguing in Publication Information Available

Library of Congress Cataloging-in-Publication Data

Weiss, Roslyn.
  Socrates dissatisfied : an analysis of Plato's Crito / Roslyn Weiss.
    p. cm.
  Originally published: New York : Oxford University Press, 1998.
  Includes bibliographical references (p.) and index.
  ISBN 0-7425-1322-X (pbk. : alk. paper)
    1.Plato. Crito. 2. Socrates. 3. Obedience. 4. Law—Philosophy. I Title.

B368 .W45 2001
184—dc21

                                                              2001049212

Printed in the United States of America

⊖™ The paper used in this publication meets the minimum requirements of American
National Standard for Information Sciences—Permanence of Paper for Printed Library
Materials, ANSI/NISO Z39.48-1992.

For George Anastaplo
—of Greek descent

It is better to be . . . Socrates dissatisfied than a fool satisfied.

John Stuart Mill, *Utilitarianism*

Acknowledgments

I am indebted both to the institutions that made this book possible and to the people who made it better than it would otherwise have been.

I am grateful to Lehigh University for granting me a year's leave, and to the National Endowment for the Humanities for the award of a generous summer stipend.

My deep appreciation goes to my husband, Sam Weiss, for his invaluable assistance in matters technical and practical and for his unflagging patience, good nature, and humor. I wish to thank those who participated in the fall 1996 Lehigh University Philosophy Department faculty seminar—Robert Barnes, Gordon Bearn, Mark Bickhard, Barbara Frankel, Alexander Levine, J. Ralph Lindgren, Michael Mendelson, and Joan Straumanis—for their animated and acutely perceptive discussion of *Socrates Dissatisfied*, as a result of which this book is greatly improved. I would be remiss not to acknowledge the loving support of my parents, Eleanor and Abraham Kestenbaum, and of my children, Miriam and Dena Weiss, and of my good friends and colleagues in philosophy Karen Bell, Patricia Kenig Curd, and, especially, Alan Udoff. The individual to whom I owe the greatest debt with respect to this project is Giovanni Ferrari, who, as reader for Oxford, read the manuscript carefully and thoughtfully, offered criticisms penetrating and precise, and took even the more outrageous of my ideas seriously enough to disagree with them without dismissing them.

Contents

SOCRATES DISSATISFIED

1

Introduction

A Dissatisfied Socrates

Is Socrates a man whose first allegiance is to his city and its laws?[1] Is he citizen first and man second? Does he refuse to escape his unjust conviction and punishment because he regards himself as morally bound to obey whatever verdicts and commands the city of Athens issues?

An affirmative answer to these questions would be unthinkable were it not for the views propounded in the speech of the Laws in the latter part of the *Crito*. Yet the unthinkable becomes thinkable if one takes those views, as many scholars do, to reflect Socrates' own beliefs.[2] In this book I contend that Socrates' first allegiance is to justice and philosophy; he is man first and citizen second; and he refuses to escape because he believes that escape would violate the moral principles to which he has always adhered. The views espoused by the Laws are the views of the Laws—not of Socrates; indeed, the moral perspective reflected in the Laws' arguments stands in stark opposition to the Socratic point of view.

My purpose in this book is to demonstrate that the Socrates who inhabits the *Crito*—no less than the Socrates who inhabits the *Apology*—is a radically independent moral agent: his moral choices are decided solely by his own reasoned calcula-

---

1. The Socrates referred to is the Socrates of Plato's dialogues. The relationship between this Socrates and the historical Socrates is not a concern of this book.

2. Although many scholars who identify as Socratic the views expressed by the Laws still resist an unqualifiedly affirmative answer to these questions, they do so at the expense of the plain meaning of the Laws' demand that the citizen do "whatever we bid."

tions with respect to justice. He will not compromise his dignity; he will be no one's—not even the city's—slave; whether he obeys or disobeys authority will turn on what he, on each occasion, holds to be best—most just and noble. As Socrates says of himself: "I, not only now but always, am such as to obey nothing else of what is my own than that *logos* which appears best to me upon reasoning" (*Cr.* 46b4–6).[3] Only in this way can a man be a man and not a slave.[4]

If Socrates in the early part of the *Crito* is a man who obeys only the principles that result from his own reasoning and recommends the same course to others, then the personified Laws in the latter part of the *Crito*, who would have men obey absolutely the city and its laws, cannot represent Socrates. These Laws, as Socrates notes, speak as orators do on behalf of the laws of the city of Athens, defending the authoritativeness of all the city's judgments and commands. Yet, if the speech of the Laws does not reflect the Socratic point of view, why, one must wonder, does Socrates invent it?

The speech of the Laws is created for Crito's benefit. It represents Socrates' last hope, now that he is at the end of his life and at his wits' end, of benefiting his friend Crito by improving his soul. Socrates has tried through philosophical argument to convince Crito of the insignificance of the opinion of the many, to arouse in him an appreciation for goods of the soul—that is, for nobility and justice—to encourage him to discard his concerns about money, reputation, and children, concerns "of the many," and to stop him from conceiving of justice in relation to friends and enemies. But Socrates fails. He fails utterly. Crito remains fixed in his belief that what is important is to save Socrates' life and thereby preserve his own reputation; that what is just is to foil the designs of Socrates' enemies; and that what counts is the opinion of the many, those who can do one "the greatest evils." Crito has known Socrates intimately for a very long time, for a whole lifetime. Yet he neither holds in esteem nor even comprehends Socrates' moral commitments. All he can finally say is: "I have no answer to what you ask, Socrates. For I do not understand" (*Cr.* 50a4–5).

The speech of the Laws, then, grows out of the increasing frustration that Socrates experiences as Crito remains unresponsive to his arguments. If Crito's moral and intellectual loyalties render philosophical investigation with him futile, how can Socrates help his friend? A despairing Socrates, no longer harboring even the faintest hope that his own preferred method of inquiry will succeed with Crito, steps aside and entrusts the discussion to someone else, to the personified Laws. It is up to them now to persuade Crito that escape would be wrong—because Socrates himself could not. But the Laws succeed where Socrates fails because the Laws offer arguments that Socrates could never offer.

Readers of the *Crito* are inclined to assume that the reasons the Laws offer against escape are Socrates' reasons. In this book I show, however, that the Laws' reasons for opposing Socrates' escape are antithetical to Socrates' reasons in both form and sub-

---

3. Translations of passages from the *Apology* and the *Crito* are based on the translation by West and West (1984).

4. Although Socrates regards himself as a man who does a service, *hupēresia*, for the god (*Ap.* 30a7), he does not conceive of himself as the god's slave, *doulos*. Indeed, as I shall argue in Chapter 2, Socrates conceives of his service to the god as his living philosophically and justly, bound to the dictates of his own reason.

stance. They reflect a moral perspective that is at its core unsocratic. The arguments that the Laws present are arguments that Crito's moral outlook can accommodate, arguments that do not demand of Crito the kind of radical overhaul of his personal moral outlook that Socrates' arguments demand. Whereas Crito and the Laws can talk to each other, Socrates remains an enigma to them both.

The rewards of resisting the assumption that the Laws' moral point of view coincides with Socrates' are significant. If the Laws' view is not Socratic, then (1) the Socrates of the *Crito* can be reinstated as a man of radical independence, the man he was in the *Apology*, (2) there is no need to reconcile the clearly authoritarian character of the Laws' speech with the Socratic view that considerations of justice must override the law, (3) there is no longer any good reason to construe the Laws' rhetorical explosion as a model of philosophical acuity, and (4) the Laws can now function as defenders of the city, leaving Socrates to champion instead the causes of justice and philosophy.

A minority of interpreters of the *Crito* have resisted the impulse to assume that the Laws are—in whole or in large part—spokesmen for Socrates: Strauss, Anastaplo, Brown, Young, Hyland, Miller, and White, among others.[5] But their view is summarily dismissed by most other scholars. Woozley, DeFilippo, and Stephens, for example, mention this alternative reading and reject it out of hand.[6] Many more do not mention it at all. In this book I lend my support to the defenders of the minority view.

In a number of ways, however, this book goes beyond the existing defenses of that view. First, the book discovers in the early part of the dialogue—that is, before the Laws even make their appearance—a complete and self-contained statement of Socrates' philosophical argument against escape, an argument that turns on the old, familiar Socratic principles rather than on the newfangled notions eventually introduced by the Laws. Second, it reveals the utter vulgarity of the Laws by showing that the term "persuade" as the Laws use it in their injunction to "persuade or obey" is but a euphemism for the kind of shameless supplication that the Laws, no less than the judges at Socrates' trial, demand of those who have fallen from favor. Third, it finds previously unnoticed or at any rate uncited indications in the text of the *Crito* itself of Socrates' disenchantment with both the style and the content of the Laws' discourse and of the Laws' deviation from Socratic views.[7] Fourth, the book stakes out an unusual position on Socrates' relationship to law: it argues that although Socrates is no anarchist, he recognizes no obligation on the part of the citizen either to commit or to suffer injustice at the behest of his polis,[8] favoring compliance with

---

5. Strauss (1983), 66; Anastaplo (1975a), 208; Brown (1992), 73; Young (1974), 2–4; Hyland (1968), 47; Miller (1996),133; White (1996), 114.

6. Woozley (1979), 29; DeFilippo (1991), 259, n. 18; Stephens (1985), 8.

7. One could say that the reading I offer recognizes in the *Crito* a meaning that lies beneath its surface. Some of the clues that I was able to discern by which Plato conveys the deeper sense of the dialogue are instances of the strategies that Strauss ([1952], 36) identifies as ways in which a philosopher reveals to just some of his readers his true intent: "Obscurity of the plan, contradictions, pseudonyms, inexact repetitions of earlier statements, strange expressions, etc."

8. It will be argued that Socrates recognizes a citizen's duty to suffer when his government so commands but not a duty to suffer when his government *unjustly* so commands. The Laws, however, say only that a citizen must do whatever the city and fatherland and Laws bid.

a government's command to suffer injustice only when the alternative to suffering it is to commit it. Finally, the book suggests fresh translations of several key passages: Cr. 50c9–d1; Cr. 51c1; Cr. 51e4–52a3; Cr. 54d5–6.

Following this introductory chapter, the book is structured as follows. Chapter 2 establishes Socrates as an independent and autonomous moral agent, utterly devoted to the pursuit of justice and truth. Chapter 3 reveals the moral chasm that divides Crito from Socrates: although Crito loves Socrates and means well, his moral views are those of the many and the "help" he offers is not of the sort that Socrates can welcome. Chapter 4 shows that the views of Socrates in the early part of the Crito are completely in accord with those of Socrates in the Apology and that Socrates' own philosophical argument against escape relies entirely upon these familiar views. Chapter 5 calls attention to Socrates' broad hint that the arguments about to be expressed by the Laws are a rhetorical, not a philosophical, defense of a view with which Socrates disagrees—that is, of the view that all the city's decrees right or wrong are valid and binding. Chapter 6 exposes the unabashed authoritarianism that pervades the Laws' arguments and reveals the logical lapses that those arguments contain. Chapter 7 argues that Socrates' choice of the Corybantic metaphor to characterize the effect upon him of the Laws' arguments indicates his lack of regard for them. It is not until Chapter 8 that the question of why Socrates has the Laws present arguments that are flawed, arguments with which he himself disagrees and of which he strongly disapproves, is addressed. Chapter 8 shows how the Laws, by speaking Crito's language—that is, by accommodating themselves to his conventional beliefs and responding to his conventional concerns—are able to accomplish what Socrates, despite his best elenctic efforts, could not: they boost Crito to a higher rung on the moral ladder. Chapter 9 reaffirms the radical independence of Socrates, who will never assume the slavish posture of obsequious reverence, deference, and submission that the Laws both crave and require.

It is a commonplace in political philosophy to point to the Crito as the locus of the first developed articulation of the view that citizens owe complete or near complete obedience to their state. Moreover, insofar as the Crito is taken to be the work that marks the start of political theory, it is generally assumed that political theory itself begins with the affirmation of the primacy of the state over the individual. If the thesis of this book is correct, however, this deeply entrenched assumption is undermined, as is the traditional conception of the history of political thought for which it provides the foundation. For this book argues (1) that Socrates affirms in the Crito the uncompromised independence and authority of the rule of reason— that is, of the rule of justice as determined by individual persons through the exercise of their own best thinking;[9] (2) that it is the Laws and not Socrates who set the state above the individual; and (3) that Socrates invents and presents the Laws and their speech only as a very last resort and only for the sake of people unwilling or unable to engage in and benefit from philosophical inquiry—people like Crito.

---

9. It is not, as I shall argue, only moral experts to whom Socrates in the Crito commends the use of reason over and above obedience to law; on the contrary, Socrates contends that it is up to all thinking individuals to reflect on moral questions and to follow the conclusions to which their reason leads.

2

Remaining at the Station

The only obligation which I have a right to assume
is to do at any time what I think right.
                        Henry David Thoreau (1989), 4

Readers of the *Crito* instinctively believe that the Socrates they encounter in this dialogue is identical with the Socrates of the *Apology*. The dramatic contiguity of the two dialogues and the life-and-death issue they share all but compel this belief. But is this assumption sound? There certainly seem to be reasons to doubt its truth: is not Socrates in the *Apology* defiant of authority, and Socrates in the *Crito* compliant?; is not Socrates in the *Apology* a man who obeys only the god, and Socrates in the *Crito* the city's obedient son? To determine whether the impulse to merge the two Socrates-characters guides us well or leads us astray, our first step will be to come to know the Socrates of the *Apology* as he relates to his city, the gods, and the court.[1]

Justice and Philosophy

Socrates in the *Apology* is the tireless and selfless champion of two causes:[2] (1) justice or virtue or the best state of the soul (*Ap.* 29d–e; 30a–b; 31b; 32a; 32b–c; 32d; 32e; 33a; 36c; 38a; 41e), and (2) reasoned inquiry or critical examination of oneself and others—that is, philosophy (*Ap.* 28d; 29d; 29e; 38a; 41b). He is on a divine

---

1. This chapter is not an exhaustive account of Socrates' views in the *Apology*. It limits its discussion to those issues that occupy both the Socrates in the *Apology* and the Socrates in the *Crito*.

2. I use the word "selfless" in the conventional sense: Socrates is neglectful of his private interests as popularly conceived (*Ap.* 23b–c; 31b).

mission (*Ap*. 23b; 28e–29a; 29d; 30a; 33c; 37e), having been sent by the god to rouse Athens from its moral complacency and to impress upon it the incomparable worth of the life of virtue and the search for truth. As the only man who thus seeks Athens' true happiness, Socrates is its greatest benefactor (*Ap*. 30a; 30d–31b; 36c; 36d). For Socrates no sacrifice is too great when justice or philosophy is at stake: he will neither do injustice nor abandon the life of philosophy though the pursuit of justice and philosophy cost him his life (*Ap*. 28b; 28e–29a; 29a; 29d; 30c; 32b–c; 32d; 38c–39b). Socrates' unwavering commitment to justice and philosophy determines his thinking on every important human question.

Authority and Law

How, according to Socrates in the *Apology*, ought one to comport oneself with respect to authority, on the one hand, and with respect to law, on the other? Let us consider first Socrates' view on the individual's relation to authority. The most striking statement in the *Apology* on the right relation to authority is the following assertion made by Socrates:

> Wherever someone stations himself, holding that it is best, or wherever he is stationed by a ruler, *archōn*, there he must stay and run the risk, as it seems to me, and not take into account death or anything else compared to what is shameful. (*Ap*. 28d6–10)

On its surface at least, this statement appears to recommend an unqualified submissiveness to authority, a submissiveness unchecked by core Socratic considerations of justice and reason. It seems to regard as shameful the sheer disobeying of authority. Moreover, as the passage continues, Socrates appears to offer himself as an example of one who has embodied this ideal — at Potidaia, Amphipolis, and Delium (*Ap*. 28e1–4). Must we not conclude that Socrates indeed favors submission to one's military commanders, no questions asked?

One reason to hesitate before concluding from this passage that Socrates endorses unreflective and uncritical submission to authority is that this conclusion neglects the passage's beginning. Indeed, the beginning of the passage speaks not about bowing to authority but about standing firm in one's own commitment: "Wherever someone stations himself, holding that it is best . . . there he must stay and run the risk . . ." (*Ap*. 28d6–8).

Taken in context, the "someone" who stations himself would seem to be Achilles, who is portrayed in the passage immediately preceding this one as a man determined to risk his life rather than "to live as a bad man and not to avenge his friends" (*Ap*. 28d1). Achilles has one thing in common with the man who remains where stationed by an *archōn*: both prefer death to dishonor. But that is where the resemblance ends. Achilles is hardly one to do as he is instructed by another: he decides to avenge Patroclus not because someone in a position of authority instructs him to do so; indeed, he so decides despite his mother's explicit warning against pursuing so dangerous a course. Achilles follows his own determination of what is to be done and at what cost. Achilles is his own man; the man who remains where stationed by an *archōn* is another's.

Which of these two paradigmatic men does Socrates esteem? Is it the man who follows orders or the independent-spirited Achilles? I shall argue that the answer to this question is neither, although Socrates certainly makes it appear as if the answer is both.

In order to see that in Socrates' estimation neither Achilles nor the man submissive to authority is ideal, we must back up to the passage immediately preceding the introduction of Achilles. In this passage, Socrates states his view on how "a man who is of even a little benefit" ought to conduct himself: rather than "take into account the danger of living or dying" (Ap. 28b6–7), Socrates says, he should "consider this alone whenever he acts: whether his actions are just or unjust, and [hence][3] the deeds of a good or bad man" (Ap. 28b8–9).

If Socrates believes that a man of even slight worth ought to consider only whether what he does is just or unjust and [hence] the deed of a good or bad man, then neither Achilles nor the man who obeys orders is in Socrates' estimation worth anything.[4] Achilles, it is true, seeks to avoid living "as a bad man" (Ap. 28d1), but, as Socrates makes clear, what counts for Achilles as living as a bad man is not the committing of injustice but rather failing "to avenge his friends" (Ap. 28d1).[5] And the man who remains where stationed by an archōn considers nothing but doing as the archōn has commanded—he gives no thought to the possibly unjust character of what the archōn commands. What, then, are we to make of Socrates' apparent approval, on the one hand, of Achilles as someone who remains where he has stationed himself and, on the other, of the obedient soldier who remains where stationed by an archōn?

The only conclusion possible, given Socrates' insistence that a man determine his course of action in light of one consideration only, that of justice, is that Socrates' apparent approval of these two types of man is merely apparent. Indeed, Socrates indicates as much through his use of the phrase "holding that it is best," hēgēsamenos beltiston einai (Ap. 28d7): for Socrates, it is neither the sheer remaining where one stations oneself nor the sheer remaining where one is stationed by a ruler that is meritorious but rather doing so "holding that it is best," where "best" is understood in the sense of "most just."

According to Woozley, the expression "holding that it is best" governs both the phrase that precedes it and the one that follows it—that is, both "wherever one stations oneself" and "wherever one is stationed by a ruler."[6] Woozley's reason for this suggestion—a reason of considerable merit—is that Socrates later presents a situation in which he defies the command of an authority because he thinks it best (that

---

3. I read "and," kai, epexegetically.

4. We may note that Socrates does not explicitly praise Achilles in the passage he devotes to him.

5. Whatever it is that motivates Achilles, it is not justice. As becomes clear in the Crito, vengeance, for Socrates, has no part in justice; it is in fact, as Socrates argues, unjust to do bad things or to commit injustice in return.

6. Woozley (1979), 49. In support of Woozley's suggestion, I should like to point out a similarly structured passage found at Gorg. 517a5–6: oute tēi alethinēi rhētorikēi echrōnto—ou gar an exepeson— oute tēi kolakikēi: "They employed neither the true rhetoric—for then they would not have been driven out—nor the flattering one." The implication here is that if the allegedly superior orators of earlier times had used either the true rhetoric or the flattering one, they would not have been driven out. The phrase ou gar an exepeson, then, governs both what precedes and what follows it.

is, most just) to do so (*Ap*. 32d4–7).[7] For me, Woozley's reading has also the great advantage of reconciling Socrates' assertion that there is but one consideration that a man must take into account if he is to have any merit—the justice or injustice of what he is about to do—with Socrates' seeming regard for both the self-determined man and the man who obeys orders. If Woozley is right, then Socrates approves of neither man unconditionally: although both have the merit of not assigning to life itself the greatest importance, neither is motivated to remain at his post by his own reasoned conviction that it is best—that is, most just—to do so. Insofar as neither Achilles nor the soldier who obeys orders gives a thought to justice, neither is, in Socrates' eyes, a true model of virtue.

If the reasoning thus far is correct, and what Socrates really means to say is that one ought always to act upon one's own determination of what is just, why, we may wonder, does he not simply say so? Why does he *appear* to advocate obedience to *archontes*? And why does he point to himself as one who obeys rulers?

It is important to remember that Socrates is on trial and facing a possible death sentence. At least until the verdict is rendered, he does what he can—without compromising his principles of justice and his sense of dignity—to impress the members of the jury favorably and to avoid antagonizing them. Here Socrates has directed the jury's attention to his patriotism and bravery—even to his submissiveness to authority. And Socrates truly is, after all, patriotic and brave. He is, moreover, submissive to authority—as long, at any rate, as *he* judges such conduct to be most just.[8] We may observe, however, that what Socrates declares would have been "terrible" (or "strange"), *deina* (*Ap*. 28d10), is not his abandoning his military post but rather his remaining at his military post when stationed there by "elected rulers," yet abandoning the philosophical post at which the god stationed him. Indeed, Socrates says not that he *would* never abandon a military post but only that in fact he never *did* do so.

Socrates, then, is no advocate of uncritical obedience to men—even in military contexts. But, we may ask, does he not endorse uncritical submission to the god? After all, he does not apply the qualifying phrase "holding that it is best" to the duty

---

7. Both in the Leon of Salamis case that Woozley cites and in the case of the mass trial of the ten generals, Socrates opposes the orders of the government. The word for government is *hē archē* (*Ap*. 32d4, 32d8), a term closely related to *archōn*. In introducing these cases, Socrates declares: "I would not yield to any one man against the just because of a fear of death, even if I were to perish by refusing to yield" (*Ap*. 32a6–9). This declaration surely serves as a corrective to the earlier declaration at *Ap*. 28d7–8 that a man must remain wherever he is stationed by a ruler. The earlier declaration would be seriously misconstrued were it taken to imply that one ought to yield to one's ruler regardless of what one believes is just. Cf. *Ap*. 33a1–3: ". . . I was the sort of man . . . who never conceded anything to anyone contrary to the just."

Woozley (1979), 49, is right to acknowledge that the phrase "'wherever he is stationed by a ruler' *might* be unqualified by the phrase about belief" (emphasis in original), but his reason for thinking it better to read it as so qualified is surely creditable.

8. Socrates is no anarchist. He is disobedient only when government orders conflict with justice. In the *Apology*, Socrates addresses the question of whether obedience is obligatory when one's government commands one to commit injustice—his answer is no; in the *Crito*, as is argued in Chapter 5, Socrates addresses the question of whether obedience is obligatory when one's government commands one to suffer injustice—his answer in this case as well is no.

of remaining where one is stationed by the *god*. If Socrates is committed to total submissiveness to the god, then does not this submissiveness contradict his earlier assertion that a man ought to act upon his consideration of but one thing: whether or not his act is just?

Since it is most likely that Socrates conceives of the god as perfectly just, it is clear that from his perspective, obedience to the god — unlike obedience to mortal rulers — could never conflict with acting according to considerations of justice. But, more than that, obedience to the god is no ordinary submissiveness, for Socrates' god is no ordinary god. Socrates' god does not issue particular directives in concrete situations. He does not make moral determinations for human beings to whom he then communicates them. What Socrates' god demands of men is that they live justly and engage in philosophical inquiry and examination. The station at which the god stations Socrates is the station of philosophy. Paradoxically, then, to do as the god demands is to be the very opposite of uncritically submissive, for what the god demands is that one make one's own moral determinations through dogged pursuit of the moral truth — through philosophy. In effect, to obey the god and to act according to one's own reasoned conclusions about what justice requires are, at bottom, the same thing.

Why, then, does Socrates call following one's own reasoned determinations about justice obedience to the god? Here, too, we must bear in mind the situation in which Socrates finds himself. He is defending himself against an impiety charge. He is also attempting to defuse the long-standing hostility that has built up against him on account of his philosophical activity. Rather than say under these circumstances that he does as he judges best, he says the same thing in other words: "I obey the god."

There remains but one further passage in the *Apology* in which Socrates seems to endorse submissiveness. At *Ap.* 29b6–7, he declares that he knows that it is bad and shameful to disobey one's better,[9] whether god or human being. To obey the god, as we have just seen, does not require submissiveness; on the contrary, to obey the god is to live philosophically — that is, to follow one's own reasoned determination of what justice demands. But what of obedience to one's *human* better?

I think it is accurate to say that, for Socrates, one can never do better than to obey a true superior. We may note in this connection the shift from obedience to one's ruler, *archōn*, to obedience to one's superior or better, *beltiōn*.[10] Given the importance of doing what is just, if there were in fact a human being truly superior in moral

---

9. The passage reads: "But I do know that it is bad and shameful to do injustice and to disobey one's better, whether god or human being" (*Ap.* 29b6–7). I read "to do injustice" as "to commit the crime," which is the way the term *adikein* is used throughout the *Apology* (*Ap.* 19b4, 24b9, 24c4, 24c5, 28a2) — that is, as a technical legal term — and I take the "and" following "to do injustice" epexegetically. So the passage states: "But I do know that it is bad and shameful to commit the crime of disobeying one's better, whether god or man."

10. The term *beltiōn* is reminiscent of the *beltiston* of *Ap.* 28d7 in the expression *hēgēsamenos beltiston einai,* "holding it to be best." As I understand that passage (following Woozley), doing what one thinks best overrides obedience to the order of an *archōn* when there is a conflict; in our present passage one is said to owe obedience to one's true better — not simply to someone with greater power. So, one must either obey one's true superior or, in the absence of a true superior, do as one thinks best. An *archōn's* command, then, takes precedence neither over the command of a true *beltiōn* nor over what one holds to be most just.

matters[11]—as opposed to a human being who is merely one's ruler—it would be incumbent upon one to submit to the guidance of this moral expert.[12] In all other circumstances, however, one must act in accordance with one's own reasoned reflections upon what is just.

The members of Socrates' jury are hardly moral experts, though they no doubt qualify as *archontes*, rulers. Their orders, therefore, carry no weight with Socrates when they conflict with the claims upon him of justice and philosophy. Only once does Socrates openly defy the members of the jury—and even then, not without first professing his love for them (*Ap.* 29d2–3): when he considers what he would do were they to release him on condition that he cease engaging in philosophy and examination (*Ap.* 29c5ff.). On this occasion he declares: "I will obey the god rather than you" (*Ap.* 29d3–4). Socrates is bound not by authority but by a god who enjoins the life of philosophy.

Socrates' view on obedience to authority may be summarized, then, as follows. Socrates maintains that one ought always to do what one judges upon reasoned reflection to be best—that is, most just. To do this is to obey the god. Only when there is a human expert available ought one to defer to the judgment of another.

Let us turn now to the question of law. Is it legitimate to suppose that Socrates would disobey *the law* as readily as he would authority? Would Socrates oppose a law that stands in the way of justice or philosophy as he would a ruler who does so? We have just seen that Socrates defiantly tells the *court* that "I will obey the god rather than you" (*Ap.* 29d3–4). Is not the thrust of this declaration that there is for Socrates a court higher than the court of men—that is, higher than the court of *law*—and that it is to this higher court that he gives his first allegiance?[13]

11. Kraut (1984), 23, n. 38, understands a *beltiōn* to be specifically a *moral* superior. And it is indeed a moral *beltiōn* that is intended here. But we must remember that, for Socrates, that one is to obey a *moral* superior is but one application of his general principle that one is to obey experts. For it is a basic tenet of Socratic thought that one's doing well in any discipline requires that one obey the expert in that discipline. What is crucial for Socrates is that one not uncritically obey another whose superiority resides merely in his greater power.

12. Socrates does not believe himself to be, nor does he know anyone who is, a moral expert. Whether he thinks there could be one, however, is a much debated question. We should note that if there could not be a human moral expert, then only the god would remain to be obeyed. But since to obey the god is to practice philosophy, all that would ultimately remain of Socrates' knowing that he ought to obey his superior—whether god or human being—would be his knowing that he ought to practice philosophy.

13. Attempts to cast the jury's order as something that necessarily falls short of being a real law and, for that reason, as something that Socrates would be prepared to disobey fail to appreciate that Socrates would not purposely anger the jury (at least before the verdict is announced), openly proclaiming to its members his readiness to defy their order and roundly asserting that he will obey the god rather than them, if in fact he would not disobey them were their order legal. If Socrates declares that the god's order takes precedence over the order of the court, he does so only because it does. It is clear from the fact that he prefaces his declaration with words of love for the Athenians that he wishes not to give offense but that he says what he says because the truth must be spoken.

For a fully developed defense of the view that this hypothetical order by the jury could not constitute a law, and that, therefore, its violation by Socrates could not constitute a genuine breach of the law, see Brickhouse and Smith (1994), 146. See also Woozley (1979), 46. On the irrelevance of the question of whether the court's hypothetical order could actually take the form of law, see Kraut (1984). Kraut says, 658: "We would be insulting his seriousness if we took him to mean that a valid legal ban is all it would take to make him renounce philosophy. . . ."

Perhaps the correct inference to draw from Socrates' declaration is that on Socrates' view one may violate the law only when it conflicts with obedience *to the god*—and not when it conflicts with one's own reasoned view of what justice requires.[14] But since Socrates specifically identifies obedience to the god as living philosophically (*Ap.* 29d4–5)—that is, reflectively and in accordance with reason—it follows that saying that one must obey the god is no different from saying that one must do what one believes to be best, in the sense of most just.[15]

Although the *Apology* certainly emphasizes those aspects of the practice of philosophy that benefit others, namely, the exhortation to virtue and the exposure of previously unrecognized and unacknowledged ignorance, these aspects ought not to be mistaken for what Socrates regards as the primary end of philosophy. Philosophy at its core is the exercise of reason for the end of attaining truth—particularly, for Socrates, moral truth. That Socrates concentrates his efforts in the *Apology* on presenting philosophy in the form of service to others is not surprising; the heart of his defense against the charge that he is a corruptive influence consists, after all, of the demonstration that as a philosopher he is actually Athens' great benefactor. Yet, that Socrates in the *Apology* portrays philosophy in its service-mode ought not to cause the reader to lose sight of philosophy's essence as reasoned reflection whose end is truth.

We may now turn our attention to the two cases in the *Apology* often cited to demonstrate Socrates' presumed fierce loyalty to law: the case of the mass trial of the ten generals (*Ap.* 32a9–c4) and the Leon of Salamis case (*Ap.* 32c4–e1). In each of these cases—touted by Socrates as proof "not in words but . . . in deeds" (*Ap.* 32a4–5) of the danger of public life to a just man[16]—Socrates relates to the court an incident in his life that purportedly helps to show why it is best that he not play a public role in the life of the city.[17] In the first case (*Ap.* 32a9–c4), the case of Socrates'

---

14. See Mulgan (1972), who argues, 210–11, that Socrates is prepared to disobey the law only when it conflicts with the god's personal command to him but that Socrates in no way recommends disobedience to law when it conflicts with "the personal moral judgement of the individual." To equate the conflict between the court and god with the conflict between the state and "one's personal moral judgement," says Mulgan, "implies that Socrates' frequent and explicit references to the god are nothing more than a metaphysical way of describing his own judgement." It is precisely this implication that I seek to defend. As I argue, since what the god commands Socrates to do is to philosophize, the god in effect commands Socrates to use his own judgment.

15. It is important to recognize (contra Young [1974], 29) that insofar as obeying the god is, for Socrates, living philosophically, and insofar as living philosophically is living in accordance with the dictates of human reason with respect to justice, it cannot be known in advance that Socrates' disobedience to law will be limited to the single case in which he is ordered to desist from practicing philosophy. For what does it mean for one to refuse to give up philosophizing? It means that one arrogates to oneself the right always to exercise and act in accordance with one's own reason. And since it is not possible to know in advance what one's reason will determine to be right in every case in which law plays a part, it is not possible to rule out in advance the chance that Socrates, when exercising his reason, will on occasion believe himself to be obligated to break the law and will, therefore, do so.

16. The court's preference for proof in deeds is in Socrates' view a vulgar one. As he says, the proofs he proceeds to offer in accordance with the court's preference are "vulgar things, typical of the law courts" (*Ap.* 32a8).

17. We may note that the second incident shows not that it is dangerous for a just man to lead a public life but simply that it is dangerous for a man to be just. Whereas in the first incident, that of the ten generals, Socrates holds a political office through which he finds himself at risk when he champi-

opposition to the mass trial of the ten generals, Socrates objects to the trial on the grounds that it is illegal—not only on the grounds that it is unjust. It has been suggested that it may therefore be concluded from this case—even if not from anything earlier—that Socrates is indeed to be regarded as a defender of law.

The first case alone, however, cannot decide this question. For although Socrates certainly denounces the mass trial of the generals as illegal, he no less certainly denounces it as unjust. Since in this case the unjust and the illegal coincide, there is no way of knowing how Socrates would have reacted had mass trials been legal: would he have been less inclined under those circumstances to condemn the trial of the ten generals? Let us consider, then, the second case.

In the second case, Socrates resists the order of the Thirty to arrest Leon of Salamis, stating as his grounds that such an arrest is unjust and impious; he does not contend that he disobeys the order because of its illegality. Despite attempts by scholars to attribute to Socrates the view that ad hoc edicts of the Thirty surely do not count for Socrates as law, we must ask if it is reasonable to believe that Socrates simply neglects to mention that the edict is in his view illegal.[18] Socrates, as we have seen, seeks wherever possible to impress upon the court his loyalty to his rulers and to the god; it is hardly credible that he would pass up an opportunity in the Leon of Salamis affair to display before the court his devotion to law: he certainly makes the most of this opportunity in the case of the ten generals. The glaring absence of any mention of illegality in this second case, especially in light of how prominently illegality is featured in the first case, can therefore only be interpreted to mean that Socrates regards as legal the command of the Thirty. He disobeys it because it is unjust.[19]

---

ons the cause of justice, in the second incident, that of Leon of Salamis, Socrates is a private citizen and is at risk even in that capacity. Moreover, by saying that "if someone who really fights for the just is going to preserve himself *even for a short time*, it is necessary for him to lead a private rather than a public life" (*Ap.* 31e4–32a3), Socrates implies that a just man will live a short life even if he lives a private life—although the life of a just man who lives a public life will be even shorter. It is interesting that elsewhere in the dialogue Socrates offers other explanations for his avoidance of the public realm. Earlier on he says: "And because of this occupation [viz., his divine mission of testing others], I have had no leisure, either to do any of the things of the city worth speaking of or any of the things of my family" (*Ap.* 23b7–9); later on he says that he "did not care for, *amelēsas*, the things that the many do—moneymaking and household management, and generalships, and popular oratory, and the other offices, and conspiracies and factions that come to be in the city. . ." (*Ap.* 36b6–9).

18. On Xenophon's account, the order of the Thirty is illegal and is opposed by Socrates on those grounds (*Mem.* IV.iv.3). Xenophon is apparently eager to show that Socrates recognizes no distinction between the just and the lawful (*Mem.* IV.iv.12). As I see it, Plato's account diverges from Xenophon's in this respect: Plato uses instances of Socrates' lawabidingness to conceal—though not completely—Socrates' radical independence; Xenophon simply expunges this radicalness from his account.

19. Woozley (1979), 54–55, seeks to explain Socrates' not having mentioned the illegality of the edicts of the Thirty as follows: "He did not *say* at his trial that their order to him was contrary to *nomos*, because he did not need to: their brief but bloody reign of terror had been so universally condemned that there was no point in his claiming that what they had ordered him to do was contrary to law; nothing was to be gained by reminding the court of that" (emphasis in original). Why does Woozley think

It is true that Socrates does not say explicitly that the order of the Thirty *is* legal. Yet Socrates' silence is in this instance easily explained. All Socrates could hope to accomplish by telling the jurors openly that he disobeyed a command he believed to be legal is to antagonize them. As we have already seen, Socrates tries, when possible—at least before the verdict is announced—to avoid provoking the jury's ill will.

We may summarize Socrates' approach to injustice and illegality, then, as follows. Socrates will not do anything unjust. Indeed, he is a man who "fights for the just" (*Ap*. 32a1).[20] Hence, he must resist any unjust command, even if legal.[21] If, fortuitously, what is illegal and what is unjust coincide, then Socrates will take advantage of that coincidence and present himself to the jury as someone who opposes illegality.[22] The mass trial of the ten generals affords him just such an opportunity, and he seizes it. The Leon of Salamis case, however, restores the criterion of justice to its exclusive sovereignty, leaving no doubt that considerations of justice will always prevail over all other considerations, including the matter of law.[23]

Gods and "The God"

The issue of Socrates' religious beliefs derives its urgency from the fact that the indictment against him contains an impiety charge consisting of two parts: that Socrates does not acknowledge the gods of the city and that he believes in novel daimonic things (*Ap*. 24b9–c1). In the *Apology*, Socrates offers no direct proof that he does

---

that "nothing was to be gained" by Socrates' reminding the court of the illegality of the Thirty's edict?; surely Socrates has much to gain—and he is quite aware of it—by representing himself as unflaggingly loyal to the law. For a view very similar to Woozley's, see Burnet (1924), 173: ". . . their [i.e., the Thirty's] arbitrary acts are evidently included among the *paranoma* referred to in *Ap*. 31e4." It appears to me, however, on the contrary, that the edicts of the Thirty are deliberately excluded from those *paranoma*. Cf. Grote (1875), I, 306, n. q: "We must remember that the Thirty had come into authority by resolutions passed under constitutional forms, when fear of foreign enemies induced the people to sanction the resolutions proposed by a party among themselves."

20. Cf. *Gorg*. 522b9–c1: "All my words and actions are prompted by justice."

21. Dover (1974), 306–307, has argued that in fourth-century Athens, to say of a *law* that it was unjust would constitute a virtual oxymoron, though it was certainly acceptable to say of verdicts or policy decisions that they were unjust. Although Socrates avoids the awkward locution of saying that a law is unjust, it nevertheless seems clear that he is skeptical of the justness of particular laws, for example, of the Athenian law mandating one-day-long capital trials. We may note that the distinction between law, on the one hand, and verdict or policy, on the other, all but dissolves when the Laws in the *Crito* speak indiscriminately of the citizen's duty to do "whatever we bid," *ha en hēmeis keleuōmen* (*Cr*. 51e4), or "whatever it [i.e., the city or fatherland] bids," *ha an keleuēi* (*Cr*. 51b4, 51b9).

22. Another occasion on which Socrates plays up his lawfulness when there is no conflict between what is lawful and what is just is in his undertaking to make his defense speech since "the law must be obeyed" (*Ap*. 19a6).

23. Whereas Socrates speaks of "preventing many unjust and unlawful things from happening in the city" (*Ap*. 31e3–4), what is critical to him is the prevention of injustice. Since what Socrates "fights for" is "the just" (*Ap*. 32a1), it is clear that when something unjust is lawful, Socrates will be obliged to oppose rather than support the lawful. Also, even in the first case, the case of the Thirty, he makes it clear at the outset that it is "against the just" that he will not yield to any man (*Ap*. 32a6–7).

believe in the gods of the city;[24] instead, he uses his belief in a private daimonic voice to establish that he is no atheist.

Socrates seeks to refute the impiety charge in his second elenctic exchange with Meletus. Having spurred Meletus to magnify the charge against him to one of utter atheism (Ap. 26c5–7), Socrates proceeds to draw from Meletus's statements the necessarily false (because self-contradictory) inference that Socrates believes both in no gods and in some gods. As Socrates reasons, if belief in daimonic things entails belief in daimons, and if daimons are either gods or children of gods, then belief in daimonic things entails belief in gods—since, of course, there cannot be children of gods without gods (Ap. 27c8–e3). Socrates does not commit *himself* to what daimons are; he seeks merely to mock Meletus's atheism charge against him on the basis of what Meletus and others must believe daimons to be.

The god, *sing.*, of whom Socrates speaks repeatedly in the *Apology*, however, is surely not simply one of the many gods whose existence Meletus suspects him of denying. Socrates' god is at first assimilated to the god of the oracle at Delphi,[25] yet we may note that Apollo is never mentioned by name, and, as the dialogue progresses, all association between Socrates' god and a god of known identity dissolves.[26] Socrates' god sends him to Athens out of concern for Athenian souls; his task is to exhort his fellow citizens to care for virtue and truth, to disabuse them of their false conceit of wisdom, and to encourage them to engage in self-examination. In other words, Socrates' god is a god who promotes—through Socrates—justice and philosophy. To obey the god, as we have seen, is to practice philosophy—that is, to guide one's conduct by one's reasoned determination of what is best in the sense of most just. The god does not serve as an alternative to human reason as a guide to moral decision making; instead, the god issues a divine mandate to use human reason as one's guide.[27] To obey the god is, for Socrates, to engage in what he believes independently to be the greatest good for a human being: philosophy. Thus, when Socrates seeks to explain why he cannot simply go into exile and "keep quiet"—that is, relinquish his practice of philosophy—he offers two reasons: first, that keeping quiet or ceasing to philosophize "is to disobey the god" (Ap. 37e6), and, second, that ". . . this even happens to be the greatest good for a human being—to make speeches every day about

24. It is surely true that Socrates performed traditional religious rites of prayer and sacrifice. Yet he does not point to these in defending himself against the impiety charge. Perhaps these activities would not suffice to establish in the eyes of the Athenians that Socrates recognizes or believes in the gods of the city. Perhaps Socrates himself does not regard these activities as proof of his piety. He believes, *nomizō*, after all, "as none of my accusers does" (Ap. 35d7). See Lofberg (1928), 603: "He [Socrates] could obviously not say anything wholeheartedly on the subject [of his orthodoxy]. Far better it was for him to trap the prosecutor into identifying unorthodoxy with irreligion and to confute him in that ground, and to keep before the jury constantly his belief in God."

25. This is the oracle, consulted by Socrates' friend Chaerophon, that proclaims that no man is wiser than Socrates.

26. See Anastaplo (1975a), 25.

27. Socrates asserts that the god's order to him to practice philosophy came to him through "oracles, and dreams, and in every other way that any divine allotment ever ordered a human being to practice anything at all" (Ap. 33c5–7). Regardless, however, of how the order is conveyed, the content of the order is always the same—to practice philosophy, examining oneself and others.

virtue and the other things about which you hear me conversing and examining both myself and others" (*Ap*. 38a2–5).[28]

Is there not, however, another divine source that Socrates regards as authoritative? Does he not, in fact, cite as just such a source his *daimonion*, the voice that began coming to him in childhood, steering him away from what he was about to do but never urging him toward any particular action or course of action (*Ap*. 31c8–d4)? Does Socrates not portray himself as obeying without question and without hesitation his *daimonion*'s warnings?

The nature of this daimonic voice and precisely how Socrates himself conceives of it are matters difficult to determine. Because the issue is difficult, and because it has engendered deep scholarly divisions, I offer the following rather lengthy discussion of it. I beg the reader's indulgence.

The *daimonion* appears to be an extrarational force—indeed, a suprarational one—that protects Socrates from bad things before he is able to or has had sufficient time to achieve understanding of their badness or inappropriateness. Anastaplo suggests that it is a "divine" substitute for the instinct that most people—but, for some reason, not Socrates—come by quite naturally.[29]

For us, the question of the *daimonion* is the question of whether, for Socrates, this divine voice constitutes a valid means separate from his own reason by which to determine what ought to be done in concrete moral situations and whether Socrates would follow its injunctions if they opposed his own reasoned conclusions.

Vlastos maintains that Socrates does not obey the *daimonion* if it contradicts his own moral reasoning, that in such a case its message would "condemn itself as a vagary of his own fancy instead of a true command of the god."[30] Vlastos contends that since the *daimonion*'s message comes without an interpretation, Socrates obeys his *daimonion* when he has either his own "independent and sufficient grounds for accepting what the voice tells him to believe" or his own "strong intuitive impression . . . that a certain belief or action is incorrect without being able to articulate his grounds for it at the moment."[31] On those occasions when the *daimonion* opposes what Socrates is about to do and Socrates obeys it, says Vlastos, Socrates has not yet reached a firm decision but is only leaning in a particular direction.[32]

---

28. Most readers will accept that, for Socrates, each of these reasons is valid—indeed, sufficient. Some readers (myself included) suspect that the first adds nothing to the second but is just another way of stating it. Reeve (1989), 72, however, contends that Socrates on his own, that is, without a divine command, would have determined only that he must examine himself and a *few* others in order to remove conceit and to test his moral views; it was specifically the god's command, he contends, that initiated Socrates' missionizing activities. Yet the phrasing of this passage suggests otherwise: Socrates determines on his own that the "greatest good for a human being" is "to make speeches every day about virtue and the other things about which you hear me conversing and examining both myself and others. . ." (*Ap*. 38a2–5). It is difficult to see how the activity of "making speeches" could refer to anything but Socrates' missionizing activities.

29. Anastaplo (1975a), 27.

30. Vlastos (1991), 286.

31. Vlastos (1991), 283.

32. Vlastos (1991), 286–87.

The contrary view—the view that Socrates, taking his *daimonion* to be a voice from god, follows it even if it opposes his own reasoned conclusions—has vigorous proponents as well.[33] It is plausibly argued that surely, on at least some of the occasions on which Socrates' *daimonion* turns him back from something he is "about to do," Socrates has devoted considerable thought to what he is about to do; yet, apparently on all occasions, including those, the *daimonion* has but to say no and Socrates will reverse his course.[34] Indeed, although all the *daimonion* does is say no,[35] offering no explanation of what is wrong with the course Socrates is poised to follow, Socrates nevertheless obeys its admonitions without hesitancy or doubt, seeking explanations only afterward.[36]

Neither of these two views seems quite right. Where defenders of the first view appear to go wrong is in undervaluing the *daimonion*'s obstructive role. According to the defenders of the first view, on those occasions when Socrates obeys the *daimonion*, the *daimonion* is either leading Socrates along the very path he would have followed even without it or guiding him in a particular direction when he has not yet decisively chosen his course. In what is evidently for them the purely hypothetical case in which there *is* opposition between the *daimonion* and Socrates' reason, they assume that Socrates would disobey the *daimonion*. It seems clear, however, from the passages in which the *daimonion* is cited, that (1) the *daimonion* stops Socrates from what he is *set* on doing, and (2) that he *always* obeys it.

Where defenders of the second view seem to go wrong is in assuming that the *daimonion* stops Socrates from his intended course of action in opposition to what Socrates' reason or sense of the matter has determined is *right*. What I shall argue is that although the defenders of the second view are correct in recognizing that the

---

33. See Reeve (1989), 70–73; McPherran (1991), 368–73; Brickhouse and Smith (1994), 190–95. Reeve contends that the *daimonion* enables Socrates "to establish truths that he could not establish in any other way" (70); he maintains, in particular, that the *daimonion*'s silence teaches Socrates the truth about the goodness of death—if only for him. Although I take up shortly the cause of the *daimonion*'s silence, it is perhaps worth pointing out here that Socrates does not regard his explanation of the *daimonion*'s silence as more than probable, *kinduneuei* (*Ap.* 40b7), and that he continues to speak, even after the "great proof" that is the *daimonion*'s silence, only in terms of having reason to *hope* that death is good (*Ap.* 40c4).

34. To the objection that Socrates says of himself in the *Crito*: ". . . I, not only now but always, am such as to obey nothing else of what is mine than that argument, *logos*, that appears best to me upon reasoning, *logizomenōi* (*Cr.* 46b4–6), both McPherran (1991), 368, and Brickhouse and Smith (1991), 193–94, respond that Socrates need not regard the *daimonion*'s admonition as being opposed to reason but may well regard it as in itself constituting a reason—indeed, a very weighty reason—to be taken into account in his reasoning. Also Reeve (1989), 70: "He [Socrates] does not need to justify each particular command and prohibition independently of the fact that he believes it to have a divine source," since his trust in the ethical reliability of such commands has been elenctically established. For an opposing view, see Nussbaum (1985), 234, who assimilates the *daimonion* to reason itself, reason being "a divine thing, a thing intermediary . . . between the animal that we are and the god that we might be." Although I think Nussbaum's view is nearer to the truth than the one it opposes, it fails to account for how differently, as it seems, Socrates experiences the *daimonion* from how he experiences reason and for its being something that, as he says, has been coming to him since childhood.

35. We do not know exactly how the *daimonion* says no.

36. See Brickhouse and Smith (1991), 192.

daimonion is indeed obstructive and that Socrates does always obey it, what we find if we look carefully at the cases in which the *daimonion* is mentioned is that the *daimonion* turns Socrates away not from doing what his reason or sense has pronounced right but rather from doing what his reason or sense has pronounced wrong.[37] What the *daimonion* opposes is not actions that are in accord with Socrates' considered judgment or sense but actions inconsistent with that considered judgment or sense. One might even go so far as to say that it is the very inconsistency between what Socrates is about to do and his own better judgment that triggers the *daimonion*.[38] The *daimonion* is not, then, a voice independent of Socrates' own thinking and intuition that instructs him to contravene their guidance but rather a voice inspired by Socrates' thinking and intuition, by beliefs that are for the moment "subconscious" — if the reader will forgive the anachronism — a voice that gives him the strength to implement these "subconscious" beliefs even when he is tempted to do otherwise. Indeed, when there is no tension between Socrates' imminent act and his deeper sense of what is right, when Socrates has no reservations, no qualms, about the course he is about to pursue, his *daimonion* is silent.

Let us consider briefly the relevant Platonic passages, ending with the passages in the *Apology*. Outside the *Apology* there are three such relevant passages.[39]

In the *Thaeatetus* (151a), the *daimonion* stops Socrates from welcoming back pupils who deserted him before his "midwifery" sessions with them had run their course. In the *Phaedrus* (242b–c), the divine sign prevents Socrates from crossing the stream until he recognizes the nature of his offense and atones for it. And in the *Republic* (II.496c), the sign keeps Socrates from abandoning philosophy.

The last of these cases is a clear and unambiguous instance of the just proposed account of how the *daimonion* works. As we know, Socrates is quite convinced that the best life for a human being is the life of philosophy. If, then, the *daimonion* stops him from abandoning the philosophical life when, presumably, attractive alternatives beckon, it surely does nothing more than help Socrates live as *he* believes he ought. Far from keeping Socrates from doing what he thinks is right, the *daimonion* keeps him from doing what he thinks is wrong.

In the *Thaeatetus*, too, it is likely that Socrates has his own sense of which of his former pupils are unworthy of renewed exposure to his maieutic art and that his

---

37. Not every matter in which the *daimonion* intervenes is one of right and wrong. In the *Euthydemus* (272e), for example, when Socrates' *daimonion* comes to him as he is about to leave the palaestra and causes him to sit right back down, there is no moral issue at hand: all Socrates achieves by staying is a chance to talk with Dionysodorus and Euthydemus. Perhaps the *daimonion* was aroused by Socrates' having subconsciously heard the group approaching. If this is so, the *daimonion* plays the same role in nonmoral situations as it plays in moral ones: it is an envoy from the "subconscious" mind to the conscious.

38. This is arguably a reasonable way to construe the manner in which the *daimonion* operates in Socrates when he is a child: the boy Socrates is attracted to a particular course of action that he believes is wrong; his *daimonion* comes to his aid to ensure that he act in accordance with the beliefs he holds and that he resist the momentary temptation.

39. I omit the *Euthydemus* passage discussed in n. 37, for the reason specified there. The other place the *daimonion* is mentioned is the *Theages*, a dialogue I consider to be spurious. For a consideration of the *Theages* passage and for a discussion of Xenophon's view of the *daimonion*, see Vlastos (1991), 281–82.

daimonion merely concretizes his own reservations about these students, stopping him from readmitting them against his better judgment.

The *Phaedrus* case is the most significant of the three. Insofar as it provides an account of the events leading up to the *daimonion*'s appearance, it actually offers a measure of proof of the thesis being proposed—the thesis that the *daimonion* reflects, rather than opposes, Socrates' own sense of what is right and wrong in the matter at hand. In the *Phaedrus*, Socrates states that his familiar divine sign, the sign that holds him back from something he is about to do, came to him, and that he thought he heard a voice forbidding him to leave the spot until he had atoned for an offense against the gods. But, he explains:

> In fact, the soul too, my friend, is itself a sort of seer; that's why, *almost from the beginning of my speech*, I was disturbed by a very uneasy feeling, as Ibycus puts it, that "for offending the gods I am honored by men." But now I understand exactly what my offense has been.[40] (emphasis added)

We see from this passage that, well before the sign forbids his movement, indeed, almost from the beginning of his speech, Socrates feels uneasy, sensing that he might be offending the gods. It is Socrates' soul that is the "seer," catching the first glimpse of the wrongness of his action; what the *daimonion* does is make audible to Socrates what his soul intuitively grasps so that his soul's quiet warning does not go unheeded. When the *daimonion* prevents Socrates from crossing the river as he intends, the *daimonion* acts upon Socrates' own feeling that he has done something wrong that needs to be rectified; it amplifies, then, his own doubts about what he is about to do. Although the sign is experienced by Socrates as adventitious, it in fact comes not from without but from within.

Let us turn now to the relevant passages in the *Apology*. The first occurs at *Ap.* 31c7–d6, where Socrates says that his *daimonion* turned him away from participation in politics. Since the question of whether or not one ought to be politically active is hardly a trivial one, it may fairly be assumed that Socrates devoted serious thought to it. Is it not therefore legitimate to infer from the *daimonion*'s turning Socrates away from politics that Socrates' own reasoned conclusion in this matter was that he ought to enter the political realm? And do we not then have ample proof that Socrates assigns priority to the directives of the *daimonion* above even the conclusions he reaches as a result of his own thinking?

There is considerable evidence in the *Apology* that Socrates, independent of, and even prior to, any warning by the *daimonion*, decides that politics is not for him. At *Ap.* 23b7–9, he says: "And because of this occupation [his service to the god], I have had no leisure, either to do any of the things of the city worth speaking of or any of the things of my family." And, later in the dialogue at *Ap.* 36b5–c3, after the guilty-verdict has been announced, Socrates, making no reference to the *daimonion*, presents his own reasons for avoiding politics and expresses his lack of interest in—even his disdain for—political affairs:

> What am I worthy to suffer or to pay because I did not keep quiet during my life and did not care for the things that the many do—moneymaking and household manage-

---

40. *Phaedrus* 242c6–d2, trans. Nehamas and Woodruff (1995).

ment, and generalships, and popular oratory, and the other offices, and conspiracies and factions that come into the city—since *I* held that I myself was really too decent to survive if I went into these things? I did not go into matters where, if I did go, I was going to be of no benefit either to you or to myself. (emphasis added)

Socrates, then, has reasons of his own that keep him from entering politics: his lack of leisure owing to his mission, his disinclination to involve himself in the sorts of occupations and intrigues that appeal to the many, his sense that, because of his decency, he would not live long if he were to be politically active, and his belief that he would benefit no one.

Of these reasons, the last two are reasons that Socrates offered earlier as a way of accounting for the *daimonion*'s opposition—namely, that no just man would live long in the public arena and that Socrates would therefore benefit "neither you nor myself" (*Ap.* 31d8–e1) if he were to pursue the political life. Although these reasons were then, as now, Socrates' own—the *daimonion*, after all, does not give reasons— one *could* say that they are reasons that Socrates adduces after the *daimonion*'s warning and in connection with it. In other words, given just these reasons, it would be possible to say that, were it not for the *daimonion*'s warning, Socrates' own prior thinking on the matter might indeed have induced him to become politically active.

But what of the other two reasons? If Socrates avoids politics because he finds himself too busy to engage in it, does he not have a reason—apart from and prior to the daimonic warning—to stay out of politics? And if Socrates has disdain for political conspiracies and factions and for public oratory, is he not, if anything, disinclined to involve himself in politics? These reasons suggest that Socrates' own thinking, apart from and prior to the *daimonion*'s influence, is far more likely to drive him away from politics than to impel him toward it. Why, then, must the *daimonion* turn him away?[41]

The answer I offer is modeled on the *Republic* passage briefly discussed earlier. I suggest that just as Socrates in the *Republic* credits the *daimonion* with keeping him from abandoning philosophy,[42] so Socrates in the *Apology* credits the *daimonion* with keeping him from entering the life of politics.[43] In both cases, Socrates clearly recognizes on his own that the life of philosophy—not of politics—is the most desirable human life; yet, in both cases, the *daimonion* must keep Socrates in philosophy and out of politics. What the *daimonion* does, it seems, both in the *Republic* and in the *Apology*, is protect Socrates from lapsing into politics—against his better judgment— in a moment of weakness. For not only must Socrates withstand constant pressures from without urging him to participate in the political life of his city, but he must no doubt withstand as well subtle pressures from within likewise urging him to do so: he is, after all, a just man who wishes to promote justice and to fight injustice in his city. It is in resisting such pressures, external but, also and more important, internal, that the *daimonion* proves useful, even indispensable: it brings Socrates to his senses,

---

41. From a rhetorical point of view, it makes good sense that Socrates would invoke the *daimonion* to soften his denunciation of politics before the verdict is reached. After the verdict is reached, however, he drops his reference to the *daimonion* and speaks openly about his dislike of political affairs.

42. In the *Republic*, it is bodily illness that is credited with keeping Theages faithful to philosophy!

43. We may note that in the *Republic*, too, the alternative occupation from which the small band of philosophers is preserved is politics.

reminding him of what he always knew—that politics is a breeding ground for injustice, that what matters to politicians is the appearance of justice but not justice itself. The *daimonion*, then, helps Socrates turn away not from something he has determined to be right and worthwhile but, on the contrary, from something he recognizes as wrong and useless.

It is interesting, and surely not purely coincidental, that although the *daimonion* removes Socrates from politics generally, it does not prevent him from serving on the very council that actually endangered his life.[44] Since, on the one hand, Socrates has no time or real regard for politics, his *daimonion* helps him resist it if it attracts him for the moment. But since, on the other hand, Socrates believes it to be his civic duty to take his place on the Council when it is his turn and since he is, moreover, not one to abdicate his responsibility, the *daimonion* is silent in this particular case of political involvement. The *daimonion* reflects Socrates' own unease or disquiet at the prospect of doing something he believes he ought not to do; when, however, he is completely confident of the rightness of what he is about to do, his *daimonion* is silent.

Toward the end of the *Apology*, Socrates appeals twice to the *daimonion*'s silence. In the first instance, Socrates interprets his *daimonion*'s silence during the trial as an indication that death is not bad but good for him; in the second, Socrates interprets the *daimonion*'s silence as evidence that it is now better for him to be dead and to have been released from troubles.[45] That Socrates' *daimonion* is silent throughout the trial and even as he is about to die is just as one would expect. Since Socrates is most pleased with the way in which he conducts himself during the proceedings, despite the great likelihood that he will die as a result of it, and since his satisfaction is unmarred by any trace of reservation or doubt, there is no uneasiness in his soul to

44. It is most surprising that scholars who hold the view that Socrates' own thinking takes precedence over the *daimonion*'s advice in the case of a conflict do not seize on Socrates' account of his service on the Council as proof that he does *not* always obey his *daimonion*: the *daimonion* warns him, after all, not to be politically active, but Socrates serves on the Council anyway. Indeed, could such scholars not reasonably maintain that Socrates' experience on the Council is what leads him to put his trust in the *daimonion*'s advice in the future? On my view, since Socrates does not relate the story of his service on the Council *as* an illustration of what happens when he fails to obey the *daimonion*'s warning, it is fair to assume that the *daimonion* issued no warning against Socrates' holding this particular public office. And, if the *daimonion* was in fact silent on this occasion, its silence can only mean that Socrates did not deem it inappropriate to take his turn on the Council—even if he thinks it generally ill advised for a just man to live a public life. I suggest in what follows why this is so. Whether Socrates was forewarned or not, however, his experience on the Council does prove that the political life is no life for a just man. Indeed, as Socrates tells the story of his service on the Council, what it is really intended to show is that, despite the personal danger to himself of fighting for justice in a public context, he will "not yield even to a single man against the just" (*Ap.* 32a6–7). Socrates, then, exploits this occasion to convey to his judges a point that is more important to him than the point that public life is dangerous for a just man—namely, that he places considerations of justice above considerations of danger.

45. It is argued later in this chapter (see the section entitled "The Penalties") that the *daimonion*'s silence does not quite establish for Socrates that death is a good thing for him; this is a conclusion that he draws for the sake of his "judges," that is, for those who voted for his acquittal. What the *daimonion*'s silence does confirm for him is that it is better now for him to be dead and released from troubles.

activate the *daimonion*. "I much prefer," he says, "to die having made my defense speech in this way than to live in that way" (*Ap*. 38e4–5). Why would the *daimonion* sound when Socrates is supremely confident of the rightness of his chosen course even in the face of death, when he believes with great certainty that it is now better for him to be dead than to pay the morally exorbitant price of remaining alive? As long as Socrates is at ease, his *daimonion* is, too.

We may conclude, then, that neither the god nor the *daimonion* functions for Socrates as a guide to moral action distinct from his judgment. If this is so, however, in what way is Socrates pious? Socratic piety consists in living philosophically and living justly. Socrates is pious not because he follows private communications from a supernatural source but because, even at the cost of his life, he does what he—as a result of reasoned reflection—believes to be right. He does not behave in court as other men do, begging and crying and parading his children before the jurors. His refusal to subvert justice in this way and to involve the jurors in this subversion is his proof that he believes in gods. But he believes, as he says, "as none of my accusers does" (*Ap*. 35d7). Socratic piety is real, but it is not conventional.

Socrates' divine mission, insofar as it consists of a charge to commit oneself to justice and philosophy, is not really confined to Socrates. It is not only for him but for human beings generally that "the unexamined life is not worth living . . ." (*Ap*. 38a5–6). Although Socrates frequently suggests that his mission is unique to him, that the god sent specifically him as a gift to Athens, it is clear that he does not mean to imply thereby that the way he lives is not for everyone.[46] Just as on Socrates' interpretation of the oracle even the name "Socrates" does not denote him uniquely but refers to men of his type—that is, to those who are cognizant of their own ignorance (*Ap*. 23a7–b4)—so, as Socrates understands it, his divine mission, the practice of examining oneself and others, is not for him alone. After all, Socrates explicitly commends to all human beings the activity of "making speeches every day about virtue and the other things about which you hear me conversing and examining both myself and others" (*Ap*. 38a1–6). Socrates perhaps is the only man at present—although he does have many young imitators—who executes the mission of the god precisely as it is meant to be executed, devoting to it unparalleled time and effort, but he surely does not see it as ideal that he alone is responsive to this mission. Indeed, Socrates bemoans the consequences the Athenians will suffer should they kill him: by killing their greatest benefactor, they will be bereft of such benefaction as he provides—until the god in his concern for the city sends another man to replace him (*Ap*. 31a2–7).

Socrates' pious mission, then, consists in his doing what all truly pious men ought to do: behave justly and practice philosophy. The life most fit for human beings generally is none other than the life the god commands Socrates to pursue. To live as one ought, guided by human reason in the pursuit of justice, simply *is* to follow the god.

---

46. For the contrary view, see Mulgan (1972), 211. Mulgan derives from the uniqueness of Socrates' mission that Socrates alone may disobey the law if it conflicts with the command of "the god"; all others must obey the law if they fail to prevail when they seek to have it changed.

Athens

Socrates, as we have seen, claims to have been sent by the god to care for his city of Athens. Socrates describes Athens as the greatest city with the best reputation, *eudokiōtatēs*, for wisdom and strength (*Ap.* 29d7–8), yet likens it for his own part to "a great and well-born horse that is rather sluggish because of its great size and needs to be awakened by some gadfly" (30e3–5).

Socrates, as gadfly, awakens his city by admonishing the Athenian people privately and one at a time (*Ap.* 31b4) for caring about money, reputation, and honor rather than about prudence, truth, and the best state of their souls (*Ap.* 29d9–e2). As gadfly, he does not stop "settling down everywhere the whole day," awakening and persuading and reproaching "each one of you" (*Ap.* 30e7–31a1). Socrates' tendance of the city is thus distributive; his care for the city is his care for the individuals who compose it and whose souls require improvement. Socrates seeks to persuade each Athenian to care for himself, for "how he will be the best and most prudent possible," before he cares for "his own things" and, similarly, to care for "the city itself" before "the things of the city" (*Ap.* 36c5–8). By the "things of the city" Socrates no doubt intends its material prosperity and power, as well as the plays for power that take place within it (*Ap.* 36b8–9); these correspond roughly to the money, reputation, and honor for which the Athenians foolishly care rather than "for themselves." By "the city itself," then, Socrates must mean what is constitutive of the city's essence, its soul, so to speak. The soul of the city is its citizens—not its docks or walls. Socrates thus exhorts the Athenians to place the welfare of their own individual souls before their material welfare and to place the welfare of the soul of their city, the virtue of their fellow-citizens, before its material welfare.

Is there reason to think that Socrates regards Athens as a better city than others? We may observe, first, that Socrates apparently has no special regard for the policies by which Athens governs its citizens. We know, in fact, of one Athenian policy of which Socrates clearly disapproves: he takes exception to an Athenian law—a law unlike the law of "other human beings"—that requires that capital trials be concluded in a single day (*Ap.* 37a7–b1). Furthermore, we may note that Socrates fails to cite Athens' superiority when giving his reasons for refusing to propose exile. Why does he not take note at that moment of Athens' presumed greater tolerance for philosophy? Why does he not proclaim then that there is no other city comparably enlightened and free? What he says instead is that if

> you who are my fellow citizens were not able to bear my ways of spending time and my speeches, but that instead they have been quite grave and hateful to you, so that you are now seeking to be released from them, will others, then, bear them easily? (*Ap.* 37c7–d3)

Although Socrates is clearly disappointed and disillusioned with his fellow Athenians, he feels this way not because he expects better of them qua Athenians but because he expects better of them qua fellow citizens. Socrates says nothing in this passage to suggest that he believes Athens to be a safe place—or even a safer place than others—for philosophy. There is no implication in this passage that Athenians are more tolerant of philosophy than are the citizens of other cities; its intent is but to emphasize how much worse it is to be a philosopher among strangers than among one's own fellow citizens. There are, however, two other passages in Plato that might be thought to suggest that Athens is a place more supportive than others of freedom of expression. Let us look briefly at these.

The first occurs in the *Meno*, where Meno, after having been subjected to a round of elenchus, says to Socrates : "I think you are wise not to sail away from here [i.e., Athens] to go and stay elsewhere, for if you were to behave like this as a stranger in another city, you would be driven away for practising sorcery" (*Meno* 80b4–7).[47] I believe the correct interpretation of this remark is that a city, any city, is willing to exercise greater forbearance toward one of its own than toward a foreigner. Indeed, later on in the *Meno* Anytus ominously says: "I think, Socrates, that you easily speak ill of people. I would advise you, if you will listen to me, to be careful. Perhaps also in another city, and certainly here, it is easier to injure people than to benefit them" (*Meno* 94e3–95a1). What Anytus says clearly suggests that Athens is no more likely than other cities to regard benignly those who dare to speak critically of its past leaders and to impugn their excellence.

The second passage, one that is quite explicit about the greater tolerance of free speech in Athens, is found in the *Gorgias*, where Socrates says to Polus that Athens is the place in Greece "where there is the most liberty to speak" (*Gorg.* 461e1–2).[48] Let us observe, however, that greater liberty to speak need not translate into greater tolerance for philosophy; indeed, it is in this dialogue that Socrates shows himself to be fully aware that "anything might happen to anyone in this city" (*Gorg.* 521c8). Athens may be more receptive than other cities to political speech, speech that is "public" and directed toward the improvement of the city as conventionally understood, but to "private" philosophy, to speech directed toward the improvement of the individual soul, it is no more hospitable. It is, after all, under Athenian law that Socrates is executed for "corrupting the young." We may note that Athens is not welcoming to sophists either, and for similar reasons, as an early exchange between Socrates and Protagoras in the *Protagoras* confirms. When Socrates introduces the young Hippocrates to Protagoras, explaining that Hippocrates wishes to become his pupil, Socrates asks Protagoras whether "you think you ought to talk about this in private, or in the presence of others" (*Prot.* 316b8–c4), to which Protagoras responds:

> You show a very proper consideration for me, Socrates. . . . A foreigner who comes to great cities and persuades the best of the young men to abandon the society of others, kinsmen or acquaintances, old or young, and associate with himself for their own improvement—someone who does that has to be careful. He becomes as a result the object of not a small amount of resentment and hostility, and of many attacks. (*Prot.* 316c5–d3)[49]

47. Trans. Grube (1981).
48. Trans. Irwin (1979).
49. Trans. C.C.W. Taylor (1991).

Not only as foreigners are sophists unwelcome; they are unwelcome as well because of what they do. Their practice of "improving" young men is as objectionable to Athens as it is to other cities.[50]

We need not believe, then, that Socrates has some special regard for Athens. Nevertheless, he does seem to have special concern for his fellow citizens. Whereas he reproaches and examines anyone he happens to meet, foreigner or fellow Athenian (*Ap.* 23b5–6; 30a3–4), he attends more to the Athenians as they are "closer to me in kin," *genei* (*Ap.* 30a4). He even goes so far as to tell the "men of Athens," that is, the jury, that he loves them (*Ap.* 29d3). And Socrates certainly goes to very great lengths to care for the Athenians. Not only does he neglect the "things of the city worth caring about," but he neglects even his own family (*Ap.* 23b9; 31b2–3). His behavior, as he says, "does not seem human" (*Ap.* 31b1), for, without receiving any sort of remuneration, he abandons his personal affairs and his family, going to each Athenian privately "as a father or an older brother might do" (*Ap.* 31b4–5). The Athenians take the place of his family, as it were; it is toward them rather than toward his own children that Socrates adopts the role of father or older brother.[51]

It is important to recognize, however, that the Socratic devotion to the Athenians is not in any way a function of their merit. On the contrary, the Athenians must be in a fairly deplorable moral state if the demands of the job of reproaching and examining the misguided and complacent among them are so great that Socrates has no time to attend to his own family. Socrates' service to the god consumes all of his time and energy because there is so much work to be done—even just in Athens among his own fellow citizens.

Socrates, then, may have affection for the Athenians, but that affection coexists with a rather thoroughgoing disapproval of, first, their attachment to and preoccupation with things of no worth and, second, their inability to find it in their hearts to tolerate him but a short while longer. To be sure, Socrates thinks that people outside Athens would tolerate him far less than his own countrymen do. Yet, as we have seen, that is not because Athenians are more tolerant than others but rather because Socrates is an Athenian. Furthermore, although Socrates sees his divine mission as a mission to serve specifically Athens, and although he sees himself as the god's gift specifically to Athens, Socrates makes it clear that (1) no matter where he lived he would do the very same things he does in Athens, namely, examine himself and others and make speeches every day about virtue, and (2) even if he lived in exile, that is, out-

50. For the view that Socrates has a high opinion of Athens as a city that allows freedom of speech and has greater tolerance for philosophy than other cities, see Colson (1989), 40–43; Kraut (1984), 222. See also Dover (1975), 54: "Tolerance of the free expression of intellectual criticism was at most times and in most circumstances a predominant characteristic of Athenian societies." We consider in Chapter 6 how the Laws characterize Socrates' view of Athens and whether or not their characterization is consistent with the characterization proposed here.

51. It is interesting that Socrates at the end of the *Apology* (*Ap.* 41e1–42a2) beseeches his condemners to reproach his sons just as Socrates reproached them, his condemners. He tells them that if they do so, he and his sons will have been treated justly by them. Socrates, as we know, neglects his sons for the sake of reproaching the Athenians. It is the Athenians with whom he busies himself as if he were their father or older brother (*Ap.* 31b4–5). What would make things right, then, would be for the Athenians to assume toward Socrates' sons the role of father or older brother and to reproach them in his place.

side Athens, his silence there, no less than his silence in Athens, would constitute disobedience to the god (*Ap.* 37e–38a). It is likely, then, that Socrates' mission to Athens has less to do with the worthiness of Athens to receive this boon from the god than with the fact that Socrates, who is this boon, happens to live in Athens.[52] Athens is not, it seems, a city with special merit, its reputation notwithstanding.

Proper Conduct in Court

At the beginning of the *Apology*, Socrates directs the jury to attend to this: "whether the things I say are just or not; for this is the virtue of a judge, while that of an orator is to speak the truth" (*Ap.* 18a4–6). Socrates assures the court many times that what he says at his trial is indeed the truth (*Ap.* 17b, 20d, 22b, 24a, 28a, 31c, 31e, 33c, 34a). From the outset, Socrates notes that it is unseemly for someone of his age to come before the court "fabricating speeches like a youth" (*Ap.* 17c5). Socrates eschews "beautifully spoken speeches" (*Ap.* 17b9) like those used by his accusers, rhetoricians whose oratory is so persuasive that "I nearly forgot myself" (*Ap.* 17a2–3).

But it is not only falsehood—and beautiful speech masking falsehood—from which Socrates is determined to refrain. There are other forms of behavior, frequently engaged in by defendants, that Socrates shuns, such as begging and supplicating the judges with many tears and bringing one's children and other family members and friends before the judges in order to arouse their pity (*Ap.* 34c2–5). Although Socrates does apprise his judges of the fact that he is human and, hence, cannot be without some human family and that, indeed, besides having had human parents, he has three sons—one a youth and two still children—he nevertheless makes it quite clear that he would not bring his children or other family members or friends into court in order to beg the judges to acquit him (*Ap.* 34d1–8).

Socrates offers two reasons for his refusal to beg and cry and bring his children before the judges to do the same. The first is that such behavior is ignoble, shameful: a person who is distinguished, as Socrates is, one who has a reputation for being outstanding, ought not to disgrace himself, his judges, and his city in this way (*Ap.* 34d8–35b8). Socrates, it appears, is more determined to protect Athens' good name than Athens itself is.

We must be careful not to confuse the concern Socrates expresses in this passage about his own reputation with the many's concern for reputation and honor, a concern that arouses Socrates' unrelenting disapproval (*Ap.* 29e1). When most people care about reputation, what they want is to appear to be virtuous, whether or not they actually are. Socrates, by contrast, cares that he and others *be* virtuous. This said, it is nevertheless the case—and there is no difficulty about it—that if one is reputed to be virtuous in some way, one ought to strive not to dishonor that reputation. Socrates does not pursue reputation; rather, he seeks to protect a distinguished reputation that he believes he has—and he encourages others in similar circumstances to do the

52. The emphasis Socrates places in the *Apology* on his service specifically to Athens may be attributed, at least in part, to his need to offset the impression the jury has of him as a man who does not serve his city properly insofar as he stands aloof from the city's political life.

same. Surely it is noble to preserve one's good name by behaving genuinely virtuously. What Socrates wants the court to recognize is the shamefulness of sullying one's good name by behaving badly.

The second reason that Socrates will not beg and supplicate his judges and induce his children to do the same is that in a court of law judges ought to acquit a man not out of pity—as a favor (*Ap.* 35c4)—but because they judge the man innocent "according to the laws" (*Ap.* 35c5). Socrates identifies two ways in which a defendant might seek to "persuade" the judges,[53] but he approves of only one of these ways as constituting appropriate conduct in court: only one of these ways helps the judges judge as they ought.

The proper type of persuasion is the one Socrates expresses as to "teach and persuade" (*Ap.* 35c2). Rather than beg, says Socrates, the defendant ought to persuade by teaching. The notion of teaching suggests an appeal to the judges' intellect, to their reason.[54] This type of persuasion, which we shall call "teaching-persuasion," takes time. Since it is this type of persuasion in which Socrates takes himself to be engaged, it is no wonder that he complains about the Athenian law that confines even capital trials to one day: ". . . if you had a law like other human beings, not to judge anyone in a matter of death in one day alone, but over many, you would be persuaded" (*Ap.* 37a7–b1).

The *improper* way of persuading is expressed as to "persuade and force you by begging" (*Ap.* 35d2).[55] Begging persuades the judges by coercing them, that is, by bypassing the cognition by which they "judge" and instead compelling their decision by working on their emotions. Such "coercion-persuasion," as we shall call it, fails to instruct the judges with respect to the truth of the matter and so makes of justice a gift that judges bestow on those whom they favor. Ironically, rather than teach the judges the facts of the case as teaching-persuasion does, coercion-persuasion would be "teaching" them, says Socrates, "not to hold that there are gods" (*Ap.* 35d3–4). In what sense would coercion-persuasion "teach" the judges not to hold that there are gods? Minimally, it would do so in the sense that it would persuade the judges to break the oath they swore to the gods to judge according to the laws (*Ap.* 35d3). But more than that, such persuasion encourages the judges to behave without regard for justice. For Socrates, behavior of this kind constitutes the very worst form of impiety, since what "the god" requires of people most of all is that

---

53. The *Gorgias* makes a similar distinction between types of persuasion, that is, between teaching-persuasion and conviction-persuasion. See *Gorg.* 454c–455a.

54. We may note that at *Ap.* 18a4, Socrates directs the judges to "apply your *mind* to this" (*toutōi ton noun prosechein*): whether what I speak is just or not.

55. For the Greeks, persuasion is ordinarily sharply distinguished from violence. See Arendt (1958), 27–28. Socrates shows, however, that both persuasion and violence may be found within persuasion itself. Persuasion itself, Socrates maintains, comprises both instructive persuasion aimed at truth and coercive persuasion aimed at conviction without regard for truth. The latter is a form of violence. Other examples of the kind of persuasion that works on the emotions rather than on the intellect may be found at *Ap.* 37d–e, where it is said that the youths in foreign cities will "persuade their elders" to drive Socrates out of their city if he drives them away, and at *Rep.* II.365e–366a, where the gods are said to be open to persuasion by sacrifices and prayers. In the *Laws* at I.634b1 we find the expression "persuade through honors," *epeithen timais*.

they care for justice, virtue, and truth. Were Socrates to beg, then, he would, as he says, be accusing himself—by his very defense—of impiety (Ap. 35d4–5).

It is in light of these two ways of persuading that it becomes possible to understand why Socrates attaches considerable moral weight to the difference between actually begging and crying and bringing his children before the judges, on the one hand, and, on the other, *informing* the court that he, too, is born of human parents and has human offspring.

It is likely that by telling the court that he has parents and children just like other men, Socrates seeks to correct an impression that he reasonably supposes the judges have of him—that he is in some sense not really human and that he is certainly not human in the way they are human: Socrates' affairs are, after all, "uncommon" (Ap. 20c6); they place his life at risk (Ap. 28b4–5); and, insofar as they cause him to neglect his own affairs and, indeed, his own children, Socrates, as he himself remarks, "does not seem human" (Ap. 31b1). If, therefore, at this moment in the trial Socrates does not beg and cry and exhibit his children before the judges as other men do, indeed, as possibly some of the judges themselves have done even in less serious trials, he runs the risk of confirming the judges in their suspicions. Under these circumstances, Socrates must persuade, must *teach*, the judges that, despite his unusual behavior, he is human no less than they.[56] By speaking the facts of his humanness, Socrates does nothing to stir up the judges' emotion; what he does is seek to remove their prejudice against him.[57]

Could the same be said if Socrates were to make, literally, a spectacle of himself and of his children? Surely such displays appeal to the judges' pity—not to their rational discernment. Such appeals are objectionable as representing the kind of persuasion that is coercive rather than the kind that is instructive. They circumvent thought and impede judgment. By refusing to beg and cry and parade his children before the court, by refusing to stoop to coercion-persuasion, Socrates forgoes the only sort of appeal that might win him acquittal: emotional appeal.

The idea that begging and crying to save one's life is disgraceful and demeaning surfaces once more in the *Apology* after the jury accepts the prosecutors' proposed penalty of death over Socrates' proposed counterpenalty of thirty minae. Socrates, in proposing his counterpenalty, announces first what he merits—namely, the highest honor of being maintained at the city's expense—and then considers and rejects exile, though he intimates that the jury would perhaps "assess [exile] as my due" (Ap. 37c5). Since the jury is not about to reward him, it will have to either fine him—or kill him. When the vote comes in favoring the death penalty, Socrates addresses those who voted to condemn him and gives them his account of why he was convicted (Ap. 38d2–e2). As Socrates understands it, his conviction resulted from his not having resorted to the kinds of things these men find gratifying: "wailing and lamenting, and doing many other things unworthy of me" (Ap. 38d9–e1), rather than from a

---

56. We may note that in two of the cases in which Socrates seems no ordinary human being (Ap. 20c4–d1; 28b3–5), Socrates introduces the complaint against him by citing what someone might say. In the third case, Ap. 31b1–5, however, Socrates himself recognizes that his activity "does not seem human." On the significance of the expression "someone might say," see Strauss (1983), 44–50.

57. This is something Socrates does as well at the beginning of the *Apology* (Ap. 18a–23a).

lack of persuasive speeches. In other words, Socrates is convicted because whereas he engages only in teaching-persuasion, the kind of persuasion that uses speech and argument, his convicters respond favorably only to begging and crying (coercion-persuasion).[58]

Whereas Socrates refuses to do things "unworthy of me" (*Ap.* 38e1) and "unsuitable to a free man" (*Ap.* 38e3), the judges, it seems, do precisely those things through which, as Socrates earlier warned, they attach shame to themselves and to the city: rather than convict the man who engages "in these piteous dramas" (*Ap.* 35b7), they convict "the one who keeps quiet" (*Ap.* 35b8). Socrates has no regrets about the speech he makes in his own defense (*Ap.* 38e3–5). He conducts himself with integrity and dignity, neither fabricating false speeches nor crying and begging and having his children cry and beg in an attempt to escape death. Death, Socrates recognizes, is not difficult to avoid as long as there is no behavior that one regards as being beneath one's dignity. Socrates, however, will not do whatever it takes to avoid death; to him, it is not avoiding death but avoiding villainy that is of paramount importance.

The Penalties

When the verdict of guilty comes in, Socrates is given the opportunity, in accordance with Athenian law, to propose a counterpenalty to the death penalty sought by the prosecution. Socrates, as we have seen, recognizes that the court would probably accept exile as an alternative to death, for the court would perhaps assess exile as Socrates' due (*Ap.* 37c5). We shall be concerned in this section to clarify why Socrates prefers death to imprisonment and exile. Let us consider, then, first, Socrates' attitude toward death.

Socrates emphasizes the following three features of death: (1) whether death is good or bad is unknown to human beings (*Ap.* 29a4–b1); (2) death is not one of the "great evils"; the distinction of being a great evil belongs to the act of committing injustice (*Ap.* 30c6–d1); (3) death cannot really "harm" a good man, "harm" being understood in its technical sense of causing injury or corruption to the soul (*Ap.*

---

58. We may compare Socrates' actual experience in court as described in the *Apology* with the experience he imagines in the *Gorgias*. In the *Gorgias*, at 521d–e, we find Socrates saying the following: "This is because the speeches I make on each occasion do not aim at gratification but at what's best. They don't aim at what's most pleasant. And because I'm not willing to do those clever things you recommend, I won't know what to say in court. . . . For I'll be judged the way a doctor would be judged by a jury of children if a pastry chef were to bring accusations against him. Think about what a man like that, taken captive among these people, could say in his defense, if somebody were to accuse him and say, 'Children, this man has worked many great evils on you, yes, on you. He destroys the youngest among you by cutting and burning them, and by slimming them down and choking them he confuses them. He gives them the most bitter potions to drink and forces hunger and thirst on them. He doesn't feast you on a great variety of sweets the way I do!' What do you think a doctor, caught in such an evil predicament, could say? Or if he should tell them the truth and say, 'Yes, children, I was doing all those things in the interest of health', how big an uproar do you think such 'judges' would make? Wouldn't it be a loud one?" (trans. Zeyl [1987])

30c8–d1).[59] What follows from these three features of death is that it is more important to avoid injustice than to avoid death, since (a) unlike injustice, death may be, for all we know, not bad or even good, (b) death is not as great an evil as injustice, and (c) death does not "harm" one, but injustice does.

Anything else that Socrates says about death in the *Apology* must be consigned to the realm of what may be hoped. Indeed, Socrates speaks optimistically about death specifically within the context of comforting those who voted for his acquittal, his "judges." He indulges them by conversing with them for as long as possible (*Ap.* 39e4–5)—by taking the trouble to offer them heartening interpretations of the events of the day. Socrates construes as "something wondrous," *thaumasion ti* (*Ap.* 40a3), the fact that his divine sign did not oppose him at any time during the trial and did not interrupt any of his speeches; for his "judges'" sake, he assigns to this wondrous thing the following meaning: "it is likely," *kinduneuei* (*Ap.* 40b7), that what has occurred to him has turned out to be a good thing, and therefore it cannot be correct to assume that being dead is bad. Socrates assures his judges that the silence of the sign constitutes a "great proof" that his impending death is something good.[60] More assurances follow. Socrates presents to his acquitters two ways of conceiving death so that they see "how great a hope there is" (*Ap.* 40c4) that it is good: either death is dreamless sleep or death is a journey to another place, Hades, where one may perhaps find "inconceivable happiness," *amēchanon . . . eudaimonias* (*Ap.* 41c3–4). Of course, Socrates does not insist that either of his depictions of death is accurate: three times during the rapturous depiction of his second conception of death, Socrates inserts the phrase "if these things are true" or "if the things that are said are true" (*Ap.* 40e5–6, 41a8, 41c6–7). But Socrates' conceptions of death are not designed to be accurate; they are designed to lift the spirits of his unhappy supporters. Finally, Socrates encourages the "judges" to adopt the following belief: that there is nothing bad for a good man, whether living or dead; that the gods are not without concern about a good man's troubles; that Socrates' present troubles have not arisen of their

---

59. Socrates does not explicitly say that by "harm" he means harm to one's soul. But since he does not deny that bad things can be done to a good man but does deny that *great* evils can be done to a good man (*Ap.* 30c7–d5), it would seem that if the bad things are things that affect the body, such things as killing, banishing, and deprivation of the rights and privileges of citizenship, then *great* evils can only be things that affect the soul. Socrates regularly reprimands the Athenians for caring about what matters little, about such things as money, reputation, and honor, rather than about what is really important—prudence, truth, and the state of one's soul. Is it not likely, then, that great evils would be those things that adversely affect the soul?

60. At most, the *daimonion's* inaction is a sign that Socrates conducted himself as he ought; for the sake of those who voted for his acquittal, however, Socrates interprets it to mean that death is a good thing for him. Yet, as Socrates has already said, and as he states yet again at the dialogue's close, he does not know if death is good or bad even for him. We may note that the "great proof," the *mega tekmērion* (*Ap.* 40c1), of the sign's not having appeared is not the kind of proof that Socrates values, for it is not a rational argument, a *logos*. It is, rather, a "proof in deed," a sign that requires no hard thinking, the kind of proof that pleases the many, the kind of proof that is ultimately vulgar (*Ap.* 32a8). One need only recall the *Phaedo* to see how Socrates uses *logoi* when comforting his *philosophical* friends concerning the nature of death. With respect to the nature of death, however, neither the "great proof" of the *Apology* nor the reasoned arguments of the *Phaedo* can do more than encourage optimism. The nature of death cannot be known.

own accord (*Ap*. 41c9–d3).[61] If the judges can trust that the gods ensure the well-being of good men, they will no doubt "be of good hope" (*Ap*. 41c8) with respect to Socrates' imminent death.

In effect, however, what Socrates offers those who voted for his acquittal is not reason to hope that death is not a bad thing, but reason to hope that *for Socrates* death will be not a bad but rather a good thing. First, the sign that fails to make an appearance is Socrates' private sign; its silence can only signify that *Socrates* is not headed for something bad, that *he* is "about to do something good" (*Ap*. 40c3). Thus, when Socrates concludes from his sign's absence that it is likely that those who assume that it is bad to be dead do not make the correct supposition, what he surely intends is that there are no grounds for the belief that to be dead is bad for everyone. Second, when Socrates describes life in Hades, he conjures up a world in which he would thrive: who else would be encouraged by the prospect of (1) meeting dead men who were unjustly judged during their lifetimes and (2) practicing elenchus to eternity? And third, even the idea that the gods take care of good men likewise says more about how Socrates is likely to fare upon his death than about the effects of death generally.[62]

To Socrates himself it is clear, *dēlon* (*Ap*. 41d4),[63] that it is better now for him to be dead because death will release him from troubles (*Ap*. 41d4–5); indeed, as he says, that is the reason his sign did not come to him. Socrates himself, we may observe, does not take refuge in the notions with which he comforts his "judges": he does not assure *himself* that the gods will care for him or that he will enjoy endless examination of others who have died. Moreover, although Socrates is confident that it is better now for him to be dead and released from troubles, he does not link this confidence to confidence in the goodness of being dead itself. We may note, too, that all that the *daimonion*'s inactivity confirms for him is that to be dead now is "better," *beltion* (*Ap*. 41d5)—not that it is good, *agathon*, as earlier at *Ap*. 40b7. As the dialogue draws to a close, Socrates, having conversed with his "friends" (*Ap*. 40a1) for as long as possible and having calmed the fears of those sympathetic jurors distressed by his impending death, reaffirms at last what he really believes—that to human beings, at any rate, it is unclear, *adēlon* (*Ap*. 42a4), whether it is better to live or die.[64]

---

61. I suggest that there should be a comma, not a semicolon, between *oude ameleitai hupo theōn ta toutou pragmata* (Ap. 41d2) and *oude ta ema nun apo tou automatou gegonen* (Ap. 41d3) so that the point about Socrates' present troubles' not having arisen of their own accord is connected to the point that the gods are not without concern about a good man's troubles: Socrates' troubles have not arisen of their own accord *because* the gods concern themselves about the troubles of good men.

62. Socrates even says: ". . . since especially for myself, *emoige kai autōi*, spending time there would be wondrous" (*Ap*. 41a8–b1). Socrates could not, and does not now seek to, convince the judges that what makes him happy—endless philosophical conversation after death—will make them happy as well. His aim is to assure them that he will be happy.

63. Rather than a comma between *gegonen* (*Ap*. 41d3) and *alla moi dēlon esti touto* (Ap. 41d3–4), I suggest a period: up to the *alla* Socrates is speaking about what the judges ought to believe; he now contrasts that which is clear to *him* with what the "judges" ought to believe.

64. I leave undecided whether the correct reading of the final sentence of the dialogue is "Which of us goes to a better thing is unclear to everyone except the god," *plēn ē tōi theōi*, or "Which of us goes to a better thing is unclear to everyone unless the god," *plēn ē tōi theōi* (42a4–5).

If it is not clear to Socrates that death is good, why *is* it clear to him that it is "better" now for him "to be dead and to have been released from troubles"? Specifically, what are the "troubles," *pragmata*, from which he believes death will release him? Socrates does not say. But what he has said—and said repeatedly—is that, regardless of what death turns out to be, it cannot fail to be better than injustice. Is not "injustice," then, the "troubles" from which Socrates believes death will free him?[65] May we not reasonably conclude that Socrates is now prepared to die because he believes that in his current circumstances it is through death, and only through death, that he can avoid "troubles," in the sense of injustice?[66] But why would Socrates be convinced that death affords him his only means for avoiding injustice?; why would he regard it as unjust to propose some reasonable alternative to death such as imprisonment or exile?

For Socrates, the injustice of proposing imprisonment or exile is related to the following two facts: (1) that he would be *proposing*—not merely submitting to—these punishments and (2) that these punishments are "bad." Let us consider the significance of each of these facts in turn:

First, Socrates is concerned above all to avoid committing injustice, including injustice to himself. By proposing as a penalty for himself something bad, he implies that he merits something bad. We recall Socrates' recognition of the likelihood that the Athenians, were he to propose exile, would probably be willing to accept this proposed penalty as an assessment of his desert (*Ap.* 37c5). Since, however, Socrates does not in fact merit something bad, for him to propose something bad is to do himself an injustice. Indeed, Socrates' first impulse is to propose as his "penalty" something good, something wonderful, in order to reflect what he believes is his true merit. Socrates does not know whether death is good or bad; it might be bad. For that reason, it is unlikely that he would have proposed death for himself were he in a position to do so. But he is not in such a position: death is an externally imposed penalty, and hence to accept it is to suffer injustice; it is not to commit it.[67]

---

65. As Socrates shifts from offering comfort to his "judges," assuring them that the gods are not without care for his "troubles," to stating what he believes—namely, that it is better now for him to be dead and to have been released from "troubles"—it is likely that the sense of "troubles" shifts as well, becoming less conventional and more philosophical.

66. At *Ap.* 39a6–b4 Socrates notes the far greater difficulty of escaping villainy, *ponēria*, than of escaping death. Socrates contrasts his fate of being "caught" by death with the fate of his accusers of being "caught" by evil, *kakias*. Insofar, then, as Socrates is caught by death, he is not caught by injustice: death releases him, as it were, from its grasp. See Calef (1992), 288–95, for a similar view of what Socrates means by being released from "troubles."

67. Some scholars have sought to make the case that Socrates' acceptance of the death penalty is tantamount to his committing injustice with himself as its victim. See, for example, Colson (1989), 35, and Woozley (1979), 58. I do not think this is a tenable position. Socrates makes it clear that it is Meletus and Anytus and those who vote against him who are the ones committing the injustice. They are "worthy of blame" (*Ap.* 41e1). Also, he contrasts himself, who is caught by death, with his condemners, who are caught by villainy (*Ap.* 39b1–4). As a further confirmation that Socrates does not regard accepting death as a form of committing injustice, we may note that in the *Crito* he sees himself as having to choose between the "committing of injustice," on the one hand, and dying "by staying here and keeping quiet or . . . suffer[ing] anything else whatever," on the other. See *Cr.* 48d4–5. If we consider in this connection the *Gorgias*'s lengthy discussion of committing injustice as compared with suffering it, it becomes even more evident that Socrates' condition is one of suffering injustice.

By contrast, Socrates *is* in a position to propose an alternative to the death penalty. If he *proposes* as a penalty something that is bad, however, then he not merely suffers injustice but actually commits it. It is therefore critical that he determine with respect to each of the counterpenalties he is considering whether it is or is not a bad thing.

Second, Socrates is not in the dark about imprisonment and exile in the way he is about death. He cannot conjure up at will visions of the joys of prison and exile—as he can of death—because he knows better (Ap. 37b7–8). The prospect of prison, of "being enslaved to the authority that is regularly established there, the Eleven" (Ap. 37c1–2), is quite repugnant to him. Nor does exile hold any attraction for Socrates: he is an old man and does not relish "exchanging one city for another, always being driven out" (Ap. 37d5–6). Since Socrates has no intention of abandoning his philosophical activity in exile, of "being silent and keeping quiet" (Ap. 37e3)—to do so would be to disobey the god and to live a life not worth living—it is quite certain that he will be subjected to the indignity of being driven from city to city, whether by the youth if he drives them away or by their elders if he does not (Ap. 37d7–e2).[68]

Since Socrates regards both imprisonment and exile as bad—and bad for quite pedestrian reasons, namely, loss of freedom in the one case and the indignity of being driven from place to place in the other[69]—he cannot propose either of them

68. It is not clear that there are no conditions under which Socrates would have proposed exile as a counterpenalty. It is conceivable that if he were younger and if there were cities receptive even to his particularly abrasive brand of philosophy, exile would have been acceptable to him: as long as exile is not something bad, he would be committing no injustice against himself in suggesting it as his desert. See my discussion of the fine that Socrates does propose.

69. Scholars have sought to explain Socrates' reluctance to choose imprisonment or exile by suggesting that these penalties would have interfered with Socrates' divine mission of practicing philosophy. But Socrates states quite plainly his objections to these potential penalties, and in the case of neither of them does he object to the penalty because it would render him unable to philosophize. Prison is objectionable because he would be enslaved. In exile he would be driven constantly from city to city. The reason Socrates fully expects foreign cities to be inhospitable to him in this way is that he has every intention of continuing to practice there the kind of philosophy he practices in Athens. For the view that Socrates rejects exile because it will impede his practice of philosophy, the activity that makes his life worth living, see Colson (1989), 37–53, and Kraut (1984), 89, n. 48. Kraut says: ". . . he thinks death preferable to the life of a homeless and rejected wanderer, since as a wanderer he could not carry out his philosophical mission." Socrates' point, however, is not that as a wanderer he could not carry out his philosophical mission; on the contrary, it is that because he *will* carry out his philosophical mission that he will be a wanderer. Had Socrates wished to say that prison and exile were unacceptable to him because they would interfere with his practice of philosophy, he surely could have; he cites just that reason for his refusal to go into exile *and remain quiet* (Ap. 37e3–38a8). For the view that Socrates rejects imprisonment because he believes the prison authorities would deny him the possibility of "holding moral conversations," see Kraut (1984), 38–39, n. 21.

There is one reason for thinking that Socrates' antipathy toward prison and exile must be connected with a belief of his that these penalties will somehow interfere with his practice of philosophy. Since Socrates says of these penalties that he knows, *oida* (Ap. 37b8), them to be bad, and since earlier he had said that what he knows to be bad and shameful is to disobey one's better, whether god or human being (Ap. 29b6–7), it seems to follow that Socrates must think that these penalties threaten his obedience to the god by threatening his practice of philosophy. In other words, if Socrates did not think these penalties would cause him to disobey the god by causing him to abandon or neglect his practice of philosophy, how would he "know" them to be bad when what he knows to be bad is to disobey the god? There is a very simple way out of this difficulty that I believe is borne out by Plato's texts. Since

as an alternative to the death penalty. As we have seen, for Socrates to propose something bad is for him to commit injustice against himself, for it is to say of himself that he deserves something bad when he does not. Let us note that, by refusing to propose either imprisonment or exile, Socrates is not in any way expressing a preference for death over imprisonment and exile. What he is expressing is a preference for submitting to death over *proposing* imprisonment or exile, a preference for suffering injustice over committing it—even against himself. There are only two things Socrates can propose without committing injustice against himself: (1) something good (hence the proposal that he be given free meals at the Prytaneum) and (2) something neutral (hence the proposal of a fine). We may observe that the good thing that Socrates proposes is not a "moral" good but a material one, just as the bad things he refuses to propose involve not moral evils but material ones. What Socrates believes he deserves is something he would enjoy; what he believes he does not deserve is anything he would abhor. Since money means nothing to him one way or the other—having a bit more of it would not be nearly as nice as being honored with free meals, and having less of it would not trouble him in the least[70]— he can propose a fine and do so with complete equanimity, having no cause to fear that, in doing so, he does himself an injustice. Moreover, since by proposing a fine Socrates does himself no injustice, Socrates can say that proposing a fine will not harm him (*Ap.* 38b2). The only real harm is harm to the soul, and harm to the soul is brought about only by committing injustice. Were the court to accept Socrates' proposal of a fine in place of death, he would be spared both the committing of injustice and the suffering of harm.

Not surprisingly, the court rejects Socrates' proposed counterpenalty. Unlike exile that would physically remove Socrates from Athens, and unlike imprisonment that would ensure that only those who deliberately sought out Socrates' company would have to endure it, a fine would do nothing to rid Athens of the thorn in its side. Socrates attributes the rejection of his proposal, as we have already seen, to his not having gratified the jury by wailing and lamenting. Since, however, he prefers to die rather than to have saved his life by engaging in such degrading behavior and since he prefers to suffer rather than to commit injustice, he agrees now to "abide by my penalty" (*Ap.* 39b6).

---

this is not the place to defend the solution I propose, however, I simply propose it here without defense. There is a difference between the technical term *oida* and the colloquial term *eu oida*. Socrates "knows," in the technical sense of "know," that it is bad and shameful to disobey one's better, but he "knows well," in a colloquial, nontechnical, sense, that prison and exile are bad. One "knows well" through ordinary, everyday experience and through "common sense"; "knowing well" implies no special wisdom. It would be odd indeed to say that experts "know well" how to perform their respective *technai*. What Socrates "knows" in its technical sense, he "knows" through his own special wisdom. I do not mean to say that *oida* or *epistamai* is never used alone yet nontechnically. These terms are used nontechnically when there can be no doubt that the kind of knowing is ordinary, common-sense knowing: Socrates readily admits, for example, that he knows, as does everyone, many trivial things— without expertise (see *Euthyd.* 293b8: "but small ones," *smikra ge*). But I do mean to say that *eu oida* is never used technically.

70. A fine would be bad only if it involved imprisonment until paid. But Socrates' friends are willing to stand as guarantors that it will be paid so that Socrates will not be forced to endure imprisonment.

Hades

Since Socrates insists that he does "not know sufficiently about the things in Hades" to be able to say for certain what death will be like or even whether it is good or bad (*Ap.* 29b5; b8–9), we would be well advised not to take too literally his depiction of Hades in the *Apology*.[71] As we saw earlier, Socrates himself does not stand by the accuracy of his portrayal. Nevertheless, his depiction is instructive in that it shows what Socrates thinks might be hoped for in life after death.[72]

The first advantage Hades has over Athens is the quality of its judges. In Athens the judges are only men "who claim to be judges"; in Hades the judges will be "judges in truth" (*Ap.* 41a1–2). Second, in Hades one would be able to associate with truly great poets: Orpheus, Musaeus, Hesiod, and Homer (*Ap.* 41a6–7); the reader suspects that Socrates means to contrast these poets of the past with the disappointing poets he has tested in his investigation into the meaning of the oracle, poets unable to speak intelligently even about their own poems (*Ap.* 22b6–8). Third, Socrates would have the opportunity to compare his experience of having been judged unjustly with that of ancient men who were similarly victims of unjust judgment, such as Palamedes and Telemonian Ajax (*Ap.* 41b1–4). But most wonderful of all, Socrates would be able to conduct his philosophical investigations in Hades with the likes of Agamemnon, Odysseus, Sisyphus, and countless others, both men and women (*Ap.* 41b5–c2); this activity would be for Socrates "inconceivable happiness," and he anticipates engaging in it in Hades without fear of being killed.

Of the aspects of life in Hades as Socrates describes it, only one has any chance at all of appealing to the "judges" in Socrates' trial: meeting and conversing with the great poets. The other aspects—better judges, the opportunity to compare experiences with others who were unjustly judged, and, of course, the possibility of unending elenctic examination—are all attractive specifically to Socrates. As noted in the previous section, Socrates designs his portrayal of life in Hades so that it will assure the men who voted for his acquittal not that *they* will be happy after death but that Socrates will. Indeed, three features of Socrates' portrayal of Hades relate to his present predicament of having been unjustly condemned by unjust judges: (1) that the judges in Hades will be "judges in truth," (2) that Socrates will meet in Hades others who experienced injustice with whom Socrates can compare his own experience, and (3) that at least in Hades one is not killed for practicing philosophy; everyone in Hades is already dead.

In his representation of Hades to his "judges," in his kind effort to give his "friends" (*Ap.* 40a1) reason to hope that there could be no "greater good" (*Ap.* 40e6–7) for Socrates than to descend to Hades at his death, Socrates clearly encourages their imagination to dwell on Hades' more attractive features, and particularly on its promising prospects for him. This deliberately selective portrayal of Hades is no doubt

---

71. We may note as well that Socrates says three times in the *Apology* that he does not know anything about what is *hupo gēs*, "under the earth": *Ap.* 18b8, 19b5, 23d6.

72. Socrates' depiction in the *Apology* of the afterlife is not at all like the account he gives of it in the *Phaedo*. The *Apology* contains no hint that death is that final release of the soul from the fetters of the body, a release for which the philosopher strives throughout his life.

intended to distract the judges from the full picture of what Hades is likely to be. For even on Socrates' account, not only the illustrious dead but all the dead are in Hades (*Ap.* 40e6). And if all the dead are in Hades, then when Socrates joins them he will encounter, besides the just judges, unjust ones; besides the great poets, the mediocre; besides those who suffered injustice, those who committed it; besides the extraordinary men and women who will serve as subjects for Socratic elenchus, the countless ordinary ones.[73] How much better, then, is Hades really likely to be than, say, Athens? Indeed, as Socrates notes with some sarcasm,[74] the reason philosophers do not get killed in Hades is that the dead in Hades cannot die again.[75]

Let us review briefly the beliefs of Socrates in the *Apology* as they have come to light in this chapter.

Socrates is fully committed to justice and to the practice of philosophy. Nothing, not even life itself, takes precedence over justice and philosophy. Socrates will therefore disobey any authority and any command, whether legal or not, if he believes it to be unjust or to represent an obstacle to philosophical pursuits. According to Socrates, the sole question to be asked before one acts is whether one's contemplated act is just. If there is a human moral superior who can say what justice demands, one must obey him in the interests of justice. If there is not, then one must obey the god, that is, one must philosophize, one must apply one's reason assiduously to questions of moral conduct, doing only what one's careful rational reflection determines that justice requires. The god does not tell one what to do on individual occasions; the god tells one to be just and to practice philosophy.

In light of these convictions, Socrates maintains that a defendant in court must refrain from untruth and from such practices as crying and lamenting and conscripting one's children to cry and lament as well, because these practices prevent the judges from exercising "judgment," compelling them instead to dispense justice as a favor to those who arouse in them feelings of pity and who please them.

Socrates does not know—and believes that no human being knows—the nature of death and whether it is good or bad. Yet, even if he knew death to be bad, he would prefer to accept a death penalty imposed upon him by the court rather than to impose upon himself the penalty of imprisonment or exile. Since he finds both imprisonment and exile repugnant, he would be committing injustice against himself were he to propose either of these penalties: he would be saying that he deserves something bad when he does not. Since in accepting the death penalty—even if death is bad—he merely suffers injustice, whereas in proposing imprisonment or exile he commits injustice, he prefers death.

---

73. Socrates acknowledges that his examination will reveal those who merely think themselves wise but really are not as well as those who really are (*Ap.* 41b6–7).

74. Dyer and Seymour (1885), 113, say this remark by Socrates is "spoken humorously and with a thrust at those who voted for his death." Also Kitchel (1898), 149: "The sarcasm is heightened to the utmost."

75. We may compare Socrates' hope in the *Apology* that in Hades he will be with better judges and better men generally with his hope in the *Phaedo* that upon his death he will be with *gods* who are "both wise and good." In the *Phaedo*, Socrates is less certain that he will dwell with good men after death than that he will dwell with good gods. Perhaps the gods he hopes to encounter are a metaphor for the Forms (*Phaedo* 63b5–c7).

Socrates shows great concern for his fellow Athenians, devoting himself to their moral improvement to the neglect of his own affairs and children. In Socrates' view, however, the city of Athens, despite its reputation for wisdom and strength, is not genuinely distinguished in any way. Moreover, it has a bad law that other cities do not have, a law that stipulates that a trial must be concluded in one day, even when the defendant faces a possible sentence of death.

3

Running the Risk for Friendship

> . . . but what he who is a friend is we have not yet
> been able to discover.
>
> Plato, *Lysis* 223b7–8,
> trans. Bolotin (1979)

Crito is a man of about the same age as Socrates, a member of the same deme, Alopece (*Ap.* 33d9), and a wealthy man (*Euthyd.* 306d). He figures importantly in the last days of Socrates' life: he is present at the trial and is one of those who stand as guarantors of Socrates' proposed fine of thirty minae; he is a regular visitor in Socrates' prison cell; it is he who tends to Socrates' needs at the final moments of his friend's life. In this chapter our aim is to become further acquainted with Plato's Crito, the Crito whose friendship for Socrates and whose generous expression of that friendship grace the Platonic dialogue named after him. Our main source is the early part of the *Crito* (up until 46a5), but we consult also the *Phaedo* and the end of the *Euthydemus* (from 304b6 on).[1]

Crito as Socrates' Friend

There can be no doubt that Crito is Socrates' deeply devoted friend. Not only does he attend Socrates' trial, stand surety for Socrates' fine, and visit him regularly in prison, but he appears in the *Crito* distraught to the point of sleeplessness (*Cr.* 43b3–4). Of all Socrates' companions, Crito, as he himself observes, will bear "most gravely

---

1. Even if the *Phaedo* and *Euthydemus* were written later than the *Crito*, there is no reason to think that Plato would not have kept Crito's character constant through the various dialogues in which he portrays him.

39

of all" (*Cr.* 43c7–8) the news portending the imminence of Socrates' death. For Crito, Socrates' death is nothing short of a "calamity," *sumphora*, for, as he puts it, it will deprive him of "such a companion as I will never discover again" (*Cr.* 44b8).

Crito acknowledges, however, a second dimension to his "calamity" as he conceives it: besides losing an irreplaceable friend, he will acquire a shameful reputation for preferring money to friends. It is this second dimension, the matter of reputation, that is at the heart of the discussion in the *Crito*:[2] whereas not another word is heard in the dialogue about Crito's losing a very dear and valued friend, we find Crito, both at the beginning of his speech (*Cr.* 44b–c; 44d) and at its conclusion (*Cr.* 45e–46a),[3] expressing and defending his anxiety over the potential loss of his good name, and we find Socrates, both in his own name and through the speech of the Laws, responding to that anxiety. What are we to think, then, of Crito's first concern? Must we regard it as unimportant, or, worse, as insincere? Perhaps not. Perhaps we are meant to surmise that Crito devoted earlier meetings to pleading his cause on the grounds of the irreparable loss he and Socrates' other friends would suffer upon Socrates' death; after all, the *Crito* is certainly not meant to be seen as Crito's first attempt to persuade Socrates to escape.[4] Moreover, since of Crito's two concerns only his preoccupation with reputation is capable of sparking a philosophical, rather than a merely sentimental, exchange between him and Socrates, is it not to be expected that this concern would be the dominant one in the *Crito*? Indeed, despite the greater prominence the dialogue accords to Crito's concern about his reputation, the fact remains that a concern for reputation could never adequately account for the profound misery and pain that Crito experiences at this moment; only Crito's love for his friend could do that.

2. Among those scholars who believe that Crito is preoccupied with reputation are Allen (1980), 67–68; Young (1974), 56 and 81, n. 5; Friedländer (1964), II, 175. E. West (1989), 72, is among those who give greater weight to Crito's caring about losing a friend. West, 72, argues that Crito's "concern about reputation springs from the slander which now threatens the life of his friend." She believes that this is the implication of *Cr.* 44d1–5: "But surely you see that it is necessary, Socrates, to care about the opinion of the many. The present situation now makes it clear that the many can produce not the smallest of evils but, I dare say, the greatest, if someone is slandered among them." I do not think West's reading of this passage is correct: the passage does not show that Crito's concern about reputation *springs from* the slander threatening Socrates' life; rather, Crito in this passage uses the fact that the many's slander now threatens Socrates' life to justify, and to convince Socrates of the validity of, his concern about reputation. West further believes that Burnet (1924), 179, shares her view, but, as I read Burnet, he does not. What Burnet says is: "Crito means that the condemnation of Socrates proves the danger of *diabolē*. . . ." One cannot infer from this statement that Burnet would agree with West that Crito's concerns about reputation *spring from* the condemnation of Socrates.

3. "So see to it, Socrates, that these things be not shameful as well as bad for both you *and for us*" (*Cr.* 46a4). In Plato, an idea to which an interlocutor keeps returning is an idea firmly rooted in him. In the *Euthyphro*, for example, no matter in what direction Socrates leads Euthyphro in their joint attempt to define "holiness," Euthyphro comes back to a conception of holiness connected with pleasing the gods. In the *Gorgias*, Polus cannot get away from the notion that being able to do as one pleases is what is most desirable.

4. That the meeting described in the *Crito* is not Crito's first attempt to persuade Socrates to escape appears to be implied by *Cr.* 44b6: "Obey me, even now." Adam (1888), 28, and Kitchel (1898), 152, make this point. Further evidence may perhaps be adduced from *Cr.* 48e1–3: "But if not, blessed man, then stop telling me the same argument again and again"; and perhaps also from *Cr.* 46a4–5: ". . . there is no longer time to take counsel—but to have taken counsel."

In hopes of staving off the double calamity he so dreads, Crito—along with Socrates' other friends—is willing to risk quite a lot for Socrates' sake; Crito mentions in particular the possibility that as a result of the informers' troublemaking, those who abet Socrates' escape will be compelled "to lose either our whole substance [i.e., property] or a lot of money, or even to suffer something else besides this" (Cr. 44e6–7). Crito urges Socrates to set aside whatever fears he may have with regard to what might befall his friends, "for surely it is just for us to save you and run this risk, and one still greater than this, if need be" (Cr. 45a1–3).[5] He then proceeds to assure Socrates that indeed he has no cause to fear: the informers are easily and cheaply bought off and there is plenty of money, both Athenian and foreign, to cover expenses. Furthermore, Crito continues, Socrates need not trouble himself about having no place to go: Thessaly is available to him. Crito has friends there; it is a place where Socrates will be regarded as important, where he will be safe, and where no one will cause him pain.

Crito, then, has gone to great lengths to ensure the well-being of his friend. His devotion is abundantly evident both in the risks he willingly assumes—loss of property and money or even something worse[6]—and in the care he takes in planning the escape, from calculating what financial resources are required and making certain that they are available to preparing a place for Socrates to go when he escapes. Yet there is something oddly amiss in Crito's efforts: he either does not see, does not quite believe, or does not fully grasp that Socrates is not like everyone else, that what Socrates fears is likely to be different from what others fear, that if Socrates is reluctant to escape he must have reasons that are beyond the reach of the quite conventional considerations to which Crito alludes. Indeed, when Socrates admits to Crito that "I am worrying over the prospect of these things, tauta" (namely, the things that Crito has just mentioned) and hastens to add, "and of many others" (Cr. 45a4–5), Crito responds: "Then do not fear these things, tauta" (Cr. 45a6), utterly neglecting Socrates' "many others." Crito does not ask what these "many others" are; does he even notice that Socrates has mentioned them? Furthermore, in proposing Thessaly as a reasonable place for Socrates to go, Crito apparently overlooks the quite extraordinary concern—a concern that he himself heard Socrates express at the trial—responsible for Socrates' refusal to propose exile: that in proposing exile he would be committing an injustice against himself. Does Crito actually think, as he suggests, that Socrates was loath to propose exile just because he "would not know what to do" with himself (Cr. 45b8)?[7] And can Crito really

---

5. The term "just" as Crito uses it here clearly means "right" or what ought to be done. The extension of the term "just" contracts when justice is but one virtue among several. See n. 31, on Cr. 45c5–6.

6. It seems that in the latter part of the Laws' speech, at Cr. 53b1–3, the Laws identify the "something else besides this" that Crito and Socrates' other friends might have to suffer as "being exiled and being deprived of their city."

7. What Crito says is: ". . . and do not let it be hard for you to accept, as you were saying in court, because you would not know what to do with yourself if you left" (Cr. 45b7–8). Congleton (1974), 441, takes this statement of Crito's as evidence of his "lack of both understanding and steadfastness." Adam (1888), 35, like Congleton, takes Crito to be freeing Socrates from remaining true to what he had said at his trial: "It may have seemed little to Crito that Socrates should be false to what was said in the excitement of his defense . . ." (my emphasis). Although I agree that Crito lacks both understanding and steadfastness, I think that his intent here is not to make light of consistency but only to assure Socrates that his earlier concern (at least as Crito interprets it) that he would not find a welcoming haven in exile but would be driven from place to place is unfounded.

believe that all Socrates requires is assurances that he will be thought important, will be safe, and will not be harmed? Is he unaware that Socrates would need to be assured that Thessaly is a place where he can freely practice philosophy?

Indeed, we may wonder generally how Crito can harbor hope that Socrates will be persuaded by the arguments he presents, arguments that stress the importance of the opinion of the many, the need to safeguard reputation, and the obligation a man has to his children. Can Crito, who has been exposed to Socrates' views in daily conversation and at his trial, fail to know that Socrates thinks the many impotent and of no real consequence; that Socrates has contempt for those who value reputation more than fact; that Socrates is not unwilling to neglect his family for the sake of a higher end? What must Crito have been thinking all these years, and especially during the trial, as he heard Socrates espouse his distinctive and unconventional views? Perhaps he simply regarded those idiosyncratic views as endearing quirks, as a bit of foolishness in his friend to be good-naturedly indulged by those fond of him.[8] Perhaps it never even occurred to Crito that Socrates' own commitment to his peculiar views might be so strong that he would stake his life on them. What Crito must surely assume is that in matters of life and death, Socrates would not defy manifest common sense for the sake of such nonsense.

If it is with thoughts such as these that Crito enters Socrates' cell to persuade him to escape,[9] then the plans he makes and the arguments he offers are signs of his generosity and sincere good will. Yet they are also signs that Crito does not really know his friend. And since he does not really know his friend, he cannot appreciate the extent to which his efforts are misguided and futile. Because he so egregiously underestimates the depth of Socrates' commitment to his moral principles, he cannot quite grasp that the help he offers is unwanted. In order to understand more clearly why

---

8. We may observe that in the *Crito*, once Socrates takes the lead in the discussion, Crito readily agrees to everything he says. Crito seems unaware of the implications of what Socrates says. Perhaps for that reason he does not quite recognize the extent to which he and Socrates disagree fundamentally in their moral perspectives. Crito agrees, for example, that only the expert's opinion is to be followed; it is only when Socrates raises an objection in the name of the "someone" who might say "but the many are able to kill us" that Crito is alerted to the fact that he disagrees (*Cr.* 48a10–11). And even this disagreement with what he agreed to earlier is expressed now as *agreement* with what someone might say. Similarly, throughout the argument that stretches from *Cr.* 49a4 to *Cr.* 50a4–5, Crito offers no resistance to anything Socrates says—until it is time to draw the conclusion, at which point Crito says that he does not understand. If Crito as participant in a philosophical conversation raises no objections and voices no disagreement even when his own views are clearly not in accord with those Socrates defends, how likely is it that he would object to Socrates' views as he hears them expressed to others?

9. It is clear that this is not the first time that Crito has tried to persuade Socrates to escape; it is also clear that he tries now yet again to persuade him, despite having already been apprised by Socrates in no uncertain terms of Socrates' decision to remain in prison. For unless Socrates had already told Crito that he was unwilling to escape, how could Crito have said at the very beginning of the plea he makes in the *Crito*, before Socrates in any way indicated at this meeting where he stands on the matter: "For the many will not be persuaded that you yourself were not willing to go away from here" (*Cr.* 44c3–4); how would he have known of Socrates' reluctance to flee? (Since Crito is himself one of the many, it is not surprising that he, too, despite what he has been told, is not quite persuaded that Socrates is unwilling to escape.)

Crito goes to so much trouble to offer Socrates help that he neither wants nor can permit, we need to become better acquainted with the unphilosophical Crito.[10]

The Unphilosophical Crito

In this section we look at the indications Plato gives us — in the *Crito*, but also in the *Phaedo* and *Euthydemus* — of Crito's unphilosophical nature. In the *Crito* there are three such indications. First, Crito is seen to regard Socrates' impending death as calamitous, whereas Socrates is serene in the face of it (*Cr.* 43b3–c3). Socrates' attitude is the "philosophical" one: it is the result of, on the one hand, his recognition that he does not know the nature of death and, on the other, his preference for death over injustice. Crito's attitude is unphilosophical: it is born of what Socrates calls in the *Apology* "that reproachable ignorance of supposing that one knows what one does not know" (*Ap.* 24b1–2).[11] Second, Crito does not wish to take counsel (*Cr.* 46a4–5); he wants only to be obeyed. Third, Socrates avoids using the term "soul" in Crito's presence, referring instead to "that which becomes better by the just and is destroyed by the unjust" (*Cr.* 47d4–5; 47e7).[12]

Since Crito is unphilosophical, his concerns are, not surprisingly, conventional: he cares about — and believes one ought to care about — what most people care about. In the *Crito*, therefore, Crito's attempt to persuade Socrates to escape from prison turns on three central considerations: money, reputation, and family. Socrates, in looking back on Crito's argument, identifies Crito's considerations with those of the many: "As for the considerations that you speak of concerning spending of money

10. See Anastaplo (1975b), 209: "We would not want Crito, feeling as he does, not to try to do something to help his friend. But does Crito understand what would be truly helpful?"

11. Since not Socrates but Crito regards Socrates' death as a calamity, and since not Socrates but Crito is overwrought at the prospect of Socrates' imminent death, we may note the unmistakable irony in Socrates' remark to Crito later on at *Cr.* 46e3–47a2: "For you, humanly speaking, are not about to die tomorrow, and the present calamity would not lead you astray." See Young (1974), 8, who regards this passage as "ironic proof that Socrates recognizes that Crito is not able to have unclouded judgment at this moment and stick to Socratic principles." The irony in this passage is even greater than Young thinks, however, because Crito has never really embraced Socratic principles at all. See the section in Chapter 4 entitled "Socrates' Procedure for Solving Moral Questions."

12. See Strauss (1983), 58: "He [Socrates] intimates in addition . . . the specific limitation of Kriton by studiously avoiding the word 'soul.'" Burnet (1924), 193, suggests that it is "the novelty of the doctrine" that makes Socrates avoid use of the word *psuchē*. But how can this be right when Socrates takes all the "doctrines" that he is now proffering for Crito's approval to be old, to be principles to which they had always in the past agreed? Indeed, how can the Socratic notion that the soul's welfare is more important than the body's be new to a man whose association with Socrates spans some seventy years? Nevertheless, it is specifically in conversation with Crito that Socrates avoids the term "soul." He uses it in the *Apology*; he even uses it in conversation with Callicles in the *Gorgias*. Indeed, although Socrates in the *Gorgias* refers to "soul" by one of the circumlocutions that he uses in the *Crito* — "what is more honorable than the body" (*Gorg.* 512a5–6) — nevertheless, in the *Gorgias*, unlike in the *Crito*, he immediately identifies the entity to which this expression refers as "the soul" (*Gorg.* 512a6). That Socrates refrains from using the term "soul" in his exchange with Crito can only attest, then, to Crito's total estrangement from philosophy.

and reputation and nurture of children, I suspect that in truth, Crito, these are considerations of those who easily kill and, if they could, would bring back to life again, acting mindlessly: namely, the many" (Cr. 48c2–6).

Let us look more closely at each of Crito's concerns. Although Crito is certainly willing to spend money in order to save Socrates' life, it is clear that the cost of freeing Socrates is a subject to which Crito has devoted much thought. When Socrates rebukes Crito, then, for appealing to considerations of the many, he does not mean that Crito sets money above all else but rather that when he reckons the course of action to adopt, money enters prominently into his calculations.[13]

We saw earlier Crito's distress at the potential damage to his reputation that Socrates' imminent death represents. There would, of course, be no truth in the perception that Crito cares more for money than for his friend, but when one is concerned about one's reputation, appearance — not truth — is what matters. Crito cares about what the many will think (Cr. 44c3–5) — namely, that Socrates died not because Socrates refused to escape but because his friends were too fond of money to help him. When Socrates challenges Crito's assumption that it matters what the many think, Crito responds: "But surely you see that it is necessary, Socrates, to care about the opinion of the many. The present situation now makes it clear that the many can produce not the smallest of evils but, I dare say,[14] the greatest, if someone is slandered among them" (Cr. 44d1–5).

Crito pleads the case of Socrates' children before their father, but Socrates regards even this way of approaching moral decisions as the way of the many. That Socrates

---

13. Adam (1888), 34, contends here that since Crito knows Socrates very well, it is not possible that he thinks Socrates might actually be worried about Crito's potential financial losses. Crito must think, says Adam, that Socrates' concerns regarding Crito's spending his own money have to do instead with his fear that the informers might make some sort of trouble for him to which foreigners would not be vulnerable. Adam's contention, however, is not borne out by the text. Crito is quite explicit at Cr. 44e2–6 that it is the loss of money and substance that he and Socrates' other friends would sustain that might be a source of worry to Socrates. And as Crito proceeds to attempt to allay Socrates' fears, he does so by pointing out to him how little money will actually be required for his escape (Cr. 45b6–8). Adam, then, gives Crito a bit more credit than he deserves: Crito does not really understand Socrates and what would and would not be of concern to him. (Socrates admits at Cr. 45a4–5 that he is worried "over the prospect of these things"; we discuss in Chapter 4 the possibility that Socrates is worried about other things besides the financial and other losses that Crito is worried about.) Crito, however, does perhaps have good reason to think, as he does a bit later at Cr. 45b2–3, that Socrates might be more concerned about his saving his money than about the foreigners spending theirs in order to pay off those who would be leading Socrates out of prison and the informers. It is likely that foreigners are less vulnerable than the Athenians to penalties in the event that the informers do "make trouble," for it is not clear how Athens could compel foreigners to pay and Athens certainly could not deprive them of their citizenship and their city. When Crito speaks, then, in the earlier passage at Cr. 44e2–3, of the trouble the informers might cause him and "the rest of your companions," he is surely alluding to the rest of Socrates' Athenian companions. Since Crito's and Socrates' Athenian friends risk more by Socrates' escape than do the foreigners, it is reasonable for Crito to assume that Socrates would wish the foreigners to be the ones to bribe the informers and the men who will lead Socrates away.

14. I translate schedon "I dare say," rather than as an adverb modifying ta megista: "nearly the greatest [evils]." It is hardly likely that Crito conceives of any greater evil than death, and Socrates does not reproduce the schedon in his rejoinder; he says only: "the greatest evils."

himself does not assign the highest priority to caring for his family is clear from his having already neglected his family for the sake of philosophy during his life.[15]

Crito, like the many, believes death to be the greatest evil. He therefore cannot understand why Socrates sleeps so serenely when he, Crito, is unable to, nor does he accept Socrates' old age as an adequate explanation for Socrates' calm: other people of Socrates' age, Crito points out, are vexed at the prospect of their imminent death (Cr. 43c1–3).[16]

Crito, we should notice, shows no sign in the Crito of holding in esteem either the city or the law. His placing higher value on helping his friend than on duty to Athens is, however, not unconventional; on the contrary, it is perfectly consonant with what was expected of an Athenian gentleman of the day.[17]

Let us turn now to the Phaedo, the dialogue that presents Socrates' philosophical discourse concerning what may be hoped for with respect to death.[18] This dialogue contains several unmistakable indications of Crito's unphilosophical nature, the most telling of which is perhaps the role Crito is assigned—and the role from which he is excluded—in this dialogue.

The first time Crito is mentioned by name in the dialogue is at Phaedo 60a7, where Socrates asks Crito to find someone to take Xanthippe home. Indeed, of the nine

---

15. We must not be too quick to assume that Socrates is devoid of concern for his children or for their education. Any plausible account of Socrates' relationship to his children would have to recognize Socrates' unconventionality. With respect to traditional forms of education, Socrates probably does not detect in himself any special abilities that would obligate him to be the one to supervise the education of his children. So, if concern for the welfare of his children does not seem to make Socrates reluctant to die, it is no doubt because he does not believe that at this time, with his children still so young, he is in a better position than anyone else to benefit them. We may note that the very last thing Socrates does in the Apology is direct his condemners to care for his children when they grow up, to reproach them then if they appear to care for unimportant things to the neglect of virtue (Ap. 41e–42a). In other words, since Socrates is about to die at the hand of these men, he thinks it only fair that they compensate him by assuming the role he would have played in his children's lives had he lived long enough to see them mature. Let us note that the same Socrates who neglects his own children assumes the role of father and older brother toward those adult Athenians, younger or older, to whom he believes he can be of benefit (Ap. 31b1–5). Moreover, Phaedo and the others present with Socrates on the last day of his life are distressed at the thought that they will be orphaned, losing a man who is like a father to them (Phaedo 116a5–7). If Socrates' children were older, there is every reason to believe that Socrates would be like a father to them, too! Indeed, that Socrates' last wish concerns his children should dispel the impression that his attitude toward them is one of callous disregard.

16. Dyer and Seymour (1885), 119, and Kitchel (1898), 152, assume that Crito simply does not take seriously what Socrates said at his trial about death's not being the greatest evil. Yet to fail to take this Socratic pronouncement seriously is to fail to take Socrates seriously; it is to fail in the most fundamental way to understand him.

17. See Dover (1974), 273; and Adam (1888), 28. Adkins (1960), 230, puts the point as follows: "The ordinary man's conception of 'the good citizen' is inadequately 'civic'. The agathos politēs is expected to help his friends and harm his enemies within the city: thus his primary loyalties are overtly to a group smaller than the state . . ." (emphasis in original).

18. The Phaedo's approach to death may be contrasted with the Apology's, for the consolation that Socrates offers in the Apology to those who voted for his acquittal is not philosophical: it contains no reasoned arguments. See Chapter 2, n. 56: Socrates' proof for his assessment of what death is likely to be is a tekmērion, not a logos. And his depiction of Hades is but a variation on "what is said" (ta legomena) about it (Ap. 40e5–6; 41c7).

men Phaedo enumerates in answer to Echecrates' inquiry at the dialogue's inception about who who was present at the scene of Socrates' death, only one is not explicitly named: Crito. He is referred to instead as Critobulus's father (*Phaedo* 59b7).

Immediately after Xanthippe is sent home, the philosophical discussion begins. Socrates starts by describing the philosopher as a man eager to die though unwilling to take his own life. Then, at the point at which Socrates is about to address the question of what sort of future is likely to await a human being after death, he pauses to find out what it is that Crito has been wanting to say. As it turns out, Crito is waiting to convey a message to Socrates from the man who is to administer the poison (*Phaedo* 63d). The message Crito conveys is a warning to Socrates to talk as little as possible, lest he become heated and have to drink the poison two or three times. Socrates dispatches Crito to inform the man to be prepared to administer the poison twice or even three times if necessary.[19] The discussion then proceeds without interruption for more than fifty Stephanus pages, during which time Crito is absent.

Crito is seen again only after the philosophical conversation is concluded. He asks Socrates for instructions with respect to Socrates' children (*Phaedo* 115b2–3); he wants to know how Socrates wishes to be buried (*Phaedo* 115c3); he accompanies Socrates when Socrates goes to bathe—the others linger behind talking with each other and reviewing what was said in the conversation that just took place (*Phaedo* 116a2–5); Socrates talks to the women and children in Crito's presence and gives them his instructions (*Phaedo* 116b2–4); Crito is charged with offering the cock owed to Asclepius (*Phaedo* 118a7–8); and, finally, once the poison has taken effect, Crito closes Socrates' mouth and eyes (*Phaedo* 118a13–14).

It is clear from the *Phaedo* that Crito is excluded from Socrates' philosophical exchanges, ministering to Socrates' physical needs but having no genuine contact with his soul. Crito tends Socrates' body and serves as Socrates' agent in matters pertaining to his family, to the city (as represented by the prison authorities), and to the gods (Crito offers the sacrifice to Asclepius). He appears both before and after the philosophical conversation; the one time he appears during it, his appearance is an intrusion.

Because of his deeply unphilosophical nature, Crito holds views, in the *Phaedo* as in the *Crito*, that are thoroughly conventional. The end of the *Phaedo* shows just how unshakable Crito remains—his association with Socrates notwithstanding—in his convictions that a man is just a body, that, therefore, when Socrates' body dies, Socrates will die (*Phaedo* 115c8–d2), and that death is a very great—indeed, the greatest—evil. Of all the friends gathered at Socrates' death scene, only one, Crito, is in danger of being "vexed *on my account* (*huper emou*) when he sees my body being burned or buried, as if something dreadful were happening to me" (*Phaedo* 115e1–3).[20] Whereas Phaedo and the others regard Socrates' death as a misfortune of the greatest magnitude, they regard it as a misfortune for *them*, insofar as they will be losing a man who was like a father to them (*Phaedo* 116a5–7). In fact, Phaedo makes explicit the distinction between being distressed on Socrates' behalf and being

19. That Socrates would prefer to take the poison two or three times rather than cease talking is reminiscent of his willingness in the *Apology* to "die many times" rather than give up philosophy (*Ap.* 30c1).

20. Translations of passages from the *Phaedo* in this chapter are by Gallop (1975).

distressed on one's own behalf: "I covered my face and wept for my misfortune—not for his, but for my own, in losing such a friend" (*Phaedo* 117c7–d1).[21]

Nowhere is the conventionality of Crito's thinking more in evidence, however, than in his attempt to persuade Socrates to delay his death for as long as possible (*Phaedo* 116e1–6):

> But surely, Socrates, said Crito, the sun is still upon the mountain; it has not gone down yet. Besides, I know that others drink the poison very late after having dinner and much wine, and sometimes intercourse with their lovers. No need to hurry. There is still time left.

Socrates is, of course, unmoved by Crito's plea. Although he readily concedes that other people behave as Crito describes "because they think that they gain by it" (*Phaedo* 116e8–9),[22] Socrates is aware that he stands to gain nothing by so behaving and will "only make myself ridiculous in my own eyes" (*Phaedo* 117a1–2) if he foolishly clings to life when it has no more to offer. Yet since Crito believes that Socrates, like all men, is only a body, he cannot but think that indulging in physical pleasure before death is a gain; indeed, he is so wedded to his unphilosophical view that he cannot imagine anyone, even Socrates, genuinely rejecting it.[23]

It is interesting that in the *Phaedo*, a dialogue otherwise replete with references to the soul, Socrates avoids using the word "soul"—as he does in the *Crito*—when speaking with Crito: when advising Crito with respect to what Crito and the others ought to care for, he tells him they should care for "you yourselves," *humōn autōn* (*Phaedo* 115b6); and when referring to that nonbodily aspect of himself that will live on after death, Socrates simply speaks in the first person singular (*Phaedo* 115d–e).[24]

Socrates does not argue with Crito in the *Phaedo*. On the contrary, he openly acknowledges the futility of using arguments to try to get Crito to adopt a new perspective: "I have made an argument for some time and at some length. . . . I seem to have spoken in vain (*allōs legein*) to him" (*Phaedo* 115d2–5). Admitting his own failure, Socrates resorts finally to asking the others to pledge their guarantee to

---

21. Crito is incapable of making this distinction; he regards Socrates' death as a calamity for Socrates (*Cr.* 43b8) as well as for himself (*Cr.* 43c6–8), even if he is well aware that Socrates does not so regard it (*Cr.* 43b8–9 and 43c5–6). Crito can distinguish only degrees of suffering in response to the calamity: Socrates suffers not at all; Socrates' other companions suffer considerably; Crito suffers most of all. See *Cr.* 43c5–8, where Crito says: "To bear a message, Socrates, that is hard—not hard for you as it appears to me, but for me and for all your companions it is a hard and grave one. And I, as it seems to me, would bear it the most gravely of all."

22. This passage echoes the passage in the *Crito* in which Crito points out to Socrates that other old men are vexed when they face death and Socrates admits that that is so. Socrates, of course, remains serene (*Cr.* 43c1–3).

23. It is true that Crito knows Socrates well enough to recognize that he would wish to continue talking even though that might interfere with the immediate effectiveness of the hemlock (*Phaedo* 63e), but this is a case in which Socrates, by doing what he wishes to do, will prolong his life, not shorten it. What Crito has difficulty accepting is that Socrates might actually wish to do something that will shorten his life.

24. Socrates does alert Crito to the bad effect of faulty language on *souls* (*Phaedo* 115e4–6), but he does not identify either what Crito and the others ought to care for or the part of himself that is not dying as "soul."

Crito that when Socrates is dead, he will not stay "but depart and be gone" (*Phaedo* 115d9–e1).

The last words Socrates speaks to Crito (before entrusting him with discharging his final religious obligation of sacrificing a cock to Asclepius) similarly betray Socrates' recognition that, with respect to Crito, he and philosophy have failed dismally. These final words are: "Obey, and do not do otherwise" (*Phaedo* 117a3). If, to the very last, Crito can recommend to Socrates the bodily pleasures of food, drink, and sex—if only indirectly by way of indicating what others in his situation have enjoyed—and the prolonging of life for a few minutes more, then, in Crito's case at least, Socrates stands utterly defeated. In these final words Socrates relinquishes his characteristic mode of speech and adopts Crito's instead: he echoes the formula that Crito himself uses twice in the *Crito* (*Cr.* 45a3; 46a8) in seeking to induce Socrates to escape: "Obey me, and do not do otherwise." Upon hearing these words, Crito stops protesting and signals the servant to fetch the man who is to administer the poison. Although Crito obeys Socrates without question, he obeys him also entirely without understanding.

There is one other Platonic dialogue in which Crito is featured: the *Euthydemus*. In this dialogue, we find Crito expressing regret over the way in which he has thus far sought to care for his children—by marrying well and amassing money. Moreover, he says of philosophy that it is "a charming thing," *charien pragma* (*Euthyd.* 304e6–7), and he worries now about his son as he begins to despair of finding a way to "direct the boy to philosophy" (*Euthyd.* 307a2).[25] Do these passages count as evidence that Crito "was attached to philosophy, at least to the extent of concerning himself in the philosophical education of his son, Critobulus . . ."?[26]

Several considerations argue against so interpreting the *Euthydemus* passages cited. The first is that the choices Crito made in the past attest to his deeply conventional thinking, to his belief that money and lineage are the means to a life worth living. Indeed, when Socrates "recommends" Euthydemus's and Dionysodorus's classes to Crito, the factor he cites as being "for your benefit especially" is that their brand of wisdom "did not in any way hinder a man from making money" (*Euthyd.* 304c3–4)! The second consideration is that Crito's concerns about the education of his sons appears to be sporadic. In particular, it seems that it is specifically when Crito is in Socrates' company that he begins to "think it madness" that he married well and made money for his children's sake but gave "no thought to their education" (*Euthyd.* 306d6–e3). Is it quite accurate to say, then, that Crito is a man "attached to philosophy"? The third consideration is that in the *Euthydemus* Crito is at sea, not knowing where to turn or who might be an appropriate teacher for his son. He rightly finds grotesque the men whose display he has just witnessed, but why does he not recognize as the salutary alternative to them the man immediately before his eyes? Why does he not see that the person to whom he ought to entrust his son is his dear friend Socrates, a man who is noble and virtuous and the philosopher par excellence? Crito's bypassing of Socrates as the best guide for his son can only make one wonder what Crito means—or, indeed, whether Crito himself has any idea of what he means—by

25. Translations of *Euthydemus* passages in this section are by Rouse (1961).
26. West (1989), 72.

seeking to "direct the boy to philosophy."[27] Although he is critical of the "philoso-phers" Euthydemus and Dionysodorus, Crito himself, as the end of the dialogue makes clear, has devoted little time or thought either to the question of what phi-losophy is or to the matter of whether it is of value (*Euthyd.* 307b–c). Whatever it is that Crito seeks, it is surely not philosophy.[28]

Crito's Conception of the Just, the Brave, and the Shameful

Crito reprimands Socrates for failing to do what is just (*Cr.* 45c5–6) and for failing to choose what a good and brave man would choose (*Cr.* 45d6–7). Furthermore, he laments the "badness" and the "lack of courage" that both Socrates and his compan-ions manifest, worrying that the bad and cowardly things they do will turn out "shame-ful as well as bad both for you and for us" (*Cr.* 46a3–4).

Terms such as "just," "brave," "shameful," "good," and "bad" are notoriously fluid: not only do they mean different things to different people, but they are also particu-larly vulnerable to manipulation and distortion. There can be no doubt that Crito understands these terms differently than Socrates does; how Crito makes use of these terms to attempt to sway Socrates is considered in the last section of this chapter.

For Crito, justice involves having no hand in the ruination of oneself, one's friends, or one's family; injustice involves being responsible in whole or in part for bringing upon oneself, one's friends, or one's family a state of adversity, as well as for furthering the malevolent ends of one's enemies. At *Cr.* 45c5–6 he says to Socrates:

> . . . you seem to me to be attempting a thing that is not even just: you are betraying yourself, although it is possible to be saved. And you are hastening the coming to pass of the very things concerning yourself which your very enemies would hasten on, and did hasten on, in their wish to ruin you.[29]

27. Even though Socrates does not do anything that can be called formal "teaching," he is clearly the man to approach for philosophic improvement. If Socrates is not the right man, then what is being sought is not genuine philosophy but rather some counterfeit version of it.

28. Miller (1996), 125, speaks of the "philosopher in Crito" who presumably resides within him alongside the utterly conventional gentleman we meet in the *Crito.* Miller believes that it is "under the tremendous pressure of the moment" that Crito lapses into "unSocratic habits of thought" (123). Yet there is no evidence to substantiate the presumption that Crito is philosophical under ordinary circumstances. The *Euthydemus* passages quoted earlier make evident that what Crito has always thought important is to marry well and amass a fortune, that he, like the notorious nonphilosopher of the *Symposium,* Alcibiades, becomes ashamed of the way he lives specifically when he is in Socrates' presence, and that he has little idea of who the true practitioners of philosophy are because he has reflected little on its nature or on its worth. We never see him participate in philosophical conversa-tions anywhere but in the *Crito,* where he nods in agreement every time Socrates asserts a principle to which he has purportedly always assented but to which, as soon becomes evident, he in fact does not subscribe. It is true that Crito "has spent years in Socrates' company" (123), but that hardly proves that he has become philosophical as a result. Indeed, it makes all the more startling just how "unSocratic" Crito is. For further discussion, see the section in Chapter 4 entitled "Socrates as Crito's Friend."

29. As E. West (1989), 73, aptly puts it: "All they [Socrates' enemies] wanted was his exile, but he is giving them his life."

Crito also extends "injustice" to cover what he perceives as Socrates' betrayal of his children.[30] In short, justice means not harming friends or self or family and not helping enemies. It is a virtue with a negative cast.

Bravery, or manliness, *andreia*, by contrast, is, for Crito, a positive virtue. It is evidenced by the attaining or preserving of a favorable condition for oneself and one's friends. To lack bravery is to fail to attain or preserve a favorable condition for oneself and one's friends when it is possible to do so.[31] Socrates and his friends, according to Crito, fail when they need not fail: Socrates is brought to trial when that could have been avoided; Socrates badly bungles his defense with the result that he is convicted and sentenced to death; and now the entire affair is about to reach an absurd conclusion in which Socrates' friends fail to save him and in which he fails to save himself. As far as Crito is concerned, the behavior of all those involved is shameful.

Several things are worth noting in the litany of complaints that Crito hurls at Socrates. First, Crito is not concerned about the effect of any of the conduct he censures—that of himself, that of Socrates' other friends, or that of Socrates—on their respective souls. Second, when he chastises Socrates for helping his enemies hasten his "corruption," *diaphtheirai* (*Cr.* 45c8), he uses "corruption" in its most vulgar sense of bodily harm. The term "corruption" is familiar, of course, from the accusation against Socrates that he "corrupts" the young, but, even in that accusation, it is used in the less vulgar sense of damaging character. Third, Crito is clearly appalled at the way Socrates conducts his defense. What does he think Socrates does wrong? According to Burnet, Crito believes that Socrates has refused to defend himself seriously and that the counterpenalty he proposed was "a mere defiance of the court."[32] According to Dyer and Seymour, what irks Crito is "that Socrates did not properly conciliate the judges."[33] As we saw in Chapter 2, there was in Socrates' estimation no way for him to win acquittal (certainly in one day's time) without degrading himself by engaging in behavior that would gratify the judges. Crito, it is clear, regards it as better—indeed, as more courageous or manly and less bad and shameful—for one to engage in such behavior if it will save one's life; what is unmanly is to allow oneself to be killed. Yet Socrates had said that men who behave in this way "are not at all

30. Crito uses the word "just" only once in this passage, but it seems to govern the entire passage of *Cr.* 45c5–d6.

31. Crito distinguishes here between justice, on the one hand, and bravery and goodness, on the other. Thus, the meaning of "just" now contracts to make room for the other virtues, and it no longer means, broadly, "right" (see n. 5 on *Cr.* 45a1–3). On this matter I disagree with Adam (1888), 36, who contends that Crito here uses *dikaion* in its wider meaning of "right" or "moral," which is "the original meaning of the word, and far more frequent than the other, i.e. just." Yet, Adam acknowledges that this virtue is one of four cardinal virtues, the others being wisdom, temperance, and courage. How then can *dikaion* have the broad sense of "right"? It seems to me that it is precisely because—and when—the virtue of *to dikaion* is one of four virtues that it cannot have its original broad sense. Generally speaking, *dikaion* in Plato shifts back and forth between broader and narrower senses. In *Rep.* I, for example, if justice is *the* virtue of the soul, the virtue by which the soul performs well its function of living, it must be very broadly meant. But later on in the *Republic*, justice is one of four cardinal virtues. At times it is synonymous with goodness or nobleness (see *Euthyphro* 7d; *Cr.* 47d; *Gorg.* 459d, 461b). Often "justice" is simply a synonym for "virtue," as in the *Apology*.

32. Burnet (1924), 186.

33. Dyer and Seymour (1885), 122.

distinguished from *women*" (*Ap*. 35b3) and "attach shame to the city" (*Ap*. 35a8) and that such conduct is "unworthy of me" (*Ap*. 38e1) and "unsuitable to a free man" (*Ap*. 38e3). And let us not forget that Socrates has no regrets about the defense speech he has made: "I much prefer to die having made my defense speech in this way than to live in that way" (*Ap*. 38e4–5).[34] Fourth, Crito makes no mention of the injustice of the accusation or the incorrectness of the verdict; for him, apparently, whether the accusation and the verdict are right or wrong is irrelevant. The fact that Meletus and Anytus accuse Socrates makes them Socrates' enemies. The fact that the members of the jury reach an unfavorable verdict and sentence Socrates to death makes them Socrates' enemies. Justice is a matter of not harming friends and not helping enemies.[35]

For all of Crito's talk of justice, it is clear that Socrates thinks that Crito has not spoken of it at all. When Socrates says at *Cr*. 48b11–c2: ". . . it must be considered whether it is just for me to try to go out of here . . . or not just. . . . As for the considerations that you speak of . . . ," he shows that, as far as he is concerned, Crito's considerations actually neglect the only important question: whether or not escape is just.[36]

Crito's Questionable Morality

We have seen evidence thus far both of the unphilosophical nature of Crito's concerns and beliefs and of Crito's failure to acknowledge the radical divergence of Socrates' views from his own. In this section we consider Crito's conduct: is Crito's conduct above reproach, and in particular above Socratic reproach, or does it exhibit what Congleton calls "tendencies to corruption"?[37]

Perhaps the best way to check a man for possible moral lapses is to look into his dealings with money. Crito, we know, is a wealthy man. We also know that Crito has every intention of bribing both those who are to lead Socrates out of jail and the informers. Furthermore, he intimates to Socrates at the opening of the *Crito* that he was permitted to enter Socrates' cell early because he had done the guard a certain "benefaction."[38] Moreover, when Crito expresses dismay at the fact that Socrates'

34. See Anastaplo (1975b), 314, n. 9: "We can assess Crito's judgment by noticing the disparaging reference he makes to the magnificent speeches recorded in the *Apology*. His concern for Socrates the friend and fellow citizen overpowers his respect for the noble and philosophical Socrates (for Socrates the human being?)."

35. See Adkins (1960), 231: "That Socrates was unjustly condemned is irrelevant . . . it is clear that Crito was bound to urge Socrates to save himself, *qua agathos* and *andreios*, whether he believed Socrates to have been wrongly condemned or not."

36. Since this chapter is concerned with Crito, I have considered in this section only Crito's conception of the just, the brave, and the shameful, without contrasting it with Socrates' conception. The next chapter concerns itself with the contrast between Crito's and Socrates' conception of these virtues. It should be evident, however, that Crito's moral views are very far removed from Socrates'.

37. Congleton (1974), 434.

38. Burnet (1924), 175, resists the most obvious meaning of Crito's expression "he has been done a certain benefaction by me," *euergetētai hup' emou* (*Cr*. 43a8), namely, that the guard has been bribed. Dyer and Seymour (1885), 115, say the guard was given "a tip," as does Adam (1888), 23, quoting Dyer;

case came to trial in the first place, he may well have been thinking, as Bonner and Smith suggest, that the trial could have — and should have — been averted by "a settlement with the accusers of Socrates."[39] Crito clearly is, as Anastaplo says, "prepared to use his wealth to get his own way."[40]

Congleton notes, with respect to Crito's bribing of the guard, that "Crito gives no indication of feeling that leading the guard into corruption is at all problematic."[41] She contrasts this attitude of Crito's toward the guard in the *Crito* with Socrates' very different attitude toward the judges in the *Apology*: Socrates, Congleton points out, was not willing "to tempt his judges to corruption."[42] Indeed, we may add that, as we have seen, Crito apparently disapproves of Socrates' refusal to gratify the judges; he regards this refusal as Socrates' mismanagement of his defense. With respect to Crito's offering the necessary bribes to spring Socrates from prison, Congleton notes that Crito has "easy familiarity with the uses and prices of sycophants, a matter about which he exhibits no concern. . . ."[43]

All these practices attest not only to a certain moral laxity on Crito's part but also to his indifference to legal prohibitions. As Congleton contends, if Crito had any sense of a principle of law, he "would necessarily find a proposed violation of law at least a little problematic, whichever way the problem might eventually be decided."[44] But Crito apparently has no compunctions about violating the law. Congleton rightly concludes, therefore, that Plato means to characterize Crito "as a man with a tendency to lawlessness."[45]

There is perhaps one additional cause for complaint. At the end of the *Phaedo* Socrates asks his friends to "stand surety for me with Crito, the opposite surety to that which he stood for me with the judges" (*Phaedo* 115d6–8). From this request we learn that Crito offered his personal assurances to the court that Socrates would not escape. For it is clear that Crito's offer to stand surety, on Socrates' understanding at least, expressed more than a bare willingness to pay should Socrates escape:

Kitchel (1898), 150, says "a trifle." Burnet translates the phrase as "I have done him a good turn" and continues: "This touch characterizes the kindly Crito at once. The man is under an obligation to him, which should not be vulgarized into a 'tip' with some editors." This is one of many instances in which scholars have gone to great lengths to find praiseworthy traits in Crito: what sort of "good turn" does Burnet think Crito could have done the guard other than paying him off in some way? We may note that it is only after Crito tells Socrates that the guard let him in early because he is accustomed to him that he admits that "besides, he has been done a certain benefaction by me."

39. Bonner and Smith (1938), II, 53. Bonner and Smith continue: "It need hardly be said that, just as Socrates rejected the idea of jail delivery, so he would not have agreed to any such financial settlement." See also Lofberg (1979), 40.

40. Anastaplo (1975b), 209. We may note that Crito's familiarity with the practice of bribery is confirmed by a story in Xenophon, *Mem.* ii.9, about Crito's having bought off some men who were harassing him by bringing frivolous lawsuits against him.

41. Congleton (1974), 434.

42. Congleton (1974), 434. It is perhaps worth adding that Socrates resists behaviors that would corrupt his judges even though he believes that such behaviors represent his only hope of securing acquittal.

43. Congleton (1974), 434.

44. Congleton (1974), 435.

45. Congleton (1974), 435.

unless Crito by his offer *vouched for* Socrates' remaining, what could Socrates mean by asking his friends to do what Crito has done? On the assumption, then, that Crito assured the court that Socrates would not escape, what are the moral implications, if any—at least from Socrates' point of view—of Crito's having offered the court these assurances?

Let us consider why Crito offered to stand surety for Socrates; what did he seek to get in exchange? Two hypotheses have been proposed: (1) that Crito sought to keep Socrates out of prison during the time he was awaiting execution,[46] and (2) that Crito sought permission to have Socrates' friends visit him in prison.[47] It apparently was standard practice in Athens at that time to imprison one who was awaiting execution;[48] it also seems that having one's friends visit one in prison was sometimes permitted and sometimes not.[49]

If what Crito asked of the court in exchange for his offer of bail was that Socrates be permitted freedom until execution, then clearly his request was denied. If what he asked was that Socrates be permitted visits by his friends while in prison, then, of course, his request was granted.[50] Regardless, however, of what Crito asked of the court and regardless of whether his request was granted, the *moral* question is whether Crito did not, in fact, intend—even as he offered to stand surety for Socrates' remaining in Athens—to help Socrates escape. If Crito never had any real intention of honoring his pledge, is it likely that Socrates would approve of his conduct?

One final point in connection with Crito's shadier side. Crito lets it be known that he has associates in Thessaly who can protect Socrates if he chooses to go into exile there (*Cr.* 45c2–4). Toward the end of the *Crito* (*Cr.* 53d2–3), the Laws repeat the point that Thessaly is a place where Crito has friends, at the same time identifying it as a place of disorder and license (*Cr.* 53d3–4). Are we to regard it as sheer coincidence that Crito's friends reside in a place known for corruption?[51]

Since it was fully expected of an Athenian gentleman that he put the welfare of friends and family above fidelity to the city and its laws, Crito's readiness to break the

46. See Seymour (1902), 202; Burnet (1924), 172; also Congleton (1974), 434–35.

47. See Adam (1888), 28: also Fox (1956), 232.

48. Seymour (1902), 202, argues that it was most unusual for a convicted man to be imprisoned until execution but that nevertheless Crito's offer was rejected and Socrates was imprisoned. But see Bonner and Smith (1938), II, 275, who cite Antiph. v.69; Xeno. *Hell.* i, 7; Plut., *Phocion* xxxvi, to show that "persons accused of flagrant crimes were incarcerated until their trial and criminals condemned to death were imprisoned until execution." See also Morrow (1960), 491: "Imprisonment was rarely used in Attic law, except as a means of holding an accused person for trial, or a condemned man for execution. . . ." Please note that T. D. Seymour is mistakenly identified by Burnet (1924), 172, as Cook Wilson, who authored the article on the facing page.

49. See *Phaedo* 58c7–9, where Echecrates asks: "Who of his friends were with him? Or did the authorities not allow them to be present and he died with no friends present?"

50. Seymour (1902), 202, contends that Socrates' use of the imperfect, *enguato*, at *Phaedo* 115d8 with respect to Crito's having stood surety to the court indicates that his request was denied, since the imperfect used here is the so-called conative imperfect. It is possible, however, that the imperfect used is the imperfect of continuance: the pledge was intended to be a long-standing one that would continue beyond the moment of its announcement.

51. See Congleton (1974), 434. Is it not likely that what a fifth-century Athenian hears when someone says: "Do not worry; I have friends in Thessaly who will protect you" is what a person today hears when someone says: "Do not worry; I have friends in Sicily who will protect you"?

law in order to save the life of his friend might well be simply the right thing to do by Athenian standards. Crito is certainly no worse from a moral perspective than his peers. And his offenses and potential offenses involve little more than fibbing and using money in mildly unsavory ways. It is shown in Chapter 4, however, that it is precisely practices such as these that Socrates seeks to discourage. Just as Socrates condemns the begging and wailing and other such behaviors that are regularly employed in court to secure life and freedom, so he shuns practices such as bending the truth and offering money for the sake of achieving similar ends. As Socrates sees it, that one indulges in behaviors such as these indicates deficiencies in one's soul.

Crito's Manner of Addressing Socrates

We conclude this chapter by getting a sense of the manner in which Crito addresses Socrates; we look at *how* Crito says what he says.

After the initial exchange in which Crito explains why he has arrived so early at Socrates' cell and expresses his great sorrow about the message he has come to deliver—that Socrates' death is but one day away—some early signs of Crito's growing impatience with his friend begin to surface. Socrates tells Crito that he has had a dream that leads him to believe that he must die not tomorrow, as Crito believes, but on the day after. Crito has put his trust in the report of the messengers from Sunium (*Cr.* 43d2–6),[52] and is not about to be deflected from the mission at hand by some Socratic dream. "The dream is strange, Socrates" (*Cr.* 44b2), he says, and, to Socrates' protest that, on the contrary, its meaning is quite evident, Crito responds, not without a trace of cynicism, "*Too* much so, as is likely" (*Cr.* 44b5). Moreover, it is specifically in connection with Socrates' report of his dream that Crito calls Socrates "daimonic Socrates" (*Cr.* 44b5), a term of affection but one tinged with irony and reproach.[53] Crito's disapproving dismissal of Socrates' dream no doubt reflects his anxiety with respect to his friend's situation: if he and Socrates do not act fast—and taking Socrates' dream seriously will surely slow them down—the moment of opportunity will pass and will be lost forever. And it is clearly the urgency of acting immediately that prompts Crito to say right after Socrates recounts his dream, "even now obey me."[54] Nevertheless, we should not overlook what the anxiety that Crito experiences at this moment reveals: it allows his underlying contempt for Socrates' private world to surface. Crito is clearly dismayed at Socrates' susceptibility to direct supernatural communiqués, particularly in the face of hard-core evidence to the contrary delivered by flesh-and-blood messengers.

Crito is unimpressed by another of Socrates' views, his view about the unimportance of what the many think—and he shows it. Crito is convinced that the opinion of the many is to be accorded considerable weight, since the many can produce the greatest evil—they can inflict death (*Cr.* 44d4). When Socrates argues that the

---

52. There can be no doubt that Crito disbelieves Socrates' dream. As he concludes his petition, he says that "all these things must be done during the coming night. If we wait any longer, it will be impossible and can no longer be done" (*Cr.* 46a5–7).

53. Adam (1888), 28; Burnet (1924), 178; T. G. West and G. S. West (1984), 101.

54. Burnet (1924), 18, renders: "even at the eleventh hour."

many are in fact impotent, that they can no more produce the greatest evils than they can the greatest goods, since everything they happen to do they do by chance (*Cr.* 44d6–10), Crito grants Socrates' point—"Let these thing be so," he says (*Cr.* 44e1)—yet he does not take it seriously; he proceeds to make his case for escape just as if this brief exchange had never taken place. Crito merely humors Socrates, in effect ignoring him.

Up to this point in the conversation, Crito's remarks merely exhibit a lack of appreciation for Socrates' views. But beginning at *Cr.* 45c, Crito's desperation to persuade Socrates to escape drives him to launch an attack on Socrates' character and moral conduct. He abandons his own idiom of money and safety and repute, and, appropriating the Socratic virtue idiom, accuses Socrates of acting in opposition to the requirements of justice, goodness, and bravery—indeed, of "choosing the most easygoing course" (*Cr.* 45d5–6). Crito associates justice, courage, and goodness with the very conventional and unsocratic goals of staying alive, caring for children, and not helping one's enemies. In his final words, he employs for his own ends a phrase Socrates uses for quite different ends in the *Apology*: when Socrates considers in the *Apology* what makes a man "of even a little benefit," *andra hotou ti kai smikron ophelos estin* (*Ap.* 28b7), he determines that it is his putting justice above life and death; by contrast, Crito says of Socrates and his friends that "if we had been of even a slight benefit," *ei ti kai mikron hēmōn ophelos ēn* (*Cr.* 46a2), Socrates' life would have been saved.

Crito's rhetoric in this final stretch of his appeal to Socrates is harsh indeed. He is, as he says, ashamed of Socrates. He disapproves of the cowardly and bad course Socrates has already taken in his trial and of the one he is about to take in refusing to escape. It is bad enough, Crito maintains, to act as Socrates has chosen to act rather than as a good and brave man would act; but, he implies in words tainted with sarcasm, it is far worse to do so "particularly if one has claimed (*phaskonta*) to care for virtue through his whole life" (*Cr.* 45d7–8).[55] Crito's insolence reaches its peak in this contemptuous phrase.

Crito desires fervently to save his friend from the worst fate he can conceive: death. At this moment, on the day Crito believes to be Socrates' last, he therefore abandons all restraint and addresses Socrates in any and every way he believes might succeed. He is at this time not even above engaging in derisive and insulting discourse.[56] He must now have his way—there is no time for counsel. "Obey me," Crito says three times (*Cr.* 44b6, 45a3, 46a8), adding twice "and do not do otherwise" (*Cr.* 45a3, 46a8).

The portrait of Crito that has emerged from the discussion in this chapter is not a flattering one. Many will think it unduly uncharitable. But Crito does not simply lack philosophical acumen.[57] His moral concerns are those of the many. He fears

---

55. Adam (1888), 37: "The touch of sarcasm in *phaskonta* is made sharper by the addition of *de*."

56. Crito's manner is quite different in the *Euthydemus*. See esp. *Euthyd.* 306d–e.

57. Despite the facts about Crito that have been disclosed in this chapter, scholars persist in their view that Crito's only defect is his lack of an astute philosophical sense. Many maintain their view even when they acknowledge some or all of the following: Crito's having bribed the guard, his willingness to engage in further acts of bribery, his indifference to an act's illegality, the predominance in his thinking of the motive of reputation, and the sarcasm with which he addresses Socrates. See in this connection fn. 2, 7, 13, 38, 53, and 55. Congleton (1974), 432–46, is the exception.

the many and is willing, therefore, to dance to their tune. His personal conduct is not, certainly from a Socratic perspective, morally impeccable. He is not deeply respectful of Socrates and even disapproves of and is ashamed of how Socrates comports himself at the trial. He cannot quite bring himself to acknowledge how broad and deep Socrates' break with conventional beliefs is or to take seriously the extent to which Socrates will cling to his distinctive moral principles even in the face of death. Crito is, to be sure, Socrates' friend, a devoted and faithful friend. He is Socrates' friend in the best and perhaps the only way he can be: he will risk everything to save his friend's life. Although his loyalty to Socrates knows no bounds, it is nevertheless misplaced: Crito is a friend to Socrates' body but not to Socrates' soul. And he is certainly no friend to philosophy.[58] If Crito were a member of the jury that tried Socrates' case — but were not his friend and fellow demesman — how, we must wonder, would he have voted?

58. See Anastaplo (1975b), 209, who understands that the association between Socrates and Crito, who are "of like age and deme," "may be based on causes to some degree accidental. They may be somewhat like the boyhood chums who continue their affection and concern for one another long after they would have ceased to find each other attractive in the guise of strangers."

4

The Philosophical Argument
against Escape

When it really happens that the just man remains
just even toward those who have harmed him . . .
this is a piece of perfection and supreme mastery on
earth. . . .

Friedrich Nietzsche (1967), 4

In the second, or middle, part of the *Crito*, *Cr.* 46b1–50a5, Socrates' moral views burst forth with clarity and force. We recognize in these pages the Socrates of the *Apology*: courageous, fiercely independent, fervently committed to justice, a man of principle. Having heard Crito's argument in favor of escape, Socrates now presents for Crito's consideration his own argument against escape; having witnessed Crito's magnanimity toward him, Socrates now returns kindness for kindness: as Crito hoped to save Socrates' life by facilitating escape, Socrates now seeks to save Crito's soul by refusing to escape.

Socrates reviews for Crito all the old *logoi* familiar to him from their long mutual association. Socrates speaks about justice, about the greater importance of the soul as compared with the body, about the worthlessness of the opinions of the many. He reminds Crito of the overriding value of living well, in the sense of nobly and justly, and of the relative unimportance of merely living. By recalling to him these old ideas, Socrates offers Crito his last hope of climbing out of the moral morass in which, to judge from the argument he has just presented, he is sunk.

On these well-worn ideas Socrates constructs his argument against escape. Socrates has no need of new notions; the old ones still work best. It is the contention of this chapter that as of *Cr.* 50a5 — that is, *before* the Laws enter the discussion — Socrates' argument against escape is complete.[1]

---

1. I agree completely with the following statement by Allen (1980), 66: "It is likely that Socrates was offered an opportunity to escape. If so, he refused. If he refused, he had reasons. If he had reasons, the *Crito* may be presumed to present them." But I do not agree with Allen that it is in the Laws' speech that Socrates' reasons are worked out. See also Allen (1984), 107.

Our first goal in this chapter is to lay bare Socrates' argument. To this end, we examine each of the following issues: (1) Socrates' procedure for solving moral questions; (2) the moral principles to which Socrates subscribes; and (3) the way in which Socrates uses his moral principles to yield the conclusion that he ought not to escape. We have a second goal as well in this chapter: to show how Socrates' decision not to escape constitutes an expression of his friendship for Crito. To this end, we conclude this chapter with a consideration of how Socrates understands friendship.

Socrates' Procedure for Solving Moral Questions

We saw in Chapter 3 that Crito wishes to dispense with counsel and be obeyed.[2] We also saw that Crito believes that a person must, when determining what course to choose, take into account the opinion of the many because, in his view, the many can produce the greatest evils if one is slandered among them (*Cr.* 44d1–5). We consider now Socrates' approach to reaching a decision with respect to moral questions, an approach very different from Crito's.

Socrates regards as the first order of business to discredit both aspects of Crito's approach to action: (1) the "obey me" aspect and (2) the aspect of attaching importance to the opinion of the many. Only after having dispensed with both of these aspects of Crito's approach does Socrates present the acceptable alternatives.

Let us consider first Socrates' rejection of Crito's demand to be obeyed. At *Cr.* 46a8 Crito says: "Obey me, and do not do otherwise." Just four lines later, at *Cr.* 46b4–6, Socrates emphatically responds: ". . . I, not only now but always, am such as to obey nothing else of what is my own than that principle that appears best to me upon reasoning."[3] Crito, being Socrates' friend, is, of course, included in "what is my own."[4] For Socrates to say, then, that he obeys "nothing else of what is my own" but the best *logos* is for him to announce quite plainly his refusal to obey Crito. The

---

2. Dyer and Seymour (1885), 125, take note of Crito's very short answers to Socrates' questions, beginning with "Nobly" at *Cr.* 47a6: "Crito's answers are brief. He cares for no discussion."

3. The term *logos*, here rendered by me "principle," is rendered variously by translators and editors. It is a term with a wide range of meanings. Burnet (1924), 188, rightly notes that the *logos* that Socrates says he obeys is the result of a process of reasoning. Hence, Burnet discounts "reason" as a translation of *logos* (this is Jowett's translation), calling this "a sense which *logos* never has in Plato." Yet cf. Burnet (1924), 196, on *Cr.* 48c6, where he renders *logos* "reckoning." (I think Burnet's generalization too hasty: *logoi*, even as principles, serve as reasons. When Socrates says, for example, at *Gorg.* 508e–509a, that his conclusions (*tauta*) are clamped down by *logoi* of iron and adamant, he means by *logoi* the principles that serve as the reasons for his conclusions.) Burnet's point seems also to discredit "argument" (Church, the Wests, Allen) or "reasoning" (Fowler). I prefer "principle" when the *logos* in question is Socrates' (Treddenick, Kitchel) because Socrates' *logos* is a reasoned conclusion. When the *logos* in question is Crito's, Burnet's term "rule" is better, for one may have a rule of conduct that is not reached by way of reasoning. Adam (1888), 40, renders *logos* "conception or definition." Although I settle on "principle" here, I do not insist that this is always the best translation of *logos*. There are times when it is more appropriately rendered "argument" or "word" or "speech."

4. Adam (1888), 40: "This is the reply to Crito's *peithou moi* (46A), for *tōn emōn* includes Socrates' friends as well as anything else that could be called his."

logos that "seems best to me upon reasoning" is the only "friend" with the authority to command Socrates' obedience.[5]

It is unusual, to say the least, to include the best *logos* among the things that are one's own—that is, among one's family and friends.[6] For Socrates, however, the product of one's thinking can be as near and dear as one's relatives and friends and certainly ought to exercise greater influence than they upon one's actions.

The only thing of "my own" to which Socrates will submit, then, is the principle reached through his own reasoning. Is there anything, however, that is not his own to which Socrates will also submit? Socrates is quite explicit at *Cr*. 47a13–48a10 that the opinion of experts is to be obeyed, that body and soul stand to be utterly ruined if expert opinion concerning what is best for them is disregarded. There is, then, one thing of his own that Socrates will obey and one thing not his own that Socrates will obey. He will obey the principle that seems best to him upon reasoning and he will obey the opinion of an expert.[7]

Let us pause for a moment to note the striking parallel between what Socrates in this part of the *Crito* will obey and what Socrates in the *Apology* will obey. We dis-

---

5. Tyler (1862), 172: "The strongest argument, in other words, the truth, as it appears to his mind, after careful consideration, is here beautifully represented by Socrates as his best *friend*, and the only one to whom he yields a controlling influence" (emphasis in original). Cf. Gandhi, ed. Merton (1964), 53: "Don't listen to friends when the Friend inside you says 'Do this!'"

6. According to Burnet (1924), 188, Kitchel (1898), 154, and Dyer and Seymour (1885), 125, the term *ta ema* embraces all faculties and functions of body and mind. But it seems to me that the most natural reading here would have *tōn emōn* refer to family and friends so that Socrates' use of this expression at this point in the dialogue to include the product of one's reasoning, as well as, later, one's body and soul (*Cr*. 47c6, 47e8–48a1), represents Socrates' deliberate extension of its scope. We may note that when the Laws use a similar expression at *Cr*. 54b7, *tōn sōn*, they clearly refer to family and friends; see also *Gorg*. 508e2, e4–5. The range of what is encompassed by the expression "one's own" is different here from what it is in the *Apology*. In the *Apology*, as we saw in Chapter 2, "his own" is distinguished from "himself," the former comprising money, reputation, and honor, and the latter, how he "will be the best and most prudent possible" (*Ap*. 36c7). It seems likely that in the *Apology* the soul just is oneself: Socrates urges in virtually the identical language care for the self and care for the soul (see *Ap*. 29e1–2: "and how your soul will be the best possible"). In the *Crito*, however, the expression "our own," *tōn hēmeterōn* (*Cr*. 47e8–48a1), insofar as it includes the soul, includes the thing that in the *Apology* is called "himself."

7. The Laws cannot qualify as another authority not "my own" that Socrates would obey. As we know from the *Apology*, the only authority not his own that Socrates would obey is someone who is his "better"—whether god or man. The Laws, of course, are neither god nor man. That the Laws are not men is underscored in the *Apology* when Socrates in his cross-examination of Meletus asks him who improves the youth and, in reply to Meletus's answer, "The laws," insists on being told what *human being* improves them (*Ap*. 24d9–e2). But even if the Laws were men, they could not qualify as Socrates' moral superior, as we shall see: they do not possess knowledge of the just and do not always do what is just; nor does it matter to them that the verdict may have been incorrectly rendered: from their perspective, it is the citizen who must avoid the injustice of doing injury to them. Furthermore, since the speech of the Laws is Socrates' own invention, it is difficult to view what the Laws say in the *Crito*, at any rate, as an authority independent of Socrates to which he must accede. Perhaps, then, the Laws' speech represents Socrates' own best *logos*? Since Socrates makes it quite clear that it is the old *logoi* that continue to seem best to him (*Cr*. 46b6–c1), he must think that the Laws' speech, rife as it is with new and unfamiliar ideas, is unworthy to displace or supersede them; how, then, could it constitute the *logos* that seems best to Socrates upon reasoning? For the view that the Laws indeed are the moral expert to whom Socrates alludes, see Bostock (1990), 17–20.

covered in Chapter 2 that Socrates in the *Apology* will obey a true superior, "whether god or human being" (*Ap*. 29b6–7). Yet, as was argued, since the god commands the practice of philosophy and the pursuit of justice, to obey the god is to obey one's own reasoned conclusion about the just. To obey a human superior, by contrast, is to follow the directives of the expert—if and when there is one. Socrates in the *Apology* does not, despite appearances, advocate "following orders"—even when the orders are legal; he believes one ought to follow orders only if they are in one's judgment just ("holding that it is best," *Ap*. 28d7). He therefore declares that "throughout my life," he has been "the sort of man" who "never conceded anything to anyone contrary to the just" (*Ap*. 33a1–3). Socrates at *Cr*. 46b1–50a5 faithfully reproduces the Socrates of the *Apology*: he will not obey Crito; rather, "not only now but always," he is "the sort of man" to "obey nothing of my own but the *logos* that seems best to me upon reasoning" (*Cr*. 46b4–6). Yet he insists, in the *Crito* as in the *Apology*, that when there is an expert, the expert must be obeyed. Like Socrates in the *Apology*, then, Socrates in the *Crito* recognizes the validity of, on the one hand, exercising one's own moral judgment when it results from careful reasoning—from philosophy—as well as, on the other, following the opinion of the expert, "if there is an expert," *ei tis estin epaiōn* (*Cr*. 47d1–2). Socrates will not, therefore, obey Crito unless Crito produces a principle superior to his (*Cr*. 46c2–3; 48d8–e1). For without a superior principle, Crito has no claim to be obeyed: on moral questions, only the best *logos* and the moral expert command obedience.

Let us turn now to Socrates' consideration of the value of the opinion of the many. Socrates contrasts the many with three types: the *epieikestatoi* at *Cr*. 44c6–9, the *phronimoi* at *Cr*. 47a10, and the *epaiōn* at *Cr*. 47b10–48a10.

The *epieikestatoi*, the "most decent" people, are those who, unlike the many, will not automatically discount the possibility that Socrates died because he refused to escape rather than because his friends were reluctant to spend the money to save him; on the contrary, they will believe "that things have been done in just the way they were done" (*Cr*. 44c8–9). What makes these men different from the many? The many are unable to believe that things happened as they indeed happened because of their conviction that death is the greatest evil; in light of this conviction they cannot conceive of a man's choosing—when given the opportunity to escape and save his life—to remain in prison to be executed. But since the most decent men do not presume death to be the greatest evil, they are able to believe "that things have been done in just the way they were done"; they are able to believe, in particular, that Socrates remained in prison because he thought it best. The opinion of the many is not to be cared about, says Socrates; it is the *epieikestatoi* to whom it is more worthy to give thought (*Cr*. 44c6–8).

The *phronimoi*, the prudent ones, are those who, unlike the many, have upright, *chrēstai*, opinions (*Cr*. 47a10), and their opinions—as opposed to the opinions of the general run of human beings—are to be honored (*Cr*. 47a2–4). Socrates does not linger on the *phronimoi* but quickly turns from them to the expert.

There are two ways in which the *epaiōn*, the expert, is distinguished from both the *epieikestatoi* and the *phronimoi*. First, the *epaiōn* is spoken of in the singular, even though there are, no doubt, more than one *epaiōn* in any given discipline. The only time the expert is spoken of in the plural is at *Cr*. 47d9, where Socrates speaks of the body's being destroyed because of a failure to obey the opinion of "the experts." But even there the implication is that in each area of expertise concerned with the body there is but a single expert: the single trainer and the single doctor together constitute the body's "experts." To speak of experts as if there is just one per field is to confer upon them an extraordinary mark of distinction.

A second way in which the *epaiōn* is distinguished from the *epieikestatoi* and the *phronimoi* is that, whereas the opinions of the *epieikestatoi* and the *phronimoi* are worthy of being given thought to and of being honored, the opinion of the *epaiōn* is to be obeyed and not disobeyed (*Cr.* 47c1, c6, d9).

For Socrates, then, in determining how one is to act, one is ill advised to look to the opinion of the many; the opinions of the most decent and prudent men are to be attended to, and the opinion of the expert is to be obeyed.

Of course, the expert concerning the just and unjust, shameful and noble, and good and bad things (*Cr.* 47c9–10) can be obeyed only if there is such a being. Yet Socrates hints that there may not be one: it is with respect to the *moral* expert alone that he says: "if there is such an expert," *ei tis estin epaiōn* (*Cr.* 47d1–2). It is clear that Socrates is not himself such an expert: he obeys the *logos* that *seems* best to him upon reasoning; he does not *know* which *logos* is best.[8] The moral expert's opinion, unlike Socrates', is the opinion that reflects the "truth itself" (*Cr.* 48a7);[9] what "seems fitting to the one" (*Cr.* 47b10), to the expert, necessarily *is* fitting.[10]

If Socrates is not a moral expert, what is he? It is likely that Socrates regards himself as one of the few *epieikestatoi* and *phronimoi*[11] and that he believes, therefore, that his opinions merit the respect and honor of other men.[12] But let us note that whereas other men owe Socrates' opinions attention and esteem, Socrates himself owes them obedience. Since these are the *logoi* that seem best to him upon reasoning, he must—in the absence of a moral expert—obey them no less than he would the opinion of a moral expert, if there were one.[13]

---

8. For the view that Socrates believes himself here to be the moral expert, see Grote (1875), I, 308.

9. It is possible to understand "truth itself" as the "expert" to be obeyed. In the absence of human experts who know the truth, one's best bet is to try to discover the "truth itself" or at least to try to get as close to it as possible. Indeed, this is the goal of the joint inquiry that Socrates will presently urge on Crito.

10. The reason Socrates speaks, even with respect to the expert, of "what seems fitting, *hēi an dokēi*, to the one" rather than of what he knows, is that the question that Socrates is addressing is whose opinion, *doxa*, one is to follow.

11. Cf. *Ap.* 36b9–c1: "since I held that I myself was really too decent, *epieikesteron*, to survive if I went into these things."

12. It may be in part because Socrates believes that his opinion is worthy of honor that he feels justified in the *Crito* in employing the rhetoric of the Laws rather than limiting himself to strictly rational means to induce Crito to acquiesce in his decision not to escape—once it becomes clear that rational means cannot succeed. The issue of why Socrates resorts to the use of rhetoric in the *Crito* is the subject of Chapter 8.

13. We may note that when Socrates says at *Cr.* 46b7 that he and Crito need to determine whether a particular *logos* is to be set aside or obeyed, the question for Socrates is whether this *logos* is the one that seems best to him, *moi* (*Cr.* 46d6): in the absence of a moral expert, one must obey the *logos* that seems best to one.

Despite all the effort that Socrates expends on discrediting the opinion of the many and urging obedience to the expert, he does not proceed to seek the advice of a moral expert on the question of escape: he is, as we have seen, skeptical about the possibility of finding such an expert. Nevertheless, he must do something. What Socrates does is embark with Crito upon a joint inquiry into the question of whether or not it would be just to escape.[14] For Socrates, inquiry of this kind is no mere academic exercise; he regards its results as binding: "Let us consider in common, my good man, and if there is some way you can contradict my *logos*, contradict it and I will obey you" (*Cr.* 48d8–e1). Socrates regards the *logos* that survives his and Crito's common deliberation as the *logos* to be *obeyed*.

Can Socrates and Crito engage successfully in common deliberation? Socrates certainly wishes to "take counsel" with Crito on the question of whether or not escape is just. He even calls what he and Crito are presently doing "taking counsel" "concerning the just and unjust and shameful and noble and good and bad things" (*Cr.* 47c9–11). Crito, as we recall, urged Socrates to take counsel no longer, contending that it is now time to be finished with taking counsel and to submit to the one counsel of escape (*Cr.* 46a4–5). But even for Socrates, who fervently desires "common counsel," *koinē boulē* (*Cr.* 49d3), there is to such counsel one insurmountable obstacle: disagreement between the deliberators with respect to a certain fundamental principle—the principle that "it is never correct to do injustice, or to do injustice in return, or to avenge oneself for bad things done to one by doing bad things in return" (*Cr.* 49d7–9).[15]

To take counsel, as Vlastos points out,[16] is not the same as to discuss something. As Vlastos correctly notes, Socrates can talk with anyone: a Polus, a Callicles, a Thrasymachus. But to take counsel is to seek to reach a decision with respect to action. It is here that not sharing fundamental moral principles presents a hurdle that cannot be overcome. For, as Socrates says, people who do not share the view that it is never right to commit injustice or to do bad things and, hence, that it is not right to commit injustice or to do bad things *in return* are bound to "have contempt for each other when they see each other's counsels" (*Cr.* 49d4–5). Crito, as we have seen, has contempt for Socrates' counsels: he calls them shameful and not what a just, brave, and good man would choose. And Socrates has contempt for Crito's counsels: he regards Crito's considerations as those of the mindless many. Yet is it not possible that Crito and Socrates share the critical view, the view that injustice, injustice in return, bad treatment, and bad treatment in return ought never to be done? If they do share this view, could they not then undertake to engage in common counsel?

That Crito does not share with Socrates the critical view in question is clear from Socrates' remark that this view is one that only "a certain few" hold (*Cr.* 49d2). Insofar as Crito shares the concerns of the many (*Cr.* 48c2–6), it is unlikely that he will prove to be on this occasion one of "the few." Moreover, Crito at *Cr.* 48a10–b2 shows

14. See Strauss (1983), 58: ". . . the agreements of two take the place of the verdicts of the single expert."

15. The term *amunesthai* need not be translated "defend oneself"; it also means "avenge oneself." The latter is clearly its meaning here.

16. Vlastos (1991), 195.

how strong his bond with the many is: even after Socrates defends at length the view that not the many but the one expert is to be heeded, Crito still finds reasonable the response, "But the fact is . . . the many are able to kill us." A man who fears the many and is receptive to the idea that their opinions are to be held in esteem because they "are able to kill us" is, in the final analysis, one of them.[17]

Since Crito shows himself to be one of the many, Socrates rightfully suspects that Crito's assent to the critical principle represents his "agreeing contrary to your opinion" (*Cr.* 49c11–d1),[18] and this despite Crito's earlier commitment to answer what is asked "in whatever way you most suppose it to be" (*Cr.* 49a1–3).[19] Socrates, we may assume, no longer harbors much hope that his attempt to take "common counsel" with Crito will yield agreement concerning the appropriate course of action to be adopted. Just as Crito had finally despaired of the fruitfulness of taking counsel with Socrates and had demanded to be obeyed,[20] so Socrates will come to realize very shortly the uselessness of pursuing the argument with Crito[21] and will resort, in his despair, to bringing in the Laws to continue the discussion. As Chapter 8 shows, the Laws, unlike Socrates, *are* able to take "common counsel" with Crito, for the Laws share with Crito the view of the many that permits generally the return of bad treatment for bad treatment.[22]

Socrates' Moral Principles

We saw in the previous section that Socrates does not put much stock in the opinion of the many. The many, he explains, cannot produce the greatest evils or the greatest goods, "for they are not capable of making someone either prudent or imprudent,

17. There can be little doubt that the hypothetical "someone" whom Socrates has raise the objection about the power of the many to kill is Crito. The objection merely reproduces Crito's earlier assertion that the opinion of the many carries weight because the many can do one "the greatest evils" (*Cr.* 44d1–5).

18. Young (1974), 6: "Crito is one of the many. The dialogue *Crito* makes this clear. For this reason there is an abyss between Crito's opinions and those of Socrates, as Socrates hints at one point in the dialogue." Young is referring to *Cr.* 49c11–d1: "And see to it, Crito, that by agreeing to this, you are not agreeing contrary to your opinion." We may observe that it is specifically because, *gar*, Socrates knows "that this seems and will seem so only to a certain few" (*Cr.* 49d2) that he worries that, in agreeing to it, Crito might be agreeing contrary to his opinion.

19. Despite, then, all Socrates' talk of things upon which he and Crito have always agreed in the past, he is not persuaded that Crito has done more than pay lip service to any of those old principles. Cf. *Phaedo* 115b5–c1, where Socrates recognizes that what Crito and the others agree to or do not agree to does not necessarily coincide with what they truly believe as attested by the way in which they conduct their lives.

20. It is unlikely that it is only the shortness of time that causes Crito to implore Socrates no longer to take counsel but simply to obey him; it is likely that he also senses the futility of ongoing discussion.

21. We noted in Chapter 3 (in the section entitled "The Unphilosophical Crito") that in the *Phaedo*, too, Socrates finally despairs of persuading Crito by argument of the worthlessness of delaying death for as long as possible and therefore finally says to him, "Obey, and do not do otherwise" (*Phaedo* 117a3).

22. The Laws do not permit the citizen to retaliate against *them*, but that is only because justice, as the Laws contend, is not equal between them.

but do whatever they do by chance" (*Cr.* 44d8–10).[23] It is clear from this passage that for Socrates the greatest good is to be prudent (*phronimos*), and the greatest evil to be imprudent (*aphrōn*).[24]

Insofar as imprudence is the greatest evil, it must be a form of corruption in the soul, for it is such corruption that, in the *Crito*, renders life not worth living. Although Socrates seems to contend as well that life is not worth living with a corrupt body (*Cr.* 47e3–5), there is reason to doubt that this contention reflects his true view. On Socrates' view, as long as a life is lived nobly and justly, it is a life well lived; he surely means nothing less than this by declaring that living well and nobly and justly are the same (*Cr.* 48b8–9). It is likely, then, that the reason Socrates suggests that life is not worth living with a corrupt body is in order to ease Crito by way of this notion, a conventional notion to which Crito is already sympathetic, into the unconventional Socratic notion that life with a corrupt soul is not worth living. Socrates reasons a fortiori as follows: since of the things that are our own, namely, body and soul, the soul is the more honorable (*Cr.* 47e3–48a4), it follows that if (as Crito believes) life is not worth living with a wretched and corrupt body, then (as Crito must agree) life is surely not worth living with a corrupt soul.[25]

Since Socrates is concerned with the soul, his considerations with respect to the matter of escape are not the same as Crito's: rather than attend to such things as

23. Many editors reject the straightforward translation of *tuchōsi* as "by chance," preferring "impulsively" (Kitchel [1898], 152) or "indifferently" (Adam [1888], 32; Burnet [1924], 180). But the sense of this term, as I see it, both here and later on at *Cr.* 45d2, is in fact "at random" or "by chance." Here, the point is that the many have no control over the effect they produce since they are unskilled. (A similar point is made at *Prot.* 320a and *Meno* 92e–93a, where the possibility of virtue's being picked up "automatically" is entertained as an alternative to its being taught and learned or coming by nature: there is a haphazardness, an unreliability, about the result.) At *Cr.* 45d2, Crito accuses Socrates of leaving his children to whatever by chance comes their way, noting that chance cannot be counted on to bring them good things. Although Crito is certainly accusing Socrates of indifference, the indifference is located in the phrase "for your part," *to son meros*, not, as Burnet maintains, in the *tuchōsi*. Socrates' complaint against the many at *Cr.* 44d8–10, let us note, is different from his complaint against them at *Cr.* 48c6, where he says that they act mindlessly, *oudeni xun nōi*.

24. In the *Apology*, Socrates regards as the greatest evil the attempt to kill a man unjustly (*Ap.* 30d4–5). For Socrates, there is a connection between being willing to commit injustice and being imprudent.

25. Socrates' discussion in the *Gorgias* of the pilot who does not congratulate himself upon bringing his passengers safely to shore works in the identical way. The pilot, according to Socrates, reckons as follows. If I save the life of a man who is suffering serious and incurable diseases in his body, I will not benefit him; therefore, if I save the life of a man who has many incurable diseases in the part of him that is more honorable than his body, namely, his soul, I will surely not benefit him. The pilot knows, says Socrates, that it is not better for the wretched man to live, "for he is bound to live badly" (*Gorg.* 512a2–b2). Here we find the identical a fortiori reasoning from the wretchedness of life with a corrupt body to the more serious wretchedness of life with a corrupt soul that we find in the *Crito*. The expression "it will not be worth it to him to live," *ouk . . . toutōi de biōteon estin*, we may observe, is here, though not in the *Crito*, reserved for the case of the wretched soul. See also *Rep.* IV.445a6–b1, where Glaucon makes the same point: "If life doesn't seem livable with the body's nature corrupted, not even with every sort of food and drink and every sort of health and every sort of rule, will it then be livable when the nature of that very thing by which we live is confused and corrupted . . . ?," trans. Bloom (1986). We may note the use of the term "does not *seem* livable," *dokei ou biōton einai*, in the case of the body. See also *Prot.* 313a1–b2. In this passage the state of the soul is said to determine one's entire faring well or ill, *pant' . . . ē eu kakōs prattein* (*Prot.* 313a7–8).

money, reputation, and nurture of children,[26] as the many do, Socrates takes into account only one thing: the justice or injustice of his act (*Cr.* 48b11–c1).[27] How does Socrates apply this single standard to the case at hand?

By way of answering this question, let us see first how Socrates understands the case at hand. From Socrates' point of view, the question that he and Crito must answer is "whether it is just for me to try to go out of here although the Athenians are not permitting me to go, or not just" (*Cr.* 48b12–c1). In posing the question in this way, Socrates recognizes a new dimension to his moral situation, a dimension that he later refers to as "unwilling Athenians" (*Cr.* 48e3; 52c5): now that the Athenians do not permit him to leave (*Cr.* 48b12–c1), since they have not been persuaded (*Cr.* 49e9–50a1), "going away" introduces moral problems different from those Socrates confronted at his trial.[28]

At the trial, as we know, Socrates had to decide whether to propose exile as an alternative to death. As he explains in the *Apology*, he preferred to accept the punishment of death rather than say falsely of himself, by proposing exile, that he deserves something bad. Socrates took himself to be choosing in accordance with the demands of justice: were he to imply that he deserves to be punished when in fact he is Athens' greatest benefactor, he would have been committing an injustice against himself. But since, as he says, exile would probably have been acceptable to the Athenians had he proposed it at his trial (*Ap.* 37c5),[29] the problem of "unwilling Athenians" did not then apply.

Now that Socrates is in prison awaiting the carrying out of his death sentence, he need not be concerned about committing against himself the injustice of proposing exile as his due: in his new context, there is simply no possibility of his *proposing* anything. Yet he does have to contend at this time with the factor of "unwilling Athenians." The Athenians, having tried, convicted, and sentenced Socrates to death, would certainly not take kindly to Socrates' having a belated change of heart on the question of exile. Escape would flagrantly contradict their will.

How does the Athenian opposition to escape shape the question that Socrates must now address? How will he apply the standard of justice, the only standard he considers worthy of application, to his moral situation as currently conceived? In order to pose the justice question with respect to his present predicament, Socrates begins by identifying two escape-related practices in which he and his friends will be obliged to engage specifically because escape defies the Athenian will—"paying money and

---

26. For a discussion of Socrates' relationship to his children, see Chapter 3, n. 15.

27. Socrates makes the same point at *Cr.* 48d3–5: "We must take nothing into account, *hupologizesthai*, compared to the doing of injustice, even if we must die by staying here and keeping quiet or must suffer anything else whatever." We may compare with these Socratic statements in the *Crito* the similar position articulated in the *Apology*: "What you say is ignoble, fellow, if you suppose that a man who is of even a little benefit ought to take into account, *hupologizesthai*, the danger of living or dying, but rather consider this alone whenever he acts: whether his actions are just or unjust, and the deeds of a good or bad man" (*Ap.* 28b5–9).

28. Colson (1989), 39–40, assimilates Socrates' question in the *Crito* of whether to escape to his question in the *Apology* of whether to choose exile. There is, however, as we shall see, a set of problems uniquely associated with the escape decision.

29. The Laws make this point as well in their speech (*Cr.* 52c3–6).

gratitude to those will lead me out of here" (*Cr.* 48c8–d1). Once Socrates identifies these two practices, his next step is to reduce the question of whether escape is right or wrong to the question of whether practices such as these are just or unjust:

> . . . nothing else is to be considered by us except . . . whether we will do just things by paying money and gratitude to those who will lead me out of here, or whether in truth we will do injustice by doing all these things — those of us who are leading out as well as those of us who are being led out. And if it is apparent that these deeds of ours are unjust, we must take nothing into account compared to the doing of injustice. (*Cr.* 48c7–d5)

Just as in the *Apology* Socrates had to consider whether or not it is just to engage in certain unbecoming behaviors, such behaviors as crying, begging, bringing in his children to beg, and proposing exile as a counterpenalty, just for the sake of remaining alive, so in the *Crito* there are unseemly forms of conduct that give Socrates pause: is it right for him and his friends, just for the sake of saving his life, to bribe and thank those men who would lead him out of prison?

Now that we see two of the practices that escaping against the will of the Athenians would necessitate, as well as Socrates' concern that such practices might well be unjust, we are in a position to clarify a passage at the beginning of the *Crito* that was left unexplained in Chapter 3. After Crito details the risks that he and Socrates' other friends are willing to run for Socrates' sake, specifically, loss of money or property or even something worse, Socrates responds as follows (*Cr.* 45a4–5): "I am worrying over the prospect of these things, Crito, and of many others." As we saw, Crito never inquires of Socrates what these "many others" are; he simply continues to discuss the financial implications of Socrates' escape for him and for Socrates' other friends. But now we know at least two of the "many others" that worry Socrates: the paying of money and the paying of gratitude to those who would lead him out (*Cr.* 48c8–d1). Socrates refers to these two things as "all these things" at *Cr.* 48d2. They clearly loom large for him.

Socrates is troubled, then, not only by the potential financial loss that Crito and his other friends might incur if they are caught but also by the demeaning acts of bribery and flattery that they will be compelled to engage in if they proceed with their escape plan. It is not surprising that Socrates recoils at the prospect of his friends' sacrificing their dignity to save his life. Socrates' friends will be, as Crito himself puts it, "stealing" Socrates "away from here," *hōs se enthende ekklepsasin* (*Cr.* 44e4). And it is precisely because Socrates' friends will be stealing him away that it will become necessary for them to pay money and thanks to the guards and informers.

Crito, of course, is undisturbed by any of the things that trouble Socrates. In the case he makes in support of escape, Crito seems to take no notice of the new set of moral issues connected with "unwilling Athenians." Instead, he considers practical matters: how the escape might be accomplished and what its risks are, and whether exile can provide Socrates with the important amenities of safety and regard. And he considers *old* moral matters — that is, matters that apply equally to the question of whether Socrates should have proposed exile at his trial and to the question of escape: ought Socrates to capitulate so readily to his enemies' designs, to abandon his children, to bring upon his friends ill repute?[30] For Crito, the new issues are of no consequence: he bribes without giving it a second thought; he thinks Socrates should have gratified the judges in order to be acquitted or at least exiled; and, since what the law forbids does not figure at all in his calculations, the fact that he and Socrates' other friends would be "stealing" Socrates away from prison is of no concern to him. And, as I argue in what follows, the aspect of escape that decisively turns Socrates against it—that it involves failing to do something just that one has agreed to do— also plays no part in Crito's considerations.

Having made clear to Crito that the only consideration that matters is justice, and having specified those aspects of escape—paying money and gratitude—that threaten to make it unjust, Socrates now proposes to Crito that they "consider in common" whether or not escape is to be pursued. In escape, Socrates faces unwilling Athenians (Cr. 48e3); in refusing to escape, he faces an unwilling Crito (Cr. 48e5). Through common deliberation Socrates hopes to persuade Crito (Cr. 48e4) of the correctness of his decision and thereby to eliminate his "unwillingness" to support it.[31]

In order to attempt to persuade Crito, Socrates reviews the principles to which they have formerly agreed, asserting that they would be acting like children were they to abandon their principles in the face of suffering or death (Cr. 49b1; cf. 46c4–5).[32] The principles to which they have formerly agreed are:[33] (1) doing injustice, adikein, is in no way good and noble (Cr. 49a5–6);[34] (2) doing injustice is in every way bad and shameful for the one who commits it (Cr. 49b4–6);[35] (3) one must in no way do

30. We recall that Crito is just as shamed by how he and Socrates' other friends managed "the affair" of Socrates up to this point as he expects to be if Socrates now refuses to escape (Cr. 45d8–e5).

31. Although Socrates will eventually despair of successfully taking common counsel with Crito, he begins their discussion on the assumption that such taking counsel together will be fruitful.

32. Socrates suggests that these principles are true "for us now more than ever" (Cr. 49b2)—that is, now that we are in a position to have to act on them.

33. We may note that, according to Socrates, all of these principles were agreed to before; none is new (Cr. 49e1–3).

34. "Justice" and "injustice" are used in a rather broad sense in Socrates' argument. It is difficult to discern—and Socrates does not give us much help in this matter—how the justice of which he speaks in this part of the Crito is related to the other virtues such as courage and temperance. It may or may not be identical with the prudence of which he spoke earlier (Cr. 44d9; 47a10), and it certainly seems to be nearly synonymous with the noble and the good (Cr. 47c9–10). Indeed, by speaking of an expert on the just, good, and noble, Socrates implies that "justice" here is not limited to a "part" of virtue. The Laws speak later of "justice and the rest of virtue" (Cr. 54a1); they also speak of piety, although they suggest at least that what is just is pious (Cr. 51a6–a9). In the Apology Socrates speaks of piety, courage, and prudence, but he does not clarify their relationship to one another or to virtue. He also speaks there of justice as if it were synonymous with virtue, when he says, for example, that the only thing one ought to consider before acting is "whether his actions are just or unjust, and the deeds of a good man or a bad" (Ap. 28b8–9). Justice in the Crito seems closest to justice in Rep. I, of which Socrates says: "But is not justice human virtue?" (Rep. I.335c4). In Book IV of the Republic, justice, though but one of four cardinal virtues, is an excellence diffused throughout the soul and not confined to one of its parts. For further discussion, see Chapter 3, n. 31.

35. See Vlastos (1991), 198–99: "In saying that it is never good [as opposed to never kalon, which has moral connotations] to do a wrong, and making this the foundational reason for breaking with the accepted morality, Socrates must be using the word in its most inclusive sense. He must be saying: 'If an act of yours will wrong another, then it is bad for you, the agent, so bad that no other good it offers

injustice intentionally (*Cr.* 49a4, 49b8);[36] (4) one must not do injustice in return, *antadikein* (*Cr.* 49b10); (5) one must not do bad things, *kakourgein* (*Cr.* 49c2); (6) doing bad things to human beings differs not at all from doing injustice (*Cr.* 49c7–8);[37] and (7) it is not just to do bad things in return, *antikakourgein* (*Cr.* 49c4–5). Three of these principles, (2), (4), and (7), are explicitly said to express views not accepted by the many. Principle (3) is derived from principles (1) and (2); principle (4) from principle (3); principle (7) from principles (4) and (6).

Principle (1) and principle (2) dissociate the committing of injustice from goodness and nobleness and associate it instead with badness and shamefulness. We may note that "bad" and "shameful," which need not necessarily be paired,[38] are paired both by Crito and by Socrates.[39] But if we look at what Crito regards as bad and shame-

---

could compensate you for its evil for you. If everything else you value . . . required you to do an unjust action, the mere fact that it is wrong would give you a final, insuperable, reason to refrain'" (emphasis in original). It is important to Socrates to collapse the distinction between *kalon* and *agathon*. This is a distinction that is made both on the popular level, in terms of what makes one admirable in the eyes of others as opposed to what serves one's best interests and, sophistically, in terms of the difference between *nomos* and *phusis*—that is, between what is conventionally right and what is right by nature. It is, I think, for this reason that Socrates links the just/unjust, good/bad, and noble/shameful in the *Crito* at 47c10, as well as in the *Euthyphro* at 7d1–2 and in the *Gorgias* at 459d1–2 and 461b6. The question of the relationship between *kalon* and *agathon* is central to much of the argument in the *Gorgias*.

36. I suspect that the "in no way," *oudamōs*, of this principle (*Cr.* 49a5) and the "in every way," *panti tropōi*, of principle (2) (*Cr.* 49b5–6) are a play on Crito's having said: "But in every way, *panti tropōi*, Socrates, obey me, and in no way, *mēdamōs*, do otherwise" (*Cr.* 46a7–8).

I have combined *Cr.* 49a4 and *Cr.* 49b8 to yield principle (3). At *Cr.* 49a4 the principle is stated thus: "In no way ought injustice to be done intentionally"; at *Cr.* 49b8 the principle is stated as: "One must in no way do injustice." We note that as stated first at *Cr.* 49a4, the principle contains the word "intentionally," *hekontas*. Yet, even when omitted, the word "intentionally" must be understood, for what purpose would be served by a principle that forbids *un*intentional action? It would seem, then, that when "intentionally" *is* stated, it is superfluous. Perhaps it is included to help us see that, whereas even unintentional injustice and doing of bad things is undesirable insofar as others suffer as a consequence of it, it is intentional injustice and doing of bad things that harms the soul of the agent.

37. The Wests translate: "For surely there is no difference between human beings doing evil and doing injustice," taking "human beings" as the subject of the infinitive rather than as its object. They do the same in the following sentence, *Cr.* 49c10–11. I prefer to take "human beings" as the object of the infinitive in both sentences because, as will become clear in my discussion, Socrates equates *adikein*, committing injustice, and *kakourgein anthrōpous*, doing bad things to human beings, in order to make the point that to do injustice is not simply to violate a rule but to seek to affect someone adversely. Others who similarly take "human beings" as the object of the infinitive think that the principle prohibits *kakourgein* with respect to human beings *as opposed to* with respect to the city of Athens and its laws. See Strauss (1983), 63: ". . . acting unjustly means inflicting evil on human beings; but the laws are not human beings." Since it is not unlikely, however, that human casualties would be a by-product of harm to laws or cities, the contrast Strauss draws is, perhaps, too sharp.

38. In the *Gorgias*, Polus seeks to separate "bad" from "shameful": whereas what is "bad" hurts one's self-interest (narrowly conceived), it may nevertheless appear noble according to conventional standards. Socrates seeks to join the two terms: both what is bad and what is shameful hurt one's self-interest—philosophically conceived. Callicles joins them as well, presumably because he accords, or says he accords, no merit to conventional standards.

39. It is interesting that for Crito "shameful" precedes "bad" and for Socrates "bad" precedes "shameful." The difference in word order may be significant, for it is possible to regard the second term as a consequence of the first. Thus, for Crito, something is shameful and therefore bad, whereas for Socrates,

ful and compare it to what Socrates regards as bad and shameful, we see how very much their moral outlooks differ. When Crito says (*Cr.* 46a3–4), "So see to it, Socrates, that these things be not shameful as well as bad both for you and for us," he implies that Socrates can avoid a shameful and bad outcome for both himself and his friends only by escaping: for Socrates to die at the hand of his enemies when means exist whereby he can be saved reflects badly on everyone involved. When Socrates says, however, "Whether the many say so or not, and whether we must suffer things still harder than these or maybe milder,[40] doing injustice nevertheless happens to be bad and shameful in every way for the one who does injustice" (*Cr.* 49b3–6),[41] he maintains that it is not dying that is shameful and bad; what is shameful and bad is to engage in whatever means are necessary to save oneself even if these means are ignoble and unjust.

Principle (3), that one must in no way do injustice intentionally, follows from principles (1) and (2). If a practice is in no way good and noble and is bad and shameful in every way for the agent, then one ought never, in any way, to do it. Since doing injustice is such a practice, one ought never, in any way, to do injustice. Socrates endorses those actions that enhance one's human excellence and improve the state of one's soul. He condemns actions that corrupt the soul and diminish one's human excellence. Principle (4), that one must not do injustice in return, follows from principle (3): if one ought never, in any way, to do injustice, then one ought not to do injustice in return, for, presumably, to do injustice in return is to do injustice in some way.

Let us see how Socrates arrives at his final principle, principle (7), that it is not just to do bad things in return. In order to arrive at principle (7), Socrates introduces the notion of *kakourgein* in principle (5), contending that one must not do bad things,[42] having up to that point spoken only of *adikein*. We may note that principle (5) lacks the "in no way" of principle (3). Of course, had principle (5) said "in no way," Socrates could have derived principle (7) from principle (5) immediately, just as he derived principle (4) from principle (3). In other words, Socrates could have derived "It is not just to do bad things in return" directly from "In no way ought one to do bad things," just as he derived "One must not do injustice in return" directly from "One must in no way do injustice intentionally." Why, then, does Socrates not say "in no way" in principle (5)?

I wish to suggest that Socrates leaves out the phrase that would enable principle (7) to be derived directly from principle (5) because if principle (7) could be derived

---

something is bad and therefore shameful. For Crito, if something one does looks bad, then it is bad insofar as it brings one a bad reputation; for Socrates, if something one does is bad, one ought to be ashamed to be doing it.

40. Since Socrates does not know the nature of death, he does not know whether something else he might be made to suffer will be milder or harsher than death.

41. I have changed this sentence from an interrogative to a declarative one.

42. I think the basic meaning of *kakōs poiein* and *kakourgein* is to do bad things—more specifically, as Socrates will soon stipulate, to do bad things to people. I try to avoid the word "evil" because of its possible moral connotations, as well as the term "harm" because "harm" may have a technical sense of harm to the soul in several at least of Plato's dialogues. I translate *kaka* at *Cr.* 44d3 and 44d7 as "evils" because of the awkwardness of saying "the greatest bad things" and because it is quite clear that the term "evils" in that context does not imply moral evil.

directly from principle (5), Socrates would have no reason to assert principle (6), that doing bad things to human beings differs not at all from doing injustice. Yet Socrates seems quite determined to assert principle (6). We may note that even though Crito agrees, indeed agrees heartily, to principle (7), seconding it with an emphatic "in no way" (*Cr.* 49c6), even without having as yet heard the principle, principle (6), on which it depends (*Cr.* 49c7–8), Socrates makes sure nevertheless to articulate principle (6).

Principle (6) contends that doing bad things to human beings differs not at all from doing injustice. Why is this principle so critical to Socrates' moral stance? It is critical because it accomplishes two important tasks. First, it deepens the notion of *adikein* by associating it not with the breach of some conventional prohibition but rather with action whose intention is to affect some human being adversely in body or soul.[43] Although, generally speaking, Socrates certainly condemns violations of ordinary moral rules, principle (6) shows that the rules are not absolute but derive their force from the harm or good at which they aim.[44]

Second, principle (6) tightens the concept of *kakourgein*. Identifying *kakourgein* with committing injustice enables it to exclude at least some things conventionally regarded as instances of *kakourgein*—namely, doing things that are painful or unpleasant but are intended to be beneficial. Thus, for example, a just judge who orders corrective punishment might be thought to have done something bad to the criminal on an ordinary understanding of *kakourgein*, but once *kakourgein* is assimilated to *adikein*, such an action no longer qualifies as an instance of *kakourgein*. We noted in Chapter 3 that the justness or unjustness of the judges' decision in Socrates' case plays no part in Crito's thinking about whether Socrates ought to escape. For Crito, that the judges sentence Socrates to death automatically makes them Socrates' enemies. By associating *kakourgein* with doing injustice, however, Socrates makes it clear that one cannot determine whether or not the judges treat Socrates badly, apart from determining whether or not they judge justly. Principle (6) asserts that if the verdict were just, the judges' condemnation of Socrates would not qualify as

---

43. As I understand him, Socrates holds one responsible for committing injustice and for *kakourgein* if what one seeks to do to someone is something that one believes will be bad for that person—in body or soul. Socrates can therefore accuse of injustice those who willingly seek to inflict upon him what they consider to be bad things, even if he is not in fact hurt by those things (*Ap.* 30d4–5; 41d7–9).

We may note the remarkable similarity between the passages *Cr.* 47d5 and 47e7, on the one hand, and *Rep.* I.335bff., on the other, with respect to their understanding of justice as necessarily beneficial. Considering the *Republic* passage Vlastos says (1991), 196–97: "The one thing that is made clear in this passage—and this is what we must settle for—is Socrates' intuition that true moral goodness is incapable of doing intentional injury to others, for it is inherently beneficent, radiant in its operation, spontaneously communicating goodness to those who come in contact with it, always producing benefit instead of injury, so that the idea of a just man injuring anyone, friend or foe, is unthinkable."

44. When ordinary rules of justice are violated in order to prevent harm and to benefit people, the violations do not constitute injustice (see *Rep.* I.331c5–9). When a rule is violated without beneficent intent, however, not only is the victim of the rule's violation adversely affected, but the soul of the person who violates the rule is damaged as well. See *Rep.* IV.443, where Socrates tests his more profound view of justice as a function of the relations between parts of the soul by "vulgar standards" (443e2): a person who is just will not steal or betray, break an oath or agreement, commit adultery, neglect parents, or fail to care for the gods.

kakourgein and would make them not his enemies but his benefactors. Socrates, let us recall, beseeches his condemners on the jury to punish, pain, and reproach his children when they grow up and concludes: "And if you do these things we will have been treated justly by you, both I myself and my sons" (*Ap.* 41e7–42a2).[45] There is then, for Socrates, no instance of *kakourgein* that is not also an instance of *adikein*, and there is no instance of *adikein* that is not also an instance of *kakourgein*.[46]

We may now state the argument for principle (7):

(4) One must not do injustice in return.

(6) Doing bad things to human beings differs not at all from doing injustice.

∴ (7) It is not just to do bad things to human beings in return.

Crito's ready acceptance of principle (7), a principle that condemns the maltreatment of any human being, including, specifically, one's enemy, arouses Socrates' suspicion: "And see to it, Crito, that by agreeing to this, you are not agreeing contrary to your opinion" (*Cr.* 49d1). The many, as Socrates points out, do not condemn retaliatory *kakourgein*, and Crito, as Socrates knows, shares the views of the many.

Let us summarize Socrates' moral considerations. One ought to consider when acting only one thing—whether what one does is just or unjust. If the action one is contemplating is unjust, one ought not to do it, no matter what one must suffer as a consequence. Since Socrates in escaping from prison acts against the Athenians' will as expressed in their verdict and sentence, the escape must be accomplished stealthily and will require "paying money and gratitude" to those who would lead him out, practices that may well be unjust. It is never right intentionally to do injustice or to do injustice in return. Since intentionally doing bad things to people—that is, doing to them things meant not to benefit them but to affect them adversely—is the same as doing injustice, it is never right intentionally to do bad things to people or to do so in return for similar treatment at their hands. There is no relation in which others can stand to one that would justify one's intentional maltreatment of them. Socrates' view is one that only "a certain few" hold; Crito is clearly not among them, however quickly he agrees to everything Socrates proposes.

---

45. Similarly, giving something "good" to someone when one recognizes that on this occasion that good thing is likely to be harmful is an instance of *kakourgein*—for example, giving "pleasant things" to patients who are ill in order to please them, knowing all the while that such treats will in fact affect them adversely. See *Gorg.* 522a2–3.

46. I understand principle (6) to equate *kakourgein* with *adikein*. I find intriguing, however, Woozley's suggestion (1979), 20, that we might understand the statement "Doing bad things to human beings differs not at all from doing injustice" on analogy with "Taking money from the church plate is the same as stealing." On Woozley's suggestion, just as one would not say "Stealing is the same as taking money from the church plate," one would also not say "Doing injustice differs not at all from doing bad things to human beings." Although Woozley's proposed reading is certainly possible, nevertheless I think Socrates' intention is to equate *kakourgein* with *adikein*. The reason principle (6) is phrased as if it is specifically about how *kakourgein* is related to *adikein* is for the sake of deriving principle (7), which is about *kakourgein*, from principles (4) and (6).

I do not agree with Kahn (1989), 34, who understands this passage as forbidding *kakourgein* when and only when it involves doing "wrongful harm." On my view, what this passage does is forbid *kakourgein* because, insofar as it differs not at all from *adikein*, it *is* the doing of wrongful harm.

Socrates' Argument against Escape

As Socrates conceives the question he must answer, it is whether it is just or unjust to engage in such practices as the paying of money and gratitude, practices necessitated by leaving prison against the will of the Athenians. In his attempt to answer this question, Socrates, as we have seen, rehearses for Crito some old Socratic principles that Socrates presumes Crito to have always endorsed. This review complements Socrates' earlier attempt to convince Crito of several others of his old views, in particular, that the opinion of the many is worthless, that the many are unable to inflict the truly great evils, and that the many's considerations of money, reputation, and children are unimportant. But how does the reaffirmation of Socratic moral principles and the deprecation of the many and their power contribute to the Socratic project of determining whether Socrates and Crito ought to be engaging in such escape-related acts as bribery and the paying of gratitude?

Let us begin with the assumption that acts of bribery and paying gratitude are prima facie unjust—they are, after all, deceitful and corruptive. What could make such acts just in the present situation? Crito thinks he has the answer, for he has *logoi* according to which it is right for Socrates to escape and right for Socrates' friends to do whatever is necessary to ensure a successful escape. How, then, can Socrates show that the prima facie unjust practices of bribery and paying gratitude are unjust in this case as well? His strategy is to undercut Crito's *logoi* and replace them with his own.

Which *logoi* are Crito's? Besides his belief that the view of the many is to be valued because of the many's power to kill one, his *logoi*, his rules, include these: (1) to help one's enemies advance their cause is in no way good and noble; (2) to help one's enemies is in every way bad and shameful; (3) one must in no way help one's enemies intentionally; (4) if someone harms one, retaliation is most appropriate; being a victim is bad and shameful; (5) if one is to be of any benefit at all, one must help oneself, one's family, and one's friends avoid being victims, insofar as being a victim is the worst and most shameful of all conditions. If Crito's beliefs and principles are sound, then the deceit involved in bribery and the corruptive flattery involved in paying gratitude would all be justified under the present circumstances: bribing the guards and the men who would lead Socrates out of prison and offering them one's gratitude would thwart the will of the enemy; moreover, such practices would help Socrates avoid the worst and most shameful of all conditions. And, of course, as a consequence of such activities, the reputation of Socrates' friends will be saved and Socrates' children will be better provided for. On Crito's view, therefore, the just course is to do whatever is necessary to facilitate Socrates' escape and thereby save his life.

But what if Crito's beliefs and rules are unsound? What if it is false that what the many believe and what the many can do to one are of paramount importance? What if it is not money, reputation, and children that matter but living well in the sense of living justly? What if it is not thwarting enemies and avoiding bodily harm and avenging such harm that is noble and good but rather avoiding doing injustice and refraining from doing bad things to anyone, even to someone at whose hands one has suffered harm? What if it is not saving one's own life or the life of one's friends that constitutes being "of benefit" but rather living justly and helping others to live justly? If it is Socrates' principles and not Crito's rules that are true, what warrant can there be for engaging in deceitful and corruptive activities? Unless there is a higher purpose that would justify such activities in Socrates' current situation—and none has been suggested[47]—then all Socrates need do to show that it is wrong for him to engage in them is to discredit Crito's *logoi*, the *logoi* that support them. Socrates, in gaining Crito's assent to principles (1) to (7) as outlined in the previous section, undermines Crito's *logoi*, thereby eroding the foundation for Crito's view that what is to be done is whatever it takes to free Socrates. Once the old Socratic principles are restored, Socrates can proceed to his conclusion that he must not escape.

Let us turn, then, to Socrates' argument against escape. As I understand the argument, Socrates appeals in it only to events and notions already familiar to Crito. His argument looks back to things that have happened of which Crito is well aware and to principles to which Crito has been exposed. Thus, when Socrates asks Crito whether someone ought to do "the things he agrees upon with someone" (Cr. 49e6) or speaks of "those to whom [bad things] ought least to be done" (Cr. 50a2), he must be understood to be referring to an actual agreement that Crito has witnessed and to people whom Crito would readily identify as "those to whom [bad things] ought least to be done." On the prevailing view, however,[48] the argument at Cr. 49e6–50a5 alludes to events and notions that are about to be—but have not yet been—elucidated; their elucidation, it is thought, awaits the speech of the Laws: the Laws will reveal what agreement Socrates has in mind and who he thinks ought least to be treated badly.[49] Yet, if Socrates' argument against escape anticipates new notions not yet disclosed, why does Socrates insist that his argument relies on old ones (Cr. 49e2–3)? And besides, how in that case could Socrates possibly expect Crito—or anyone else, for that matter—to follow his argument? Socrates, having discredited the *logoi* to which Crito appeals in his argument, having reviewed the old *logoi* to which he and Crito have presumably always agreed, and having received Crito's assurances that he indeed abides by these old *logoi*, expects now that Crito will be able to see that escape would be wrong. When, therefore, Crito fails finally to understand Socrates' argument (Cr. 50a4–5), he fails to understand an argument he could have and should

47. There is nothing to ennoble the practices in which Socrates and his friends would be engaging: the purpose of these practices is no higher than to save life and reputation. Cf. *Gorg.* 512d6–8, where Socrates says to Callicles: "But no, blessed man. See if what is noble and good is something else besides preserving life and having it preserved," trans. Irwin (1979). By contrast, the lie in the *Republic* that is advanced for the sake of promoting the virtue of the citizens and the city and, hence, for the sake not of mere life but of the good life is a "noble lie." As I shall argue, Socrates himself engages in deception in the *Crito* by not explicitly dissociating himself from the argument of the Laws to which, as I contend, he is actually quite unsympathetic; yet he presents the Laws' argument, as will be shown, for the sake of improving Crito's soul. Therein lies its justification.

48. I call this view "the prevailing view," but it is in fact the only view that I have encountered.

49. It does not follow from the fact that the Laws' speech builds upon ideas it borrows from Socrates' argument at Cr. 49e5–50a3 that Socrates' argument relies upon or anticipates the Laws' version of those ideas. I argue in Chapter 6 that the Laws distort such Socratic notions as that one ought to do what one has agreed to do and that one ought not to do bad things "to those to whom they ought least to be done."

have been able to understand, if only he truly understood what Socrates had been saying all along.[50]

Here is the skeletal argument that Socrates presents for his conclusion that he ought not to escape: (1) one ought to do the things one agrees upon with someone, as long as those things are just, *dikaia onta* (*Cr.* 49e6), and (2) one ought not to engage in deceit, *exapatēteon* (*Cr.* 49e6–7); (3) if we go away from here not having persuaded the city, then (a) we do bad things to those to whom such things should least be done (*Cr.* 49e9–50a2) and (b) we fail to abide by the things we agreed upon—those things being just, *dikaiois ousin* (*Cr.* 50a2–3).[51]

On the assumption that this argument relies only upon old ideas and upon events with which Crito is familiar, I interpret it as follows.

(1) One ought to do the things one agrees upon with someone, as long as those things are just.

This proposition states a general rule. Is there a particular application of this rule that Socrates has in mind in positing it? Is there something that Socrates has agreed upon with someone, something that he would fail to do were he to escape? There is in fact something—something of which Crito is well aware—that perfectly fits this description: the thing that Socrates has agreed upon with the Athenians is that he will "abide by my penalty," *kai egō te tōi timēmati emmenō* (*Ap.* 39b6).[52] If one ought to do the things one has agreed upon with someone, Socrates ought surely to abide by his penalty and ought not to escape.

The obligation to do what one has agreed upon is binding, however, only when what one has agreed upon is just. Was Socrates' agreement to abide by his penalty a

---

50. What happens here in the *Crito* is different from what happens in other dialogues in which Socrates' interlocutors have difficulty understanding him. In other dialogues such as the *Euthyphro*, the *Gorgias*, the *Meno*, and the *Republic*, it is clear that there is a difficult point being made and that it will take some effort on Socrates' part to get his interlocutor to understand it. In the *Crito*, however, Socrates has already exerted considerable effort—he has cleared away all Crito's false premises and has laid out in their place the requisite true ones—and is therefore ready now to draw his conclusion. Crito can reasonably be expected at this point to be able to follow the argument.

51. The participial phrase *dikaia onta* at *Cr.* 49e6 I render "as long as those things are just." This seems to be the phrase's most likely sense when it appears in a question concerning whether certain things ought to be done. Note that I understand this phrase to refer to the substance of the agreement, not to its procedure. See Woozley (1979), 25–26, who similarly regards the substantive reading as the more natural one. Woozley also notes that the substantive reading accords better than the procedural one with Socrates' absolute principle that under no circumstances ought one to do what is unjust. Burnet (1924), 199, points out that "Socrates is always represented as making this reservation" (that is, of *dikaia onta*) and cites *Rep.* I. 335c5ff., where Socrates insists that it is not right to return a weapon to a friend who has gone mad when he asks for it or to tell him the truth.

The phrase *dikaiois ousin* at *Cr.* 50a3 I render "those things being just" because here Socrates' question implicitly accuses himself and Crito of doing something wrong insofar as they fail to abide by the just things they agreed to. Young (1974), 11, renders *dikaiois ousin* similarly: "things which are *dikaia*."

52. See E. West (1989), 78: ". . . we remember that Socrates participated in selecting his verdict and agreed to obey it." Cf. White (1996), 118: "By failing to ask for exile . . . Socrates has waived his right to it and in this sense has agreed to his punishment. . . . If the thrust of Socrates' own position were legalistic, it could perhaps rest on this waiver without more." The fact is, however, as we shall see, that in Socrates' statement that he will abide by his penalty there is more than just a waiver.

just one? Crito may well regard it as unjust: he says explicitly in making his case for escape that Socrates' helping his enemies in this matter is "not even just," *oude dikaion* (*Cr.* 45c5). And, more generally, Crito rebukes Socrates for lacking the courage to handle the judicial contest itself properly (*Cr.* 45e4–5)—that is, by gratifying his judges and thereby securing an acquittal. For Crito, it is always best to save oneself: it does not matter how old one is; it does not matter what means one must use; nothing else is of comparable importance. Furthermore, Crito apparently does not understand what makes exile so repugnant to Socrates: he does not see, any more than do Socrates' judges, why Socrates cannot just keep quiet and live out his days peacefully in another city. The injustice of Socrates' agreement with the Athenians to abide by his penalty lies for Crito in its helping Socrates' enemies to end his life.

But how does *Socrates* regard what he has agreed upon with the Athenians? Does he think that what he has agreed upon with them is unjust? Socrates believes that he has acted the part of a good and free man; he has maintained his dignity and refrained from disgraceful conduct, even though such conduct would have gratified the judges and saved his life. He compromised neither his own integrity nor that of the judges; consequently, he has no regrets concerning the conduct of his trial: "I much prefer to die having made my defense speech in this way than to live in that way" (*Ap.* 38e4–5). Nor is he sorry that he did not propose exile as a counterpenalty: insofar as exile is a bad thing, he could not have proposed it without thereby committing against himself the injustice of suggesting that he merits something bad when what he merits in fact is something wonderful. Indeed, as Socrates notes, his *daimonion* opposed neither the deeds nor the speeches connected with the trial (*Ap.* 40b). At the point at which Socrates declares that he will abide by his penalty, all other options have been exhausted: he has spurned begging and wailing and otherwise gratifying the judges; he has refused to propose prison or exile; and the fine he does propose is rejected. Preferring death to injustice, Socrates abides by his penalty; his accusers, Socrates notes, who much prefer injustice, abide by theirs as well (*Ap.* 39b6). Since of the two penalties, death and injustice, death is the better,[53] there is, as Socrates says, "due measure" in that he, the better man, incurs death, while his accusers, the worse men, incur injustice (*Ap.* 39b7–8).[54] But Socrates does not merely incur death; he chooses it.[55] He goes to his death not a mere victim of injustice—though a victim of injustice he surely is—but a champion of justice as well. His decision to abide by his penalty,

53. Socrates says, moreover, at *Ap.* 32d1–3: "I do not care about death in any way at all—if it is not too crude to say so—but . . . my whole care is to commit no unjust or impious deed."

54. By way of introducing the notion of "due measure," Socrates remarks: "Perhaps these things even had to be so" (*Ap.* 39b7). Socrates here acknowledges the unhappy reality that in an unjust city there is little chance that a just man will flourish; the "due measure" lies in his suffering the lesser of two evils—death rather than injustice.

55. There is choice implicit in the term "abide by"; otherwise, Socrates could have stopped after saying: "And now I, since I am slow and old, am caught by the slower, while my accusers, since they are clever and sharp, are caught by the faster, by evil. And now I go away, having incurred at your hand the penalty of death, while they have incurred at the hand of the truth wretchedness and injustice" (*Ap.* 39b1–6). By going on to say that he abides by his penalty as his accusers do by theirs, Socrates casts himself and his accusers not as passive victims of their respective penalties but as active participants in them. Socrates prefers death to injustice; his acccusers prefer injustice. In the *Crito*, the term "abiding by" has the active sense of firmly standing by a principle.

therefore, takes the form not of quiet resolve but of a veritable proclamation.[56] To choose death over injustice is the mark of a free man,[57] and Socrates asserts his freedom in making this choice.[58] What Socrates chooses—to abide by his penalty—is the just choice; it is the only choice a just man in his situation could have made.[59]

To reach the conclusion now that escape would be wrong, all Socrates must do is apply the general principle that one ought to do the things one has agreed upon with someone, as long as they are just, to the particular thing he has agreed upon, namely, to abide by his penalty. Since by escaping Socrates fails to abide by his penalty in accordance with his just agreement to do so, it would be wrong for him to escape. Both at his trial and after it, the cost for Socrates of securing exile is too high: in both cases it requires doing something unjust. In the absence of any higher purpose to justify Socrates' breaking his word, and without the support that Crito's *logoi* would provide, the ordinarily unjust act of breaking one's agreement remains unjust. Socrates may not escape.

(2) One ought not to engage in deceit rather than do the things one has agreed upon with someone, as long as they are just.

Because escape defies the will of the Athenians, the alternative to Socrates' doing what he has agreed upon with the Athenians is for him to engage in deceit. We al-

---

We may note that Socrates never says that he abides by his penalty because it is the law or because the court has so decided. If there is any place in the *Apology* where one would expect to find Socrates asserting his willingness to suffer any penalty the court decides upon because he accepts the legitimacy of its authority, this is it. Yet he says no such thing. We may contrast Socrates' conspicuous silence about the government's authority to punish him as it sees fit with his explicit recognition of their authority to try him (*Ap.* 19a6–7).

56. This proclamation is what the Laws will denounce later as Socrates' having "plumed himself" (*Cr.* 52c6).

It is possible that Socrates' proclamation has yet another—though surely very secondary—purpose. We know that Socrates does not wish to go to prison; he does not even wish to go to prison until he can pay a fine; undoubtedly, then, he prefers not to go to prison to await his execution. Moreover, Crito, as we know, offers to stand surety for Socrates' not escaping, probably in order to keep him out of jail. (See the discussion of this issue in the section of Chapter 3 entitled "Crito's Questionable Morality.") By declaring for all to hear that he will abide by his penalty, Socrates in effect assures the court that he will not escape; perhaps he hopes that the court will then see fit not to imprison him. Even if Socrates does entertain this hope, however, his declaration is nevertheless no mere ploy; he is perfectly sincere in asserting his choice. His decision is categorical and not made to depend on what the Athenians decide with respect to imprisoning him. How, then, will Socrates not be violating his agreement with them if he escapes?

57. We may note that Socrates chooses not death over exile but death over injustice. Socrates spurns exile only because to propose it would be to commit injustice against himself; it is not because exile is less desirable than death that he spurns it.

58. For Socrates, it is those who choose injustice in order to avoid death who are the slavish ones. See *Gorg.* 510a–d.

59. See Friedländer (1964), II, 178: "The fact that the philosopher dies voluntarily, as a logical consequence of the way he has lived, needed to be confirmed even after the *Apology*. Otherwise, the objection that death was forced on him by external compulsion could not be refuted. Hence, it must be shown clearly that Socrates' death was an act of free choice." The *Crito*, as I argue, shows that, in refusing to escape, Socrates again makes the choice to abide by his penalty, the choice required by the principles by which he lived.

ready know the implications of deceit: Socrates will have to be "stolen" out of prison (*Cr.* 44e4), and he and the others will be obliged to pay money and gratitude to those who will lead him out (*Cr.* 48c8–d1). Yet, as Socrates has said, if "all these things" are unjust, that will count decisively against escape—there will be nothing else to consider (*Cr.* 48d2–5).

It is quite evident that deeds of stealth, bribery, and obsequious flattery do not normally recommend themselves to Socrates. As Socrates says in the *Apology*, "there are many other devices to escape death in each of the dangers, if one dares to do and say anything at all" (*Ap.* 39a4–6), but "neither in a court case nor in war should I or anyone else devise a way to escape death by doing anything at all" (*Ap.* 38e5–39a1). Just as for Socrates in the *Apology* it was just to accept the penalty of death rather than degrade himself and encourage the judges to substitute favors for justice, so too in the *Crito* he regards it as just to remain in prison and die rather than demean himself (and his friends) through the practices associated with deception. Both Crito and the Laws think Socrates should have accepted exile when the Athenians were willing (*Cr.* 45e4–5; 52c3–9); indeed, Crito thinks he should choose exile even now that they are unwilling and despite the fact that the choice of exile will involve stealth and bribery. Socrates, however, having earlier agreed to "abide by my penalty" rather than sacrifice his dignity, corrupt the judges, or commit injustice against himself in order to secure exile, will hardly seek now to secure the same end by deception. In the absence of any higher purpose that would justify Socrates' engaging in deceptive practices, and with Crito's rules defeated, Socrates can only conclude that to escape would be unjust.

(3a) If we go away from here not having persuaded the city,[60] we treat badly those who ought least to be so treated, *hous hēkista dei* (*Cr.* 50a2).

To whom does Socrates refer by the phrase *hous hēkista dei*? If Crito is to have any chance of following the argument, Socrates must be referring to those people whom Crito would acknowledge to be least deserving of bad treatment. If Socrates were referring instead to the city and its laws, entities not even mentioned yet in the dialogue, how could Crito—how could anyone—be expected to grasp his meaning? Moreover, if Socrates thought that it was the city to which bad ought least to be done, how could we account for his conspicuous shift to an unidentified plural "some," *tinas*, immediately after having explicitly mentioned the city? Having said, "If we go away from here not having persuaded *the city*," would he not most naturally have

---

60. The expression *ek toutōn dē athrei*, "observe [what follows] from these things" (*Cr.* 49e9), suggests that what follows refers back to the previous sentence. It is likely, therefore, that the "going away from here not having persuaded the city" constitutes a violation of the duty just mentioned—the duty to do the things one has agreed upon and not evade them by deception. The most direct way in which "going away from here not having persuaded the city" can constitute a violation of the duty to keep one's agreement and not evade it by deception is if what one has agreed to is, specifically, not to go away from here without having persuaded the city. It is precisely this that Socrates' agreement to abide by his penalty amounts to.

There are two ways in which Socrates, were he to escape, would be going away "not having persuaded the city": he would not have persuaded the judges by teaching, as he would have liked, because a one-day trial provides too little time for that; and he would not have persuaded them as they would have liked, by saying and doing what would gratify them.

continued "do we do bad to some*one*, *tina* [fem. sing., referring to "the city"] — indeed to one to whom, *hēin* [fem. sing.] it ought least to be done — or not?"[61]

Those whom Crito would recognize as least deserving of harm are surely oneself, one's family, and one's friends.[62] And it is not unlikely that Socrates would concur — in some sense. For even though Socrates holds that no one is to be treated badly, he may well look out first and foremost for the well-being of his own soul and those of his friends: we may recall that Socrates tells us in the *Apology* that he rebukes most of all those closest to him by kinship, *genei* (*Ap.* 30a4), and in the *Gorgias* Socrates says: "This must surely be the help that it is most shameful to be unable to render to one's friends and relatives ..." (*Gorg.* 509b6–8). If, then, Socrates in the *Crito* is worried about doing bad to those to whom it ought least to be done — namely, himself and his friends — what he is worried about is involving them in injustice.[63] Injustice is "in every way bad and shameful for the one who does injustice" (*Cr.* 49b4–6); it corrupts the soul (*Cr.* 47d5; 47e7); corruption of the soul is far worse than corruption of the body (*Cr.* 47e6–48a4); it makes life not worth living (*Cr.* 47e6–7).[64]

(3b) If we go away from here not having persuaded the city, then we fail to abide by the things we have agreed to — those things being just.

What are the "things" that we have agreed to? Are they the same things as those discussed earlier, in (1) and (2)? Whereas it is certainly not impossible that Socrates here merely recalls his earlier principles — that (1) one ought to do what one has agreed upon with someone as long as it is just and (2) not evade it by deception — concluding now that escape would violate those principles, there is reason to think that the "things we agreed to" here are distinct from the earlier "things he agrees upon with someone." For, first, if these things are the same as those, why does (3b) not follow immediately upon (1) and (2)?; why would Socrates break the flow of the argument by interposing (3a)? And, second, there are two differences between the "things we agreed to" as found in (3b) and "the things he agrees upon with someone" as found in (1) and (2). One

---

61. Although one could say that Socrates uses the plurals *tinas* and *hous* to include not only the city of Athens but its laws as well, it remains odd that he would bypass the obvious antecedent *tēn polin*, "the city," and allude instead to the hitherto never mentioned "laws" by only a plural indefinite pronoun.

62. According to Dover (1974), 275, the expression "whom it is least appropriate" is a "stock phrase" meaning family. In support of this point, he cites Antiphon, i.1; Euripides, *Bacchae*.26, *Electra*.1012, *Iphigenia at Aulis*.487; Demosthenes, xlviii.1. There is no reason to doubt that Socrates and certainly Crito would easily extend the expression to include self and friends. Crito speaks of being ashamed "for you and for us, your companions" (*Cr.* 45d8–e1) and of Socrates' not escaping as shameful and bad "both for you and for us" (*Cr.* 46a3–4). As Socrates considers the possibility of escape, he is surely concerned most about himself and his friends, rather than his family, since it is he and his friends who are in a position to commit injustice and whose souls are therefore most in danger and most in need of protection.

63. In the *Gorgias*, Socrates says he is most afraid of not being able to help himself and others refrain from doing injustice in word or deed against gods or men: if he could not provide this help, then, he says, "I would indeed be ashamed" (*Gorg.* 522d3–7).

64. The notion that among people there are some who ought least to have bad things done to them reminds us that within a single individual as well there is a part that ought least to be corrupted, a part that is "in no way ... more paltry" than the body, a part that is "more honorable" than the body, the part of us that "the unjust maims and the just profits" — the soul (*Cr.* 47e6–48a4).

difference is that in (1) and (2) the things agreed upon are things that *one* person agrees to do, whereas in (3b) the things agreed upon are things that "we" — that is, two people together — agree upon. A second difference is that in (1) and (2) Socrates affirms the importance of his doing, *poiēteon* (Cr. 49e6), what he has told someone else he would do; in (3b) Socrates is concerned lest "we" — that is, he *and Crito* — fail to abide by, *emmenomen* (Cr. 50a2), what they have agreed upon with each other.

We need look back no farther than Cr. 48b11–c1 to confirm that the "things we agreed to," the things "we" would fail to "abide by" should the escape take place, are the *logoi* to which Crito and Socrates have mutually consented. At Cr. 48b11–c1 Socrates begins his deliberations with respect to escape as follows: "Therefore," he says, "from the things agreed upon, it must be considered whether it is just for me to go out of here although the Athenians are not permitting me to go, or not just." The "things agreed upon" are clearly the principles just established as principles that "abide," *menei* (Cr. 48b5–7, 9–10),[65] "for us," *hēmin* (Cr. 48b5), for Socrates and Crito — namely, that it is not living but living well that is to be regarded as most important and that living well and living nobly and justly are the same. Given these things to which Socrates and Crito have agreed, *tōn homologoumenōn* (Cr. 48b11), it is now to be determined whether trying to go out of here without the permission of the Athenians is just or unjust. When Socrates asks, then, in (3b) whether "we abide by the things we agreed to" if we go away from here not having persuaded the city, what can he be asking but whether by escaping he and Crito remain true to the principles to which they have both agreed? Indeed, Socrates returns to the theme of "what we agreed to" at Cr. 49a5–7, where he asks Crito whether doing injustice is in no way good or noble "as we have often agreed in the past," continuing to ask at Cr. 49a6–7 whether "all those former agreements of ours have been poured away in these few days." These agreements are, moreover, agreements that Socrates explicitly expects Crito to *abide by*; only if he does abide by them will Socrates proceed to the final stage of his deliberations: "But if you abide by, *emmeneis* (Cr. 49e2), the things from before, hear what comes after this" (Cr. 49e2–3). Since Crito affirms that he does abide by them, *All' emmenō* (Cr. 49e4), is it any wonder that Socrates asks at Cr. 50a2–3 if, by escaping, "we abide by, *emmenomen*, the things we agreed to — those things being just — or not"?

Socrates' concern in (3b), then, is not identical with his concern in (1) and (2). Whereas in (1) and (2) he fears that by escaping he will engage in deception in order to avoid keeping his word, in (3b) he fears that for him to escape in accordance with Crito's wishes is for him and Crito to legitimate the considerations advanced by Crito in his speech and to abandon the principles which they, together, have always endorsed. There are at least five such principles: (i) that the opinion of the many is unimportant (Cr. 44c6–7; 48a5–10); (ii) that life is not worth living with a corrupt soul (Cr. 47e6–7); (iii) that it is not living but living nobly and justly that is most important (Cr. 48b5–10); (iv) that the only consideration to take into account upon acting is justice (Cr. 49d3–5); (v) that committing injustice is in every way bad and shameful for the agent (Cr. 49b4–6).

65. Cf. *Gorg.* 480b2–3: ". . . or what else are we saying, Polus, if our previous agreements, *homologēmata*, remain firm, *menei*?," trans. Irwin (1979).

We may now state, then, Socrates' argument against escape:

(1) If Socrates attempts to escape with Crito's help, Socrates will fail to do what he agreed with the Athenians to do—that is, abide by his penalty—even though what he agreed to do is just.

(2) If Socrates does not do what he agreed upon with the Athenians, Socrates will be involved in the injustices of deceit—that is, in stealth and paying money and gratitude to those who would lead Socrates out of prison.

(3a) Since it is unjust to fail to fulfill one's just agreement and engage instead in deceit, Socrates and Crito, by involving themselves and their friends in the attempt to escape, would be doing bad things to, in the sense of damaging the souls of, those to whom bad things ought least to be done: oneself and one's friends.

(3b) Since escape will involve Socrates and Crito and their friends in injustice, Socrates and Crito, by attempting Socrates' escape, will fail to abide by the just principles upon which they have agreed with each other, principles that would forbid such action.

Crito does not understand the argument (*Cr.* 50a5). It is not that he understands it somewhat and requires only clarification; he does not understand it at all: he finds himself utterly unable to respond. Crito cannot see how saving one's own life or the life of one's friend and thereby protecting the reputation of oneself or one's friends can possibly be construed as treating badly those people who ought least to be so treated. Crito's concern with the body and with things associated with the body prevents him from appreciating the havoc that such acts as breaking an agreement, cheating, bribing, flattering, and stealing someone away from prison can wreak upon the souls of those concerned. Crito does not understand Socrates' argument because he shares to the end the moral perspective of the many.[66]

Socrates' argument against escape is complete as of this point. He has given his reasons in terms of the injustices that escape would involve and in terms of just principles to which he has adhered unwaveringly throughout his many years. The reasons Socrates offers reflect the commitment to justice and to the use of one's own reason so characteristic of Socrates in the *Apology*. The Socrates of the second part of the *Crito, Cr.* 46b1–50a5, is indeed completely consistent with the Socrates of the *Apology*. This Socrates obeys his own reasoned conclusions with respect to justice and will die rather than abandon those conclusions. He is fiercely independent, loyal

---

66. On the view presented here, Crito fails to understand the argument not because he is unable to decode Socrates' esoteric expressions but because he does not share Socrates' moral outlook. It is interesting to see how common is the view among commentators that the reason Crito says he does not understand is that he understands all too well. Adam (1888), 60, says: ". . . the words are full of pathos: Crito sees but too clearly what the conclusion will be." Kitchel (1898), 157, implies that Crito fears what will follow if he does understand and reply accordingly. Also, Dyer and Seymour (1885), 135: "Crito seems afraid of understanding what is meant; the consequences alarm him." By contrast, Congleton (1974), 435, accepts at face value Crito's inability to understand, attributing this inability to Crito's "innocent lawlessness." Like Congleton, Strauss (1983), 60, also takes seriously Crito's inability to understand, but he attributes this inability to Crito's belief that in assisting Socrates in escaping from prison "neither he nor Socrates would . . . inflict evil on human beings, and least of all on those whom one ought least to harm, *i.e.*, relatives and friends."

only to the *logos* that appears best to him upon reasoning. It is this *logos* that determines his decision not to escape: to escape is for him to fail to do what he agreed to do though it was just; it is to be engaged in unseemly deceptive practices; it is to abandon without justification principles to which he has always subscribed; it is, therefore, to treat himself and his friends very badly, for it is to cause injustice to take root in their souls.

Socrates as Crito's Friend

In Chapter 3 we saw the way in which Crito seeks to give expression to his feelings of devotion, friendship, and love for his lifelong companion, Socrates. Crito, we observed, is prepared to sacrifice much—his money and property, perhaps even his citizenship—in order to save his friend. But all his sacrifices aim at securing the well-being of Socrates' body: his life, his safety, his reputation.

Why does Crito insist on helping Socrates achieve an end Socrates does not want through means of which Socrates disapproves? Because Crito is so thoroughly convinced of the truth of his unphilosophical and utterly conventional views that he cannot quite believe that Socrates, in his heart of hearts, does not share those views. He does not, as we have seen, really know Socrates.

Socrates is no less a friend to Crito than Crito is to him. He, too, goes to great lengths to save his friend, although what he tries to save is not Crito's body but Crito's soul. Socrates expends considerable effort in correcting what he believes to be Crito's current misconceptions about the power of the many and about what is truly just, noble, and good; he seeks to replace Crito's popular and conventional concerns about money, reputation, and children with the single concern of justice.

Nor is this all. As we have seen, featured prominently in his argument against escape is Socrates' special regard for the welfare of his friends: he worries lest by escape he and Crito will do bad things to "those to whom they ought least to be done"—to Socrates himself and to his friends. Socrates, it is clear, does not hold the view that one should concern oneself equally with the welfare of everyone. Although Socrates does not say—and, indeed, would never say—that one may do injustice or bad things to anyone, he does say that there are some to whom one may *least* do such things. For Socrates, however, the things that one should do least to oneself and one's friends are things that adversely affect the soul.

We may now ask regarding Socrates the same question we asked regarding Crito: Why does Socrates insist on helping Crito achieve an end Crito does not want through means of which Crito disapproves? And we may give a parallel answer: because Socrates is so thoroughly convinced of the truth of his philosophical and startlingly unconventional views, that he cannot quite believe that Crito, in his heart of hearts, does not share these views. Does Socrates, then, know Crito no better than Crito knows him?

Perhaps we should not expect Socrates to know just how conventional Crito is. But why does he take it for granted, as he certainly appears to in the *Crito*, both that Crito is sympathetic to his moral views and that he has come to be sympathetic to Socratic views as a result of having talked with Socrates? Specifically, what justifies

Socrates' frequent references in the *Crito* to his and Crito's past agreements? By what right does he say, for example, that "at our age, Crito, we old men have long been seriously conversing with each other" (*Cr.* 49a9–b1)? Is Crito a regularly active participant in Socratic philosophical discussions? Plato certainly does not portray him that way. And even if Crito is often present when philosophical discussions take place between Socrates and others, that in itself would hardly constitute evidence of his general concurrence with Socratic views.

Indeed, Socrates knows better than to regard Crito as someone who shares his views. In the *Euthydemus*, as we have seen,[67] Socrates is well aware of Crito's fondness for money—a trait that is, certainly for Socrates, a sure sign of a nonphilosophic disposition. And, as we know from the *Crito*, Crito has by the time of the *Crito* already offered Socrates "the same argument"—the same conventional argument— "many times" (*Cr.* 48e2–3). Moreover, Socrates in the *Crito* betrays several times his suspicion that Crito is one of the many. First, there is Socrates' ironic remark at *Cr.* 46e3–47a2: "For you, humanly speaking, are not about to die tomorrow, and the present calamity would not lead you astray."[68] Second, Socrates, fully expecting Crito to take the bait, dangles before him at *Cr.* 48a10–11 a possible objection that "someone" might raise to his just completed argument for the importance of heeding expert advice rather than the opinion of the many—that "the many are able to kill us." As expected, Crito takes the bait. Third, Socrates admonishes Crito at *Cr.* 49c11–d2 not simply to agree to whatever Socrates says: "And see to it, Crito, that by agreeing to this, you are not agreeing contrary to your opinion. For I know that this seems and will seem so only to a certain few." In this third instance, Socrates shows not only that he suspects Crito of being one of the many but that he is not sure that he can take even Crito's explicit agreements at face value. Nevertheless, it is not until *Cr.* 50a4–5, where Crito finally confesses that he cannot answer because he does not understand, that Socrates faces squarely the reality that he cannot fruitfully conduct with Crito a philosophical investigation into the question of escape.

Until it is absolutely beyond doubt, then, that joint philosophical inquiry between Socrates and Crito is impossible, Socrates does all he can to persuade Crito of the wrongness of escape by using standard Socratic elenchus and relying on Crito's presumed endorsement of standard Socratic views. Socrates, like Crito, pursues his end as if unaware of the inevitable resistance he will encounter. Socrates, like Crito, is determined, however unrealistically, to give his friend the benefit of the doubt. For to Socrates, just as to Crito, the issue at hand is far too critical and the stakes far too high for him to admit before he absolutely must—even to himself—the hopelessness of his cause.

The stakes for Socrates are nothing short of the well-being of Crito's soul. It is all-important, therefore, that he help Crito, that he get him to think not about how to avoid death but about how to avoid dishonesty, stealth, deception, and corruption. Crito, however, can neither comprehend nor accept help of this kind. When he says finally, "I do not understand," what he does not understand is simply this: how Socrates can think that by getting himself killed and soiling the reputation of his friends he

---

67. See the section in Chapter 3 entitled "The Unphilosophical Crito."
68. See Chapter 3, n. 11.

will not have done bad things to those to whom such things ought least to be done. But it is precisely this that Socrates fervently hopes Crito would by now understand: that what is of utmost importance is the well-being of the soul, that the well-being of the soul is threatened by injustice, and that insofar as escape involves injustice, the very best thing Socrates can do for them all is to refuse to escape.

Socrates' hopes fade in the face of Crito's admission that he does not understand. Socrates can no longer ignore the gulf that separates Crito from him. He accepts now, for the first time, that Crito will not be persuaded through rational argument. It is at this point that Socrates makes the greatest sacrifice for his friend: he steps aside, transferring the argument to the Laws. The Laws will speak to Crito in a way that Crito understands; they will produce a "willing" Crito. But they will not engage Crito in elenctic exchange, and they will not defend Socratic principles. Why Socrates surrenders the argument to the Laws and how that surrender constitutes a supreme act of kindness on behalf of his friend Crito is discussed in Chapter 8.

5

"Especially an Orator"

> So, if oratory is used to defend injustice, Polus,
> one's own or that of one's relatives, companions,
> or children, *or that of one's country when it acts un-*
> *justly*, it is of no use to us at all. . . .
>> Plato, *Gorg.* 480b7–9, trans. Zeyl (1987);
>> emphasis added

Cr. 50a6–d1 contains a rather heated opening exchange between Socrates and the Laws. With the advent of these new speakers come radical changes in tone, in style, in substance. The torrent of words unleashed on Socrates by the Laws constitutes an unsettling departure from Socrates' far less strident mode of discourse. In place of Socrates' rather civil "considering in common," we find a veritable verbal assault by the Laws; in place of Socrates' question-and-answer style of *Cr.* 47a2–48b11, 49b3–c8, and 49e5–50a5, we find the Laws' lengthy harangues replete with accusations and threats;[1] in place of Socrates' long-held principles, we find the Laws' presumption that the city's claim upon its citizens is absolute.

The Laws are introduced into the *Crito* at the point at which Socrates' method, principles, concerns, and argument have failed to persuade Crito of the wrongness of escape. Crito, as he himself says, does not understand (*Cr.* 50a5); Crito, it seems, cannot understand. Yet Socrates, as we saw earlier, "regard[s] it as important to act after persuading you, not while you are unwilling" (*Cr.* 48e3–5). The Laws' speech represents, then, Socrates' new way of trying to get through to Crito. This new way, however, as we shall see, abandons all that is recognizably Socratic.

Three features of the section *Cr.* 50a6–d1 alert the reader to the discontinuity between what precedes this section and what follows it: (1) that Socrates shields Crito from the Laws' attack; (2) that Socrates links what the Laws say to what orators would

---

1. Grote (1875), I, 302, calls the speech of the Laws a "rhetorical harangue."

say; and (3) that Socrates differs with the Laws concerning what a citizen "agrees to." Let us consider in turn each of these features.

Protecting Crito

Considering Socrates' firmly held conviction that to escape would be wrong, perhaps the most striking feature of the introductory exchange is the Laws' opening words: "Tell me, Socrates, what do you have in mind to do?" (Cr. 50a8–9). Even though Socrates portrays the Laws and the community of the city as coming and standing before "us" (Cr. 50a6)— before him and Crito—he portrays them as *addressing* him. Yet, what Socrates has in mind to do, as we well know, is to remain in prison and abide by his penalty; it is Crito who has escape in mind.[2] By right, then, the Laws' rebuke should have been directed at Crito, the advocate of escape.[3] Nevertheless, from the very beginning of the Laws' speech to its very end, Socrates ensures that he alone bears the full brunt of the Laws' reprimands.[4]

We may note that before the Laws are introduced into the dialogue—that is, for as long as Socrates is still addressing Crito directly—Crito is cast in the role of instigator and Socrates, if he goes along with Crito, in that of mere capitulator: Socrates speaks of escape as his "yielding" to Crito (Cr. 46c3) or "obeying" him (Cr. 48e1). Moreover, Socrates consistently includes Crito as a full participant in the deed: "whether we will do just things by paying money and gratitude . . ." (Cr. 48c8–d1); "those of us who are leading out as well as those of us who are being led out" (Cr. 48d1–2); "if we seem to be doing unjust deeds" (Cr. 48d3); "do we do evil to some?" (Cr. 50a1); "And do we abide by?" (Cr. 50a2). Socrates, then, when inquiring with Crito into the rightness or wrongness of escape, treats the escape as a joint venture, initiated by Crito. The Laws, however, no longer inquiring but reprimanding, direct their ire solely at Socrates. That the Laws assign full responsibility to Socrates for the escape plan, though Socrates himself assigns responsibility to Crito, is one clear sign that the Laws are not simply a new voice taking up the old Socratic line.[5]

2. Burnet (1924), 199–200, speaks as if Socrates uses the Laws to make the case against himself: "The personification of the Laws . . . allows Socrates to invest the declaration of his principles with a certain emotion . . . the style of this passage is remarkable. Plato aims at representing the Laws as pleading earnestly with Socrates (in fact, of course, Socrates is pleading with himself . . .)." But do the Laws need to plead with Socrates or Socrates with himself? Socrates has already decided not to escape. The Laws, then, can only be pleading with Crito—though indirectly, through Socrates.

3. At the end of their speech, even the Laws acknowledge this fact, saying: "But let not Crito persuade you to do what he says rather than what we say" (Cr. 54c8–d1).

4. The Laws, of course, must speak to Socrates and must consider Socrates' agreements and obligations in order to determine that it would be wrong for Socrates to escape. But the opening charge that they level against Socrates, "What do you have in mind to do?," is clearly misdirected, given the fact that escape is Crito's idea.

5. Both Kitchel (1898), 157, and Dyer and Seymour (1885), 135, think that Socrates has the Laws address him alone because Socrates recognizes that it is really he who would be at fault if he were to escape. Kitchel: ". . . this change from *hēmin* . . . indicates that Socrates feels that he is individually responsible, mainly, in this matter"; Dyer and Seymour: "The somewhat abrupt transition from *hēmin* alone to *ō Sōkrates* suggests the fact that in this matter Socrates considered himself alone responsible to the Laws." It is evident, however, that Socrates did not earlier regard himself as "alone responsible."

The Laws as Rhetoricians

Of what do the Laws accuse Socrates? They accuse him of destroying them and the whole city "as far as it lies in you" (Cr. 50b2)[6] and of doing so, specifically, by destroying "the law that orders that the judgments reached in trials be authoritative" (Cr. 50b7–8). According to the Laws' reasoning, since a city whose judgments are disregarded by private citizens cannot survive, the law that declares all such judgments authoritative is an indispensable one whose violation will destroy the city. As the Laws continue their argument, they make a case not only for the authoritativeness of all the city's judgments, but also for the authoritativeness of all orders of any kind that the city issues.

Although Socrates has, as we know, no intention of escaping, it now devolves upon him to produce a defense of his alleged attempt to destroy the city by way of destroying the law that legitimates all verdicts.

Before considering the defense that Socrates offers, it is important to raise the question that will occupy us throughout the rest of the book: For whom do the Laws speak? Virtually everything to be said as the book continues will bear in some measure on this question. Nevertheless, the most powerful hint as to the identity of the Laws is to be found in this introductory section.

The hint is contained in four words in Greek, *allōs te kai rhētōr*, three in English, "especially an orator" (Cr. 50b7). Through these words Socrates makes it known that he regards the Laws' speech as a rhetorical display, a display in defense of the authority of all official verdicts.[7] After the Laws' initial outburst, in which they demand to be told what Socrates thinks he is doing if not destroying the laws and the city as far as it lies in him, Socrates turns to Crito and asks how they ought to reply to "these and other such things" (Cr. 50b6). "These" can only refer to the eruption just past and "other such things" to the speech of the Laws yet to come. And Socrates continues: "For someone, especially an orator, would have many things to say on behalf of this law that is being destroyed—the law that orders that the judgments reached in trials be authoritative" (Cr. 50b6–8). It is clear that Socrates identifies "these and other such things"—that is, the things the Laws have just said and the things they are about to say—with the "many things" that an orator would say on behalf of the law rendering all verdicts binding. The Laws, then, are the oratorical champions of the law that legitimates all judgments rendered by the city.[8]

6. The phrase is *to son meros*, a phrase used earlier at Cr. 45d2. We discuss it later in Chapter 6, n. 4, and in the section in Chapter 8 entitled "Engaging Crito."

7. Instead of just presenting, through the agency of the Laws, a rhetorical case against escape, Socrates calls attention to its rhetorical nature by his use of the expression "someone, especially an orator." The reader becomes obliged, therefore, to consider the import of Socrates' characterizing the Laws' speech in this way. See White (1996), 114.

8. We may note that by equating destruction of the single law that renders all judgments authoritative with destruction of the city, the Laws indeed speak as "someone, especially an orator," would. See Grote (1875), I, 302: "It is a doctrine which orators of all varieties (Perikles, Nikias, Kleon, Lysias, Isokrates, Demosthenes, Aeschines, Lykurgus) would be alike emphatic in upholding: upon which probably Sophists habitually displayed their own eloquence, and tested the talents of their pupils. It may be considered as almost an Athenian common-place." Also Woozley (1979), 111: "The claim that to break the law is to destroy the law is a familiar theme of public rhetoric." According to Burnet (1924),

What is the significance of Socrates' identifying the Laws' discourse with what an orator would say on behalf of the law establishing the authority of all verdicts? First and foremost, by linking what the Laws say with what an orator would say, Socrates decisively dissociates himself from the speech of the Laws.[9] Socrates in the *Apology* fervently denies his accusers' "shameless" characterization of him as a clever speaker— "unless of course they call a clever speaker the one who speaks the truth" (*Ap.* 17b4– 5). Since, of course, nobody calls the one who speaks the truth a clever speaker, Socrates can only mean to contrast what he does, namely, speak the truth, with what orators are in the business of doing—persuading without regard for truth.[10] More-over, Socrates distances himself from what the Laws say not only by identifying it as what "especially an orator" might say but also by relating it to what "someone," *tis* (*Cr.* 50b6), especially an orator, might say. It is, as we recall, "someone" who might say: "But the many are able to kill us" (*Cr.* 48a10–11). "Someone" is not Socrates; "someone" is one of the many.[11]

Second, that Socrates associates the Laws with rhetoricians is Plato's way of warn-ing the reader not to be too easily taken in by what they say. As Socrates in the *Apol-ogy* warns the judges not to be seduced by the eloquence of his accusers who "speak so persuasively" that "I nearly forgot myself" (*Ap.* 17a2–3), so Plato, in the *Crito*, by having Socrates characterize the Laws as orators, cautions the reader against being seduced by them. The accusers in the *Apology*, insofar as they are orators, persuade, but "they have said little or nothing true" (*Ap.* 17b7).[12] If the Laws' speech in the *Crito* is what "someone, especially an orator, would say,"[13] the reader had best be on guard; there is danger ahead.

201: "This refers to the practice of appointing advocates . . . to defend laws which it was proposed to abrogate."

9. Kitchel (1898), 157, contends that Socrates hints by the words "especially an orator" "that he has not the gifts or training in public speaking of professional orators." But what point would there be in his hinting that he has no such skill when he is about to display it? The only point there can be is to remind the reader that he is only imitating orators—he is not one of them. And he is not one of them because, whereas orators speak without regard for truth, he himself, when he speaks in his own name, speaks with the utmost regard for truth.

10. Socrates uses interchangeably the terms "clever speaker" and "orator" (see *Ap.* 17b4–6).

11. We noted in Chapter 2 (see n. 56) Socrates' use of "someone might say" in the *Apology* at 20c4 and 28b3 to signal in both cases an objection that might be raised by one who is so clearly affiliated with the many that the philosophical life is incomprehensible to him.

12. We may note that in the case of the mass trial of the ten generals to which Socrates objects on the grounds that such a trial is both illegal and unjust, it is "the orators" who are ready to indict and arrest him (*Ap.* 32b).

13. Allen (1984), 108, contends that the kind of rhetoric that the Laws employ is the good rhetoric described in the *Gorgias*, a kind of "philosophical rhetoric aimed at excellence of soul, indifferent to whether it gives pleasure or pain to the hearers, and directed toward producing that order of soul asso-ciated with lawfulness and law." It is clear, I think, that Socrates could not, when speaking in the *Crito* of the many things that "someone, especially an orator" would have to say on behalf of the law legiti-mating all verdicts, be thinking of the theoretically conceivable philosophical oratory envisioned at *Gorg.* 503a–b, about which he says to Callicles: "But a rhetoric such as this you have never seen" (*Gorg.* 503b1). Rather, Socrates is surely alluding to the ordinary orators who abound in Athens. Allen's char-acterization of the Laws' speech as "philosophical rhetoric" is discussed further at the beginning of Chapter 8.

The Citizen's Agreement

When the Laws enter the discussion, they do not simply replace Socrates as Crito's interlocutor; Socrates does not relinquish his voice to them. On the contrary, Socrates maintains a voice distinct from theirs for the duration of their speech; indeed, at its inception he even raises his own voice in opposition to them. The Laws assume the role of Socrates' accusers, and Socrates defends himself against their accusations.

To the Laws' charge that by escaping, Socrates destroys the city by way of destroying the law that upholds the legitimacy of all verdicts, Socrates offers the following justification: "For the city was doing us injustice and did not pass judgment correctly" (*Cr.* 50c1–2). Socrates does not deny that he is destroying the law that renders all verdicts legitimate; on the contrary, by offering a justification for escape, Socrates indicates that, in fact, he rejects that law: if he grounds the justification for his act in the incorrectness of the verdict, then he must regard incorrect verdicts as invalid and, hence, as not authoritative.

Many commentators on the *Crito* have suggested that Socrates' response to the Laws' charge is the response he assumes Crito would favor, that it does not represent Socrates' own view.[14] And, indeed, Socrates does ask Crito, "Shall *we* say this, or what?" (*Cr.* 50c2), to which Crito does reply enthusiastically: "Yes, this, by Zeus, Socrates!" (*Cr.* 50c3). Nevertheless, there are strong reasons for doubting that Socrates' proposed response is best ascribed to Crito.

First, we recall from the discussion in Chapter 3 that the incorrectness of the verdict plays no role in Crito's thinking as he seeks to convince Socrates to escape. This is how Crito conceives Socrates' refusal to escape: "And you are hastening the coming to pass of the very things concerning yourself that your very enemies would hasten on, and did hasten on, in their wish to ruin you" (*Cr.* 45c6–7). Crito complains not of the jurors' injustice and of their having rendered an incorrect judgment but of their wish to ruin Socrates.[15] For Crito, the Athenians who condemned Socrates are Socrates' enemies—and they are his enemies regardless of the rightness or wrongness of their verdict. Nevertheless, it is no wonder that when Socrates proposes to Crito that they oppose the Laws' charge that Socrates is attempting to destroy the law that authorizes all the city's verdicts, with the countercharge that the city's verdict was incorrect, Crito heartily approves. For Crito must surely expect that even Socrates would regard it as shameful to submit meekly and passively to the injustice of a faulty verdict. The answer that Socrates advances thus affords Crito hope that Socrates may have found grounds for escape after all.

Second, we know from the *Gorgias* that, for Socrates, suffering injustice is the lesser of two evils when the other evil is committing injustice. But there is no doubt

---

14. See, e.g., West (1989), 77.

15. The danger of conflating wrong verdicts with unfavorable ones is not avoided by even the meticulous Kraut (1984), 184: "Consider, for example, the Athenian statute that gave authority to the courts. That law orders the citizens to accept any lawful verdict brought by a jury, whether that verdict is favorable or unfavorable to the defendant. If someone objects to this, and says that he would like to live in a city where verdicts are enforced only when they are favorable to the accused, we would strongly suspect him of insincerity. For his proposal would in effect destroy the legal system of the city, and any sane person can be expected to see this." See also Kraut (1984), 36, 37.

in the *Gorgias* that Socrates would wish to avoid suffering injustice as long as in so doing he did not commit it: "I would want neither of them. But if it were necessary for me either to do or to suffer injustice, I would elect to suffer injustice rather than to do it" (*Gorg.* 469c1–2). There is, then, nothing unsocratic in the claim that one is under no obligation to suffer injustice.

Third, it is worth noting that even if Socrates includes Crito in his response to the Laws, Socrates does speak here in his own name. He need not have done so: he could have had recourse to a "someone" to voice this response, for, as we have seen (most recently at *Cr.* 50b6), it is not unusual for Socrates to invoke a "someone" to raise objections that are not his.[16] But he does not choose this course.

Fourth, Socrates elsewhere gives us reason to suspect that he does not recognize the city's authority to punish him unjustly. In the *Apology*, when Socrates announces at last that he will abide by his penalty (*Ap.* 39b6), he says nothing about the obligation of a citizen to submit to the penalty the city imposes; his stated reasons for abiding by his penalty have to do only with his unwillingness to say or do whatever is necessary—no matter how unjust or shameful—to save his life. Yet, early on in the *Apology*, when Socrates begins his defense speech, he explicitly says that he does so because "the law must be obeyed" (*Ap.* 19a5). The conspicuous absence of this reason in Socrates' decision to abide by his unjust penalty suggests that it plays no part in that decision.[17]

Finally, the Laws direct their reply to Socrates alone: "Socrates, is it this too that has been agreed to by us and by you [sing.]?" (*Cr.* 50c4–5). Of course, the Laws direct their entire speech to Socrates alone, but at this point they are responding to an answer that Socrates has offered on behalf of both himself and Crito: "Or shall *we* tell them, 'The city was doing *us* injustice . . .'?" (*Cr.* 50c1). As if deliberately discounting Socrates' use of the first person plural, the Laws respond in the second person singular. The Laws thus make it clear that, as far as they are concerned, Socrates' answer is his alone.

Despite all these reasons for thinking that Socrates' response is indeed Socrates' and not Crito's, the reader may well object that this response cannot possibly represent Socrates' true view because we know that he does not condone retaliatory injustice or harm.[18] For someone who does not condone retaliatory injustice or harm, how could the fact that the city ruled incorrectly and thereby committed an injustice against him justify his destroying it in return?

Two replies may be made to this objection. The first reply is that Socrates never concedes that he is destroying the city. Although the Laws do their best to imply that he is, he never confirms them in their accusations. The Laws attack him with a barrage of questions: "what do you have in mind to do?"; "what do you think you are doing if not destroying us and the whole city . . . ?"; "or does it seem possible to you for a city to continue to exist . . . ?" (*Cr.* 50a9; 50a9–b2; 50b2–3). Socrates does not reply directly to any of these questions; he is not given a chance to reply. The ques-

16. See n. 11.

17. See Chapter 4, n. 55.

18. That there is retaliation involved in Socrates' proposed response is clear from the term *gar*, "for." See Adam (1888), 62.

tion he does answer is the implicit one: "What justification do you offer for destroying the law that orders that judgments reached in trials be authoritative?" By answering this question, Socrates concedes in effect that he does destroy this law. But whereas the Laws assume that insofar as it is this law that sustains the city, anyone who destroys this law destroys the city, it is by no means clear that Socrates would agree.

The second reply is that, as we saw in Chapter 4, Socrates does not count all acts that cause pain or damage as unjust or as instances of doing bad, *kakourgein*. Painful or destructive measures, when administered justly and for the purpose of benefiting rather than harming their recipients, are good things rather than bad. If, as the quote from the *Gorgias* with which this chapter opens suggests, Socrates believes that one ill serves one's country by helping it to get away with injustice, then he must believe that by repaying his country's attempt to destroy him by destroying the law that legitimates even unjust verdicts, he repays evil with good, injustice with justice.[19] Socrates does nothing to hurt his city.

Indeed, Socrates must believe that the particular law that his escape would threaten is a law that fosters and breeds injustice. In fifth-century Athens, verdicts reached by heliastic courts could not be appealed to a higher court, jurors were not held accountable for their actions, and there were no retrials.[20] Among the complaints lodged against the judicial system in antiquity were that: (1) the trial itself did not provide opportunity for deliberation among the judges or for the questioning of witnesses and principals before the verdict was rendered; (2) the jurors were susceptible to flattery and emotional appeals and were vulnerable to misrepresentation of law and fact;[21] (3) jurors voted anonymously and were thus individually immune to attack or criticism.[22] Socrates in the *Apology* protests against several aspects of the system to which he is subject: the danger that popular prejudice will affect verdicts, the one-day duration of capital trials,[23] and the practice of bringing children into court. Socrates also worries that as judges become accustomed to granting acquittal or a lighter sentence "as a favor," they regu-

---

19. See White (1996), 110: "One could well imagine Socrates . . . responding that if the laws or other actions of the city are unjust, the city is not injured but helped by disobedience." Also 113: "...it may well be argued that to disobey an unjust law is to do the city, and the laws themselves, a service."

20. Dover (1974), 292, and MacDowell (1978), 258. Dover cites Dem. xliii.15; Isok. xx.22, xxi.18; Lys. xiv.4.

21. Dover (1974), 292, notes that "the question before a jury, as representing the people, was not exactly, 'Has this man, or has he not, committed the act with which he is charged?' but rather, 'What should be done about this man, who has been charged with this offense?'"

22. Morrow (1960), 253. Morrow cites Aristophanes, *Wasps*; Xenophon, *Apol.* 4, *Const. Ath.* 1, 18; Thuc. III, 38, VIII, 68; Isoc. VII, 54, VIII, 129–30, XV, 142. Plato criticizes the Athenian judicial system at *Gorg.* 454b; *Rep.* 405c, 492ff.; *Laws* 766d, 876b. See also Bonner and Smith (1938), II, 293–306. Bonner and Smith point out that "the dicasts did no wrong, the unscrupulous prosecutors were responsible for all miscarriages of justice" (II, 298). Bonner and Smith reject the common view that in *The Wasps* Aristophanes criticizes dicasteries; they see *The Wasps* as "really an attack on the demagogues who exploited the dicasts for their own political purposes" (II, 299). But even if this is so, the dicasts are not above reproach insofar as they allowed themselves to be exploited.

23. See *Theaet.* 201b, where Socrates makes the point that it takes a long time to teach the jury about the truth; it cannot be done "while a little water is flowing in the hourglass." No one, says Socrates, no matter how clever, can teach the truth so quickly, but orators and lawyers can quite quickly persuade the jurors to adopt their opinions.

larly violate their oath.[24] In the *Laws*, Plato seeks to correct these defects by instituting a higher, more selective, review court and provision for appeal. The members of this higher court are to be as incorruptible as possible (*Laws* 768b) but are also to be subject to prosecution if the guardians believe that they have deliberately judged falsely in the case before them (*Laws* 767e). Moreover, proceedings and voting are to be open.[25] Until such time as improvements like these are implemented, however, defendants — and Socrates among them — are at the mercy of a system wide open to abuses. Under these circumstances, a law that legitimates all verdicts is a law that sanctions gross injustice; it is, therefore, a law to which a just man will not readily bind himself. Indeed, insofar as orators have much to say in defense of this law, they promote the vulgar interests of their city at the expense of what ought to be its overriding interest: justice.

To review. The Laws charge Socrates — and only Socrates — with attempting to destroy the Laws and the city by destroying the law that legitimates verdicts reached in trials. Socrates does not deny that he destroys this particular law — though he does not admit that he thereby destroys the city. On behalf of himself and Crito, Socrates defends his destruction of this law by pointing to the incorrectness of the verdict and the injustice against him (them) that an incorrect verdict represents.

The Laws now turn to Socrates and once again, addressing him alone, challenge the defense he has offered: "Socrates, is it this too that has been agreed to by us and by you, or to abide by whatever judgments the city reaches in trials?" (*Cr.* 50c4–6). What do the Laws mean by this question? In particular, what do they mean by "this too," *kai tauta* (*Cr.* 50c5)?

In order to ascertain the meaning of the Laws' question, let us consider it in context. As the Laws see it, when Socrates says in his defense, "The city was doing us injustice and did not pass judgment correctly," what he is saying in effect is that he regards himself as bound only by correct verdicts. Socrates' protestation that the city did not judge correctly and hence treated him (and Crito) unjustly implies that he would not protest but would rather readily submit were the verdict correct. The Laws therefore demand to know if the agreement between Socrates and them entails "this too" — that is, that Socrates will submit to verdicts subject to his determination that they are correct — or if the agreement is simply that Socrates will abide by whatever, *an* (*Cr.* 50c6), verdicts the city reaches in trials, regardless of whether they are (in Socrates' judgment) correct or incorrect.[26]

24. Although the oath as preserved by Demosthenes in his speech against Timocrates (xxiv.149–51) does not represent what the oath was at all periods, "the promise to vote according to the laws and decrees of the Athenian people and the council of the five hundred, the promise not to accept bribes, the promise to listen impartially to both sides of the case" are probably included at every period (Bonner and Smith, [1938], II, 155). It seems likely that in the *Apology* Socrates refers to the first part of the oath as preserved by Demosthenes: "I will vote according to the laws and the decrees of the Athenian people and the council of the five hundred," for what he says is that the judge has sworn "to give judgment according to the laws" (*Ap.* 35c5).

25. Morrow (1960), 253–64; Bonner and Smith (1938), II, 232ff.

26. The phrase *kai tauta* is understood similarly by Adam, Burnet, and Dyer and Seymour. Adam (1888), 62, understands the phrase *kai tauta* to indicate "the reservation that you were to question our decrees and disobey them if they seemed to you wrong." Burnet (1924), 201, says nearly the same: "that the justice of the decision should be open to question." Also Dyer and Seymour (1885), 136: "i.e. that in certain cases the sentence of the laws might be set at nought."

Since Socrates apparently does indeed think that a citizen is bound only by correct verdicts, it is no wonder that when the Laws suggest that, on the contrary, citizens agree to abide by "whatever" verdicts the city reaches, Socrates is surprised, *thaumazoimen*.[27] He may include Crito in his surprise—he uses the first person plural[28]—but it is surely he who is surprised.[29] Indeed, the Laws, turning yet again to Socrates alone, say: "Socrates, do not be surprised at what is said."[30]

Socrates, as we know, is committed to the principle that one must do what one has agreed to as long as what one has agreed to is just (*Cr.* 49e6). Is it not unreasonable, then, to think that he would agree in advance to abide by all verdicts—right or wrong—issued by his city?[31] Is it plausible that a man who "obeys nothing of my own but the *logos* that seems best to me upon reasoning" (*Cr.* 45b4–6) is a man who would consent to forgo subjecting verdicts to review and would submit without reflection to whatever verdicts the city reaches? Surely this is not what Socrates *does*. Socrates reaches the decision to abide by his undeserved penalty only after giving careful consideration to how each of his options measures up against the standard of justice. His decision is grounded in the principles that he has embraced throughout his life. Socrates conducts himself not as a man bound to submit, not even as a man who has bound himself to submit. He says nothing about accepting his punishment because the law must be obeyed or because he, qua citizen, has agreed to accept whatever

27. Socrates is surprised not at the notion of agreement itself but at the notion that he has agreed to abide by whatever judgments the city reaches. Had Socrates been surprised at the notion of agreement, there would have been no point to the Laws' contrasting two alternatives: (1) the agreement to "this too," that is, that one may determine for oneself the limits of one's obedience to the city's judgments, as opposed to (2) the agreement to abide by whatever judgments the city reaches in trials. Indeed, what the Laws go on to argue is that Socrates has agreed to abide by "whatever" the city and fatherland bid, *ha an keleuēi hē polis kai hē patris* (*Cr.* 51b9–c1), and by "whatever we bid," *ha an hēmeis keleuōmen* (*Cr.* 51e4)—not simply that Socrates has agreed to *something*.

28. Socrates in this instance does not even consult Crito in order to gauge his reaction; he merely speaks for them both.

29. Even though Crito, as we know, does not feel particularly bound by any verdict, right or wrong, there is no reason to think that he would find surprising the notion that all verdicts are binding—especially when this notion is represented as being espoused by the Laws and the city.

30. Kraut (1984), 35, says: "Someone might think that Socrates is too impressed with this point," that is, with the point that he has agreed to abide by whatever the courts say. But we may note that Socrates is not impressed; he is surprised.

31. Many scholars think that, although Socrates would not agree to be the perpetrator of anything unjust, he might well agree to be the victim of injustice. But since Socrates does not believe that one ought to be the victim of injustice except when the only alternative is to be its perpetrator, it is difficult to see why he would agree in advance to his possible victimization by an incorrect verdict: since it is by violating an agreement to abide by all verdicts that Socrates runs the risk of committing injustice, he can spare himself that risk by not making such an agreement in the first place. See Martin (1970), 32: "We might grant that if one has made an agreement to abide by all laws then it is morally right to keep it; but we need not grant that it is morally right to *make* such an agreement in the first place. I find it paradoxical to say that *making* such an agreement is morally right" (italics in original). We have no more reason to believe that Socrates agrees in advance to suffer injustice at the hand of the city than that he agrees in advance to commit injustice at the city's behest. We cannot rely upon the Laws' assertion at *Cr.* 50c4–6 that the citizen agrees to obey all verdicts, for, if we rely upon their assertion here, we must similarly rely upon their later assertion, at *Cr.* 51e3–4, that the citizen agrees to do "whatever we bid."

punishment the court metes out to him. On the contrary, Socrates conducts himself as a man free to give thought to his options, free to consider them in light of his moral principles, and ultimately free to determine for himself what he ought to do. It is indeed altogether consistent with everything we know of Socrates—even from just our review of the *Apology* and the first two parts of the *Crito*—that he would be quite taken aback by the Laws' insinuation that he has agreed to abide by whatever judgments the city reaches in trials.[32]

If it is true, as was argued in Chapter 4, that Socrates comes to a decision about his own case by attending to all relevant moral factors yet not to any presumed moral obligation to comply with the court's decree per se, it is clear that he is unaware of ever having agreed to obey any and all judgments right or wrong. How could he have made a blanket agreement of this kind if he must always retain his freedom to follow the dictates of reason and to act in accordance with the demands of justice? In the absence of a moral expert, Socrates may obey nothing but his own carefully considered judgment; for him to sign on in advance to "whatever judgments the city reaches in trials" is for him to relinquish his ultimate authority—and duty—to judge. The Laws and Socrates stand opposed to one another, then, on the question of precisely what it is that a citizen has agreed to, the Laws maintaining that a citizen has agreed to obey all verdicts, correct or incorrect, Socrates maintaining that a citizen has agreed to obey all verdicts that are correct and hence just—even if unfavorable. The battle lines are drawn, and Socrates and the Laws are adversaries.

As the Laws proceed, they command Socrates to answer, "since you have been accustomed to make use of questioning and answering" (*Cr.* 50c3–4). That the Laws make this demand of Socrates in no way indicates that *they* mean to adopt the Socratic method of question and answer. Whereas Socrates subjects both Crito's views and his own to examination—they consider together the question of the importance of the opinion of the many, the magnitude of the evil of death, the meaning of justice, the rightness or wrongness of inflicting retaliatory harm[33]—the Laws neither examine Socrates' view nor submit their own view to his examination. Indeed, the Laws do not even give Socrates the opportunity to answer: before Socrates can say what it is that he takes himself to have agreed to, the Laws are asking their next question.[34]

---

32. Several commentators defend this view on its merits, independent of whether the view was Socrates'. Allen (1980), 75, says: ". . . when a man signs on to sail on a ship of state, he does not thereby contract to be thrown overboard at the whim of other passengers, and there is no apparent justice in abiding by agreements which carry the consequence of innocent death." Woozley (1979), 109, says: "If a man has agreed to do what the law tells him to do (provided that what he has agreed to do in agreeing to do what the law tells him to do is just), he does not thereby give the law a blank cheque in telling him what to do. . . . And he [Socrates] could have argued that abiding by the verdict and sentence of an unjust and politically fixed trial was not among the things that he had agreed to in agreeing to obey the law. . . ." On my view, this is precisely what Socrates does argue.

33. Socrates' three somewhat protracted speeches appear only as introductions to elenctic exchanges (*Cr.* 46b1–47a2; 48b11–49b2) or, in one case, as the summation of a preceding elenctic exchange (*Cr.* 49c10–e3).

34. Kitchel (1898), 158, misses the Laws' sarcasm and their baiting of Socrates in this passage: "Socrates represents the Laws as pursuing his own method in argument." Allen (1984), 110, seeks to characterize the Laws' speech as "both rhetoric and dialectic—dialectical rhetoric—even though only

The new question to which the Laws now demand an answer, *ti engalōn hēmin kai tēi polei epicheireis hēmas apollunai;* (*Cr.* 50c9–d1), is rendered as follows in the West translation: "What charge are you bringing against us and the city that you are attempting to destroy us?" All the translations I have consulted translate the passage similarly. I wish to suggest, however, that if this translation were correct, the Laws would be asking a question to which they have already been given the answer. For Socrates has already specified the charge that he is bringing against the Laws and the city: it is that "the city was doing us injustice and did not pass judgment correctly." I propose, therefore, instead of the standard translation, the following one: "Why [reading *ti* absolutely[35]], [thus] charging us and the city, do you attempt to destroy us?" What the Laws demand to know, according to this translation, is why Socrates, believing that his case was incorrectly decided by the Laws and the city, regards this belief as sufficient justification for attempting their destruction; the Laws know what the charge is but challenge its adequacy as a warrant for what Socrates is doing.

To summarize. The opening exchange between Socrates and the Laws sets the stage for the speech of the Laws to follow. It shows that the Laws' perspective on the duties of citizenship is not only independent of Socrates' view but, indeed, stands in opposition to it. As the Laws see it, a citizen is obligated to submit to whatever verdict the city issues—it is to this that a citizen agrees; on Socrates' view, a citizen must obey only correct verdicts—it is to this that a citizen agrees.

In this section, Socrates also alerts the reader to the rhetorical nature of the speech to come: the Laws are about to say the kinds of things that orators would say, in defense of a view that orators would defend, namely, the view that a citizen must comply with all the city's commands. Since orators are skilled at persuasion but not bound by truth, it is most important that the reader be forewarned.[36]

Socrates, like the Laws, believes that he ought not to escape. But his reason, as was argued in Chapter 4, is that he will not violate the specific agreement that he has made in his particular situation, the agreement to "abide by my penalty" despite the wrongness of the verdict, and will not engage in deceitful and corruptive practices such as bribery and "paying gratitude." His decision not to escape has nothing to do with any general agreement on his part to abide by all verdicts of the city. Were it not for Socrates' specific agreement in this case, were it not for the ignoble acts that escape necessitates, he would not, on his view, be bound to submit to his verdict and, hence, would not be bound not to escape. Socrates does not believe that people must accept injustice; they must submit to injustice only when there is but one way to avoid suffering it—that is, by committing it.

---

intermittently cast in dialogue form." Let us note, however, that once the Laws secure at *Cr.* 50d5 and 50e1 Socrates' assent to their initial premise—that the laws concerning marriage, nurture, and education are noble—the Laws pose only rhetorical questions that require no answer. It is Socrates who twice interrupts the rush of their rhetoric, at *Cr.* 51c3–5 and 52d6–7, turning the Laws' merely rhetorical questions directed at him into a real question that he directs to Crito: "What shall we say in reply?"

35. *Ti* is used absolutely at *Cr.* 43c4, *alla ti dē houtō prōi aphixai;,* "But why have you arrived so early?" and at 44c6–7, *Alla ti hēmin . . . houtō tēs tōn pollōn doxēs melei;,* "But why do we care in this way . . . about the opinion of the many?"

36. In Chapter 7 we shall see how Socrates' reaction to the Laws' speech confirms that it is but an oratorical tirade containing arguments to which he is not sympathetic.

Socrates is no anarchist. He is patriotic, brave, and submissive to authority—but only up to the point at which injustice, whether as something to be committed or as something to be endured, comes into play. Socrates could readily agree in advance to do whatever the city commands as long as it does not command injustice; he could similarly agree in advance to accept the city's verdicts as long as its verdicts are not unjust. Socrates is obedient to his city, and he is willing to suffer and even to endanger his life when it so demands—but not when it so demands unjustly.

6

"Whatever We Bid"

*La loi doit toujours être respectée avec humeur parce
qu'elle ne peut pas être complètement respectée.*
Jean-François Lyotard (1983), 208, #208

In their speech, the Laws address but one question: is it just for a citizen who has been ordered by the city—whether correctly or incorrectly—to suffer something at its hand to disregard that order? They do not, let us note, consider either of the following two questions that have nevertheless been attributed to them: (1) whether a citizen who disobeys an unjust law because he believes it to be unjust must submit to punishment for his disobedience; (2) whether a citizen who protests a law he believes to be unjust by disobeying either that law or some other law must submit to punishment for his disobedience. The reason the Laws do not deal with these questions is simply that neither one applies to Socrates' situation. Socrates is not in the position of someone who has violated a law on principle and now faces punishment for that violation. Socrates is completely innocent; he has violated no law.[1] Therefore, the question the Laws confront is whether even an innocent man, falsely accused, convicted, and sentenced, must suffer whatever the city orders him to suffer.

The Laws, as we saw in Chapter 5, take the view that a citizen must, indeed, obey all verdicts, whether just or unjust. The Laws support their view by characterizing acts of disobedience as acts destructive of both them and the city: no city, they assert, can long survive acts of that sort. Yet, even if we grant the Laws, for the moment, their dubious characterization of disobedience as destruction, does it follow that Socrates' disobedience is unjustified? Are all destructive acts necessarily unjust? Do even the Laws repudiate all acts of destruction? If they do not—and, as we shall see,

---

1. That Socrates believes he has violated no law makes it awkward and inaccurate to characterize Socrates' case, as is often done, as an instance of "civil disobedience" as this term is ordinarily understood.

they, in fact, do not[2] — they must say why it is that acts of disobedience/destruction of the kind that Socrates is poised to commit are wrong.

The Laws offer two reasons for condemning specifically this type of destructive activity: (1) the citizen is our offspring and slave, and, therefore, justice is not "equal" between him and us, and (2) the citizen, by remaining in Athens when he could have left, has agreed to do "whatever we bid." Since the Laws do not recognize exceptions to the obligations entailed by (1) the nature of the relationship between citizen and city and (2) the citizen's having made an agreement with his city, they consider both of these sources of obligation to be particularly well suited to serve as reasons against escape.[3] Presenting these reasons occupies the Laws from Cr. 50d1 to Cr. 53a7. When the Laws conclude at Cr. 53a6–7 that Socrates can avoid becoming "ridiculous" only if he obeys them and does not escape, they introduce what is in effect the theme of the rest of their speech, namely, that for Socrates to escape would render him an object of derision: he would benefit no one — not his friends, not himself, and not his children.

In the second part of their speech, then, from Cr. 53a8 on, the Laws consider such questions as how the choice of exile will affect Socrates' friends financially and politically, what sort of reception Socrates can expect if he goes to a lawful city and what sort if he goes to a lawless one, how his children will fare, and what awaits him in Hades when he dies. The focus in this final section of the Laws' speech shifts from the question of justice that is Socrates' concern to the more "practical" issues that had occupied Crito at the beginning of the dialogue.[4] The Laws, we may note, con-

---

2. The Laws believe that retaliatory destruction is justified when the parties are equals and that acts of destruction by superiors to inferiors — whether justified or not — do not constitute injustice. See the amplification of propositions (2), (6), and (7) of the Laws' first argument against escape in the following section, "The City as Parent and Master."

3. Woozley (1979), 110, thinks that Socrates' reason for not escaping is ultimately independent of agreement and is rather a matter of destruction of the law, particularly the law requiring that all verdicts be upheld: "Even if there is no such thing as an agreement, it might still be true that disobedience to law is destructive of it." Cf. Allen (1980), 76, who argues that "the wrongfulness of escape will be found to consist, not in breach of agreement, but in the fact that such breach implies injury to the legal order, the Laws of Athens, by denial of its authority." In other words, for Allen, were it not for the citizen's agreement by which he becomes subject to the authority of a particular set of laws, a citizen's escape could not constitute an injury to that set of laws and to the city whose laws they are. But, for Allen, the wrongfulness of the escape is to be found in the injury it causes to the laws. On my view, although the Laws clearly regard escape as destructive of the Laws and the city, they locate the source of the wrongfulness of such destruction in (1) the unequal relationship between Socrates, on the one hand, and the Laws and the city, on the other, and (2) Socrates' presumed agreement to do whatever the city bids. Thus, from the Laws' perspective, it is not the destruction per se that makes escape wrong; indeed, were conditions (1) and (2) not satisfied, escape would not be wrong, despite the injury to the Laws that it entails.

4. According to Irwin (1986), 406, that the Laws use these "supplementary arguments" implies that they recognize conditions under which escape would be acceptable and, hence, that they do not regard as "overriding and conclusive" the "absolute and invariable obedience" prescribed in the speech's central arguments. But perhaps there is a simpler account of why the Laws append these "supplementary arguments." Insofar as the central arguments are arguments about justice and as such address typically Socratic concerns — albeit, as we shall see, for Crito's benefit — there is a good chance that they alone will not satisfy Crito, whose own concerns are indeed sorely neglected until Cr. 53a8. If, as we said earlier, the target of the Laws' argument, despite appearances, must be Crito, the sole proponent of escape, we can make sense of their turning finally to the concerns he had expressed.

clude each of the two parts of their speech by appealing to Socrates to obey them and be persuaded by them (*Cr.* 53a6, *Cr.* 54b2, c8–d1); they conclude their speeches, then, just as Crito concludes his (*Cr.* 46a7–8).

As we turn now to a detailed analysis of the argument contained in the speech of the Laws, we seek to understand it in terms of its basic structure: (1) on the assumption that a citizen's disobedience to the city destroys it, it is unjust for Socrates to escape because (a) Socrates is the city's offspring and slave, and (b) he has agreed to obey the city no matter what it commands; and (2) escape is ridiculous for Socrates because through it he does neither his friends nor himself nor his children any good.

The City as Parent and Master

The Laws contend that Socrates, by escaping, seeks to destroy, to the extent of his ability, *to son meros* (*Cr.* 50b2),[5] the city and its Laws. On their view, a city cannot survive if private citizens—that is, citizens acting outside the political process[6]—render judgments ineffective and corrupt them. That Socrates' act is destructive of at least the law that validates all verdicts is not challenged by Socrates;[7] yet he does challenge—through his protest that "the city was doing us injustice and did not pass judgment correctly" (*Cr.* 50c1–2)—the assumption that his act is unjustified: must a citizen submit to and comply with incorrect verdicts as he surely must with correct ones, or does the very incorrectness of the verdict provide just cause for Socrates to escape?

In response to Socrates' challenge, the Laws' first move is to seek to ground the unjustness of a citizen's attempt to destroy the Laws and the city in the citizen's relationship to the Laws and the city, a relationship that, because it is hierarchical, is one in which justice is not "equal" between the parties to it. They argue as follows: (1) Socrates seems to believe that the city's attempt to destroy him warrants his de-

5. This phrase is used by Crito to accuse Socrates of allowing his children, "as far as lies in you," to be subject to whatever might befall them (*Cr.* 45d1–4). Its import seems to be that even if the dire consequences predicted do not materialize, and even if Socrates is not directly and unilaterally responsible for them if they do, nevertheless he makes it possible, to the extent that he can, for forces to be set in motion that could, theoretically, bring about an undesired and undesirable state of affairs. See the section in Chapter 8 entitled "Engaging Crito," for a fuller discussion of this phrase.

6. The Laws worry about how the city's power might be weakened *hupo idiōtōn*, "by private men" (*Cr.* 50b4). The notion of a "private" man has important Socratic resonances: in the *Apology* Socrates says of himself that he has long carried out privately, *idiāi* (*Ap.* 31b4–5), his mission of improving souls, that he is a busybody in private (*Ap.* 31c4–5), and that it would be dangerous for him to be a public man because a public man who is also just will not survive (*Ap.* 31d6–32a3). The notion of privacy can also suggest the kind of independence shown by a man who will do only what is right in his own judgment (when no expert is available).

7. The Laws do not give Socrates a chance to object to their characterization of escape as an act destructive of the city. Of course, that does not mean that he would not object to it if he had the chance. By offering a justification for his alleged intention to escape, however, Socrates implicitly concedes that he would be destroying the particular law that authorizes all the city's verdicts and judgments. As was argued in Chapter 5, Socrates need not believe that even destruction of the city necessarily counts as *adikein* or *kakourgein*: if there were some way in which his escape might improve the city's "virtue," Socrates would no doubt consider his escape a great benefit—even if the power of the city were lessened and even if the city considered it an injury.

struction of the Laws and the city. (2) But the attempt by the city and the Laws to destroy Socrates would only warrant Socrates' destruction of them if justice were equal between them. (3) Certain laws enabled Socrates to be born, nurtured, and educated. (4) Socrates agrees that (a) the laws concerning marriage, laws through which his parents bore him, and (b) the laws ordering his father to nurture and educate him in music and gymnastic, are noble ones. (5) He must therefore admit that both he and his forebears are the Laws' offspring and slave. (6) Hence, justice is not equal for him and the Laws: what the Laws and the "fatherland" do to him—namely, attempt to destroy him, "believing it to be just"—he cannot justly attempt to do to them. (7) There is, then, no justification for Socrates' escape, for his attempt to destroy, "to the extent that you can," *kath' hoson dunasai* (*Cr.* 51a5), [8] the Laws and the city.

Let us look more closely at each step of this argument:

(1) The Laws do not say of themselves that they do injustice to Socrates. Whereas Socrates has charged the city with committing an injustice against him (and Crito) by having judged his case incorrectly, the Laws speak only of the city's—and their own—attempt to destroy him.

(2) The Laws regard as unjust Socrates' attempt to destroy them in return because, as they say, justice is not equal between Socrates and them. Insofar as the Laws ground the injustice of retaliation in the unequal status of the parties involved, they reveal themselves to be opposed not to retaliation per se but to retaliation taken by an inferior against a superior.

(3) If the Laws are to prove that escape is unjustified, they must establish the hierarchy that exists between themselves and the citizen. In order to do so, they appeal to a certain very small set of laws—the laws concerning marriage and the laws ordering fathers to provide for their children's nurture and education. The particular laws selected are not arbitrary; they are not just any benefactions for which the Laws are owed a debt of gratitude. On the contrary, they are specifically related to the Laws' putative role as the citizen's "parents."[9]

---

8. The expression *kath' hoson dunasthai* operates in much the same way as the expression *to son meros* (*Cr.* 50b2). See n. 5.

9. The most common way by far to interpret this argument by the Laws is as an argument from gratitude. The Laws, it is thought, maintain that they can claim obedience from citizens, just as parents can from children, because of the benefactions they provide. A straightforward gratitude argument, however, would not require a parent-child analogy: the Laws could simply list their many benefactions and speak of how much the citizen owes them in return. What the Laws do instead is point to the laws concerning marriage, nurture, and education and assert that, because of those laws, they stand in a parental, hence hierarchical and unequal, relation to the citizen. Whereas I would not go so far as to say that there is no "look-what-we-have-done-for-you"-message at work in the Laws' argument, the main point of the Laws' argument is to establish the superior position they occupy in the hierarchy. (See Woozley [1979], esp. 63–64 and 70–71, for the view that there is a distinct and independent "Filial Gratitude Argument" that "merges" at *Cr.* 50e with the "Parental Authority Argument.") The benefaction message is accorded a measure of prominence at *Cr.* 51c9–d4, where the Laws link their having begotten, nurtured, and educated Socrates to their having given all citizens a share "in all the noble things we could." But it may be assumed that the phrase "all the noble things we could" refers back to the "noble" marriage laws through which Socrates was born (*Cr.* 50d4) and the laws "nobly" ordering Socrates' father to educate him in music and gymnastic (*Cr.* 50d7).

(4) The Laws ask Socrates to confirm that the marriage laws through which his parents bore him are noble ones and that "nobly" did certain laws command Socrates' father to nurture him and educate him in music and gymnastic. Socrates agrees. The Laws do not ask, however, and Socrates does not say, whether he found the education he received satisfactory.[10] The Laws' interest lies primarily in having Socrates acknowledge the rightness of their assuming the role of parents—not in having him thank them for the benefits he received.[11]

(5) Having elicited Socrates' acknowledgment of the nobleness of the laws concerning marriage and the nurture and education of children, the Laws go on to infer that Socrates must, therefore, admit to being their offspring. The Laws, to be sure, cannot maintain literally that these few laws actually bear, nurture, and educate Socrates; giving birth to him and nurturing and educating him are things his real parents do. What the Laws wish nevertheless to maintain is that, insofar as they have a hand in these parental activities, they are themselves "parents." Yet the Laws also infer from Socrates' acknowledgment of the nobleness of the laws concerning marriage and the nurture and education of children that he must concede that he is their *slave*—and not only he but his forebears as well. No argument is offered—indeed, nothing is said at all—to support the idea that Socrates, let alone his forebears, is a slave of the Laws and the city. It appears that the Laws just tack the master-slave idea onto the parent-child idea, like an unpopular rider on a popular bill.

(6) Taking for granted Socrates' acquiescence in their characterization of him, the Laws proclaim the inequality of justice for him and for them. What does it mean to say that justice is unequal for Socrates and the Laws? What it means is that there obtains between Socrates and the Laws no mutuality of duties as obtains between equals. What the Laws may do to the citizen, the citizen may not do to the Laws. And when the Laws do something disagreeable to a citizen, a citizen has no remedy in the form of redress or retaliation. Just as one may not return to one's parents or one's master—if one has one—"whatever" one has suffered at their hand, so, the Laws reason, a citizen may not attempt to return to the city and to the Laws the suffering that they attempt to inflict upon him, believing it to be just. The force of the qualifier "believing it to be just," *dikaion hēgoumenoi enai* (Cr. 51a4), is that the Laws may do whatever they *think* is just—even if it is, in fact, unjust—and the citizen must comply; once a verdict has been rendered, the citizen must submit to punishment even if the verdict is incorrect.

(7) Since justice is unequal for the two parties to the citizen-city relationship, the city's attempt to destroy Socrates does not justify Socrates' attempt to destroy the city in return. The Laws make it quite clear that it is specifically retaliation undertaken by an inferior (such as a child or slave or citizen) against a superior (such as a parent or master or city) to which they object—not to retaliation per se. It would appear that, for the Laws, retaliation between equals and, a fortiori, retaliation undertaken by a superior against an inferior are not unjust. Having already character-

---

10. According to Colson (1989), 41, "perhaps the education in music and gymnastics provides the necessary foundation on which a life in pursuit of virtue can be built." Yet, Colson himself admits that Socrates in the *Protagoras* "doubts that this form of education is able to instill virtue."

11. See Woozley (1979), 63–64, for the contrary view.

ized Socrates' escape as his attempt to destroy the Laws and the city (*Cr*. 50b1–2, 50b5, 50d1), the Laws can now conclude that Socrates' escape cannot be justified.[12]

In this argument, the Laws fashion themselves honorary parents who, as such, are entitled to an extraordinary measure of restraint on the part of each individual citizen whom they mean to harm. As mentioned earlier, in our explication of step (4) of the Laws' argument, the Laws do not cite a host of benefactions to ground the citizen's duty toward them; rather, they cite specifically those that help establish them as the citizen's parents. It is as parents, then, and not as mere benefactors, that they make their demands upon the citizen.

One must wonder why the Laws portray themselves not only as the citizen's "parents" but as his master as well. As we saw above, in (5), the Laws provide no grounds at all for the master-slave analogy.[13] Moreover, any free Athenian is bound to find such an analogy offensive.[14]

That the Laws portray themselves as parents *and masters* is no accident. The Laws' adoption of this dual image suggests that they model the relationship between city and citizen on the Greek household, in which the head of the household exercises tyrannical rule over its other members, whether children or slaves.[15] Since the Laws are about to make increasingly stringent demands upon the citizen, they require a model that can bear the weight of those demands.[16] The Laws begin with the duty to refrain from retaliatory acts, a duty forbidding children or slaves to return "whatever"

12. The analogy between parent-child and city-citizen conceals an interesting disanalogy between them. The acts that the Laws seem to regard as destructive of parents (and masters) are acts that cause them to suffer: beating them in return, speaking ill of them in return, and other such things. It would be odd indeed to characterize disobedience to parents or refusal to submit to whatever unjust suffering they inflict as "destructive" of them. Yet the Laws regard the citizen's disobedience to the city and refusal to submit to whatever it inflicts as destructive of themselves and the city: "By this deed that you are attempting, what do you think you are doing, if not destroying us Laws and the whole city, as far as it lies in you? Or does it seem possible to you for a city to continue to exist, and not to be overturned, in which the judgments that are reached have no strength, but are rendered ineffective and are corrupted by private men?" (*Cr*. 50b2–5). Thus the Laws, by arguing both (1) that a child ought not to return to parents what they do to the child, specifically, that a child ought not to cause parents to suffer in return or beat them in return, and (2) that a citizen's sheer disobedience to the Laws threatens to destroy them, conclude (3) that a citizen ought not to attempt to destroy the Laws in return—by *disobeying* them and not submitting to the suffering they inflict.

13. The master-slave analogy, we may note, is wholly incompatible with the common interpretation of this argument as an argument from gratitude for benefactions. It is not as if it is because of the many benefits his master bestows upon him that the slave may never retaliate against his master.

14. To recommend that a free citizen do what a slave does is to recommend that he be anything but an *agathos*. See Adkins (1960), 263–64.

15. According to Arendt, the characteristic feature of the household—as opposed to the *polis*—is that there is in the household no equality and hence no freedom. As she says (1958), 32: ". . . the household was the center of strictest inequality . . . within the realm of the household, freedom did not exist." And, indeed, the Laws' first inference from the household model is that justice is unequal between citizen and city.

16. The Laws apparently do not regard even their contention at *Cr*. 51a8–b3 that they are more to be revered than biological parents or ancestors—presumably at least in part because they make the parental and hence the ancestral relation possible—as sufficiently strong to bear the weight of the demands they place on the citizen. Only the master-slave model, operating silently in the background, can adequately support their demands.

they suffer to the parent or master: they may not speak ill in return; they may not beat in return (*Cr*. 50e7–51a2). The Laws' next step is to require that citizens endure all suffering imposed by an angry fatherland: they must "keep quiet and suffer if it [the city] orders one to suffer anything" (*Cr*. 51b4–5).[17] Finally, the Laws demand that the citizen obey the city's every command, whether in war or court or anywhere else (*Cr*. 51b5–9).[18] The city-citizen relationship can sustain the Laws' most exacting demands only if it is like a parent-child relationship that is itself assimilated to a relationship between master and slave.[19] Readers of the *Crito* would do well to take their cue from the Laws' use of the master-slave analogy and resist sentimentalizing the Laws' conception of the relationship between city and citizen.

Kraut seeks to limit the application of the master-slave analogy to the issue of violence, as if the only point the Laws seek to make through it is the following: just as a slave may not use violence against a master despite having suffered violence at the master's hand, so a citizen may not use violence against the city and Laws despite having suffered violence at their hand.[20] In no other respects, Kraut maintains, do the Laws liken the city to a master and the citizen to a slave. There are, however, several considerations that work against this view. First, and most important, unless the Laws characterize generally the relationship between city and citizen as a master-slave relationship, on what grounds can they maintain that in the specific matter of violence a citizen's relationship to the city is like that of slave to master? And, in fact, the Laws do establish the general analogy between themselves and the citizen, on the one hand, and master and slave, on the other: they explicitly and directly affirm of Socrates that he regards himself, insofar as he has been born, nurtured, and educated, as the Laws' offspring *and slave* (*Cr*. 50e2–4). Second, it is unclear what Kraut means by speaking of the Laws' restricting of the master-slave analogy to the matter of violence as opposed to that of disobedience.[21] For, in the current context, the "violence" Socrates would be doing in return to the city and the Laws is nothing but the disobedience through which he presumably attempts to destroy them: the Laws make quite clear that they regard Socrates' disobedient act as an act of destruction (*Cr*. 50a9–b5). Finally, if the Laws appeal to the master-slave analogy in order specifically to make the point that a citizen may not return violence for violence, it is odd that at *Cr*. 51c2–3, when the Laws speak of the impiety of doing violence to the fatherland, they invoke not the master-slave analogy but the parent-child one. One can only conclude, contra Kraut, that the master-slave analogy does more than forbid violence; the Laws rely upon it to support the very stringent demands they make on the citizen's compliance and submission.

---

17. At *Gorg*. 483a8–b4, Callicles contends that by nature only a slave would allow himself to suffer injustice.

18. We discuss presently the alternative to obeying that the Laws permit: "persuading."

19. If the parent-child analogy alone and not in conjunction with the master-slave analogy cannot sustain the inequality of justice required for the Laws' argument, it is highly unlikely that an argument from benefaction could: does one's conferring benefits upon others entitle one to the beneficiaries' absolute obedience and to their submission to all suffering one inflicts upon them?

20. Kraut (1984), 105–108.

21. Kraut (even 1984), 108.

Socrates, we may note, agrees in his own name to nothing beyond (1) the nobility of the marriage laws that made possible his birth, and (2) the nobility of the laws that ordered his father to attend to his nurture and education. Only in relation to the nobility of these laws does Socrates say "*I would say*," *phaiēn an* (*Cr.* 50d5; 50e1).[22] As for the other points made—that Socrates and his forebears are the Laws' offspring and slave and that it is unjust to do back to a father, master, or fatherland what one has suffered at his/its hand—these are imputed to him by the Laws. Moreover, the tone with which the Laws dictate to Socrates what he must believe is sneering and scornful: "Could you say, first, that you are not ours, both our offspring and slave. . . . And if this is so, do you suppose that justice is equal for you and for us? And do you suppose . . . ?" (*Cr.* 50e3–5). The disrespect for Socrates manifest in the Laws' manner of addressing him reaches a peak at *Cr.* 51a6–7: "And will you say that in doing this you are acting justly, you who in truth care for virtue?,"[23] followed by: "Or are you so wise . . . ?" (*Cr.* 51a7).[24]

We may now consider how the Laws develop the parent-child analogy and what implications they draw from it. Having proclaimed the injustice of attempting to destroy the Laws and fatherland in return, the Laws' next step is to instruct as to the proper attitude the citizen ought to adopt, and the appropriate way he ought to behave, toward an angry fatherland:[25] since the fatherland is more honorable than father, mother, and other forebears,[26] as well as more venerable, more holy, and more esteemed among gods and intelligent human beings, the citizen must revere the fatherland—that is, yield to and fawn upon it when it is angry even more than a child must with respect to a father when he is angry (*Cr.* 51a8–b3).[27]

Is the Laws' view reasonable? Is it a view that Socrates would endorse? Even if the attitude of reverence, *sebesthai*, is appropriate not only for a child toward his parent but for a citizen toward his city, it is surely doubtful that the behaviors that the Laws regard as expressing reverence—yielding, *hupeikein*, and fawning, *thōpeuein*—even

22. These are the only occasions during the entire speech of the Laws in which Socrates agrees in his own name to what they argue. At *Cr.* 52a6 he asks a question in his own name, *egō eipoimi*, but otherwise throughout the Laws' speech Socrates asks Crito how they should respond, and the actual response is Crito's. I argue in Chapter 7 that Socrates offers in the concluding section of the dialogue fairly clear hints that he is unimpressed with the Laws' argument.

23. Many commentators have noticed the harsh and derisive tone of the Laws here. See Burnet (1924), 202: "a scornful reference to the Socratic doctrine of *psuchēs epimeleia*"; Adam (1888), 66: "*tēi aletheiāi* is bitterly sarcastic"; Tyler (1862), 176, says this phrase "is added in bitter irony."

24. Adam (1888), 67, says: "It is clear from *Apol.* 18B that *sophos* (like *phrontistēs*) was almost a nickname for Socrates. Here of course the word is used with bitter irony, as indeed it often was in Socrates' time." See n. 106.

25. See Dover (1974), 218–19: "On the assumption that devotion to one's parents is virtuous, patriotism can be justified by treatment of our own land as a parent."

26. It is possible to see now why the Laws went so far as to say that Socrates must agree that not only he but his forebears as well are the Laws' slaves. Since reverence for parents and forebears is a duty that Socrates would no doubt acknowledge, if the Laws wish to maintain that Socrates owes even greater reverence to the fatherland, they must make the point that Socrates' forebears are themselves slaves of the fatherland.

27. The sentence reads: ". . . to revere is obligatory, *dei*, and more to yield to and fawn upon fatherland when angry than father." If the first "and," *kai*, is taken epexegetically, the yielding and fawning with respect to an angry fatherland together constitute "revering" the fatherland.

if they are proper responses to an angry parent, are at all desirable with respect to an angry fatherland. Socrates in the *Apology* declares that he would not yield, *hupeikathoimi* (*Ap.* 32a6), to any man against the just, regardless of the fatal consequences to him of refusing to yield, *hupeikōn* (*Ap.* 32a7); as proof that he has comported himself in accordance with this declaration, he cites his refusal to obey the unjust commands *of his government* (*Ap.* 32a9–e1). Moreover, as far as fawning is concerned, Socrates makes clear in the *Apology* that such behavior is repugnant to him, that he will not cry and beg and lament before the judges (*Ap.* 34b7–35d8), even if refraining from such behavior costs him his life; he does not do things that he regards as unsuitable to a free man (*Ap.* 38e2–3). Yet the Laws in the *Crito* regard a citizen as the city's slave and, therefore, precisely because the Laws understand fawning, *huperchomenos*, as behaving slavishly, *douleuōn* (*Cr.* 53e4), they insist that fawning is fitting and even required behavior for a citizen toward his fatherland.

The Laws continue to prescribe what the citizen is to do when the fatherland is angry with him. He is required, they say, either (1) to persuade, or (2) to do whatever it bids, quietly submitting to any suffering that it orders, whether in the form of being beaten or being bound (*Cr.* 51b3–5). The meaning of the second of these two alternatives, to do whatever the fatherland bids, is quite clear.[28] The meaning of the first, however, "to persuade," *peithein*, is less so. In order to discern its meaning, we must look to its context. The Laws have just specified the two forms that proper reverence takes: (1) *hupeikein*, yielding, and (2) *thōpeuein*, fawning upon, flattering, wheedling.[29] As the Laws go on to amplify their meaning, they require of the citizen that he either persuade the city or do whatever it bids. If, as is plain, the demand that the citizen "do whatever it bids" corresponds to *hupeikein*, the first form of reverence, then surely "persuade it" corresponds to *thōpeuein*, the second form of reverence. In context, then, what the Laws require of the citizen is either that he do as he is told or that he "persuade" — entreat the fatherland by way of flattery and fawning in the hope of prevailing upon it either not to reach an unwelcome decision or to reverse that decision before it is too late. The sense of "persuade" as "prevail upon by entreaty" is quite standard,[30] and its use in this sense in Plato is not uncommon.[31]

Support for the idea that "prevail upon by entreaty" is the likely meaning of persuasion when the Laws propose persuasion as an acceptable alternative to obedience is supplied by the *Apology*.[32] Socrates refuses in the *Apology* to "persuade" in the way the judges desire: he refuses to wail and lament, to be daring and shameless; he is

---

28. Although this expression is quite unambiguously unrestricted, we shall see shortly the ways in which many commentators on this dialogue seek to restrict it.

29. Liddell-Scott-Jones (1966), s.v. *thōpeuō*, "flatter, wheedle." For *thōpeuein* as "fawn" or "flatter," see *Rep.* VIII.563a4; *Rep.* IX.579a1; *Rep.* IX.590c5; *Theaet.* 173a2; *Laws* I. 643a3.

30. Liddell-Scott-Jones (1966), s.v. *peithō*, A.2. Also II.1: "in bad sense, talk over, mislead"; and II.2: "bribe." The *Apology* contains several instances of II.1: at 18b4–6; 18d2–4; 19e4–20a2.

31. See *Ap.* 37d7–8: "And if I drive them away, they themselves will drive me out by persuading (*peithontes*) their elders"; also *Rep.* II.366a3–4: ". . . and by praying when we transgress and sin we shall persuade (*peithontes*) them and escape unpunished." In the *Laws* (I.634b1), we find the expression *epeithen timais*, "persuade through honors." Adam (1888), 67, notes that Plato sometimes opposes persuading to compelling, as at *Rep.* VI. 488d, but sometimes links them, as at *Gorg.* 517b.

32. Woozley (1979), 141, argues that there is nothing in the *Apology* about persuading, so that, in that dialogue, if a command of the city is unjust, the citizen's only recourse if he wishes to avoid doing

unwilling to say "the sorts of things to you that you would have been most pleased to hear" (*Ap*. 38d8). He recognizes that it was not for lack of *logoi* that he failed to persuade and was convicted but for lack of precisely this daring and shameless behavior (*Ap*. 38d6–8). Socrates refuses to engage in the only kind of persuasion that the city appreciates, the persuasion that we earlier called "coercion-persuasion," and he bemoans his having insufficient time to persuade as *he* would like: it would take longer than the single day allotted to him for him to present the facts and arguments that would successfully reverse the effects of long-standing rumors about him.[33]

"Persuading," then, is not, for the Laws, the sheer presenting of a defense that, if successful, spares the citizen the need to submit but, if unsuccessful, results in the citizen's being required to submit. "Persuading" is, rather, the alternative to submission: if one does not wish to yield, one must entreat by way of fawning and flattering.[34] The Laws in the *Crito* expect of the citizen precisely what the judges in the *Apology* expect of Socrates.

The Laws proceed: if the fatherland—no longer necessarily an angry fatherland[35]—leads one into war to be wounded or killed, one is to go; one must not yield or retreat or leave one's station, but, in war and in court and everywhere, one must do whatever the city and fatherland bid. The Laws, in these cases as well, provide persuasion as an alternative to obedience:[36] *ē peithein autēn hēi to dikaion pephuke* (*Cr*. 51c1).

---

what is unjust is to disobey the law in the name of obedience to the god. But the *Crito*, he thinks, appears to offer the option of disobedience in the case in which the citizen engages in "publicly protesting, or trying to persuade the authorities of the injustice." On my view, the *Apology* and the *Crito* are in complete accord as long as the Laws are seen to be on the same side as the judges, and Socrates to be opposed to both: both the Laws and the judges require obedience but provide groveling as an alternative—it is when the citizen defiantly refuses to adopt the appropriately abject posture that the Laws and judges demand obedience. Since, for Socrates, "persuading" in the sense of entreaty by way of fawning is not a viable option, he must decide whether to obey or disobey, taking into account considerations of justice alone.

33. See the discussion in Chapter 2 of *Ap*. 35c–d, where Socrates speaks of (1) "to teach and to persuade," which we there called "teaching–persuasion," as contrasted with (2) "persuade and force you by begging," which we there called "coercion–persuasion."

34. Kraut (1984), 54–60, is right to understand *peithein* as a genuine alternative to obedience and, therefore, to reject the more common understanding of *peithein* as the offering of a defense, which, if unsuccessful, necessitates obedience to the city's ruling or command. As he notes, 83, n. 40, the Laws regard the citizen's not persuading as a second, distinct ground of complaint, most clearly at *Cr*. 52a2–3. As Kraut says, 67–68, when the Laws complain that Socrates did not "persuade," they clearly cannot mean that he failed to offer a defense, nor is it likely that the source of their complaint is that his defense was unsuccessful. Contra Kraut, however, I would contend that *peithein* is an option open to a citizen for as long as it remains possible for the city to spare him. Once the city's decree is final, it is too late for "persuasion."

35. It is not generally out of anger that the city sends a citizen into battle. We may note the seamless transition from the angry fatherland to simply the fatherland.

36. It may seem odd that the Laws offer the citizen the option of "persuading" in the sense of begging, if he wishes, say, to avoid being sent to war once he has been ordered to go. Yet it seems even more odd that the Laws would provide the citizen the opportunity to discuss with them questions of justice when the city has ordered him to serve in a war. Some have sought to construe what the Laws say in this passage as their offering the citizen the opportunity to debate before the fact the question of whether his city should enter a war. This construal, however, does not fit the text; it is quite clear that the Laws state the options the citizen has once he has been ordered to fight.

As this alternative is traditionally rendered, it offers the citizen the opportunity to persuade the city "what the just is by nature," *hēi to dikaion pephuke*. On the traditional reading, this alternative can only be taken to signal the city's openness to instruction and criticism by its citizens, indeed, to instruction and criticism by them with respect to natural justice.[37]

Is it really possible, however, that the Laws seek to be instructed and enlightened by the citizen with respect to what is just by nature? Is it not the Laws who instruct Socrates with respect to what justice requires? Would it not be odd indeed for them to seek moral guidance from him? The Laws have their own understanding of justice. According to them, justice is not equal for the citizen and the city any more than for a child and father or a slave and master; on the Laws' understanding of justice, it is unjust for a citizen to do to a city in return what a city does to him. Having made their view of justice clear, they dare Socrates to dispute it: "And will you say that in doing this you are acting justly, you who in truth care for virtue?" They demand to know, further, if Socrates' wisdom is such that he would overturn what is from their perspective virtually self-evident—that the citizen's demeanor with respect to the city should manifest abject humility and submissiveness. Indeed, the Laws explicitly pronounce on the requirements of justice: ". . . Or if it leads one into war to be wounded or killed, this must be done, *and this is the just, kai to dikaion houtōs echei* . . ." (*Cr.* 51b5–7).[38] This pronouncement by the Laws regarding what is just makes it most unreasonable to think that they offer as an alternative to obedience that the citizen teach *them* what is just. How then can we explain the Laws' saying: "or else persuade it what the just is by nature"?

There is, fortunately, another way of interpreting the Laws' words, *ē peithein autēn hēi to dikaion pephuke* (*Cr.* 51c1), a way that preserves both the meaning I proposed earlier for *peithein*, to seek to prevail by way of entreaty and supplication and fawning, and the despotic character of the Laws. No more is required for this alternative interpretation than the insertion of a comma after *autēn*.[39] With the insertion of this comma, the passage no longer reads, implausibly, "or else persuade it *what* the just is by nature,"[40] but rather, "or else persuade it, *as* is just by nature."[41] On this reading the Laws remain in character, continuing to dictate to Socrates the requirements of justice: justice by nature, they inform him, requires that the citizen be submissive to the father-

37. If correct, this traditional understanding of the passage would, of course, undermine my interpretation of *peithein* as related to fawning rather than to rational discourse.

38. Note that I connect the phrase "and that this is the just," *kai to dikaion houtōs echei*, to what precedes it rather than to what follows it. It is quite awkward to try to connect "and that this is the just" to what follows it, because of the *kai*, "and," that intervenes.

39. I found this comma in two of the editions I consulted, in Kral (1885) and in Goebel (1893).

40. If the Laws wished to be persuaded about justice, perhaps they would have used the expression in the *Gorgias* at 455a1–2, *peri to dikaion te kai adikon*. But the Laws do not seek to be "persuaded" *about* something; they seek to be "persuaded" in the sense of entreated. We may note that on none of the other occasions when the Laws demand persuasion as an alternative to doing as they say (*Cr.* 51b3, 51e7, 52a2) do they speak of persuading them *about* something. One advantage , then, of my interpretation is that it makes this instance consistent with the others.

41. Goebel (1893), 136, supports this reading of *hēi to dikaion pephuke*; he is, however, the only editor I could find who does. On my reading, the Laws say the following: "Or are you so wise that you have been unaware that . . . if it leads one into war to be wounded or killed, this must be done and this is the just, and that one is not to give way or retreat or leave one's station, but that in war and in court

land either by obeying it or else by "persuading" it. The Laws go on to complete their lecture with a lesson on piety, affirming the greater impiety of doing violence to one's fatherland than to one's mother or father.[42]

As the Laws portray the city or fatherland, then, it certainly does not look to the citizen for guidance with respect to justice.[43] Because of the hierarchical relation in which the fatherland stands to its citizens, nature itself—no less than the gods (Cr. 51b1)—approves of the total submission of the citizen to the city. This submission, whether in the form of obedience or in the form of "persuasion," is what is "just by nature." In this context, "persuasion" can only mean humble supplication.[44] On the household model, inasmuch as it conceives of citizens as children and slaves, the last thing the city would tolerate, let alone encourage, is persuasion that takes the form of instruction with respect to what justice requires.[45]

In addressing Socrates, the Laws limit their discussion to situations comparable to his. They envision cases in which the city causes the citizen to suffer in some way or orders him to endure something painful or confront something dangerous. The Laws do not discuss such questions as what a citizen ought to do if he regards a particular law as unjust or how he ought to proceed in the Assembly to prevent unjust laws from being passed or to have already existing unjust laws repealed.[46] The Laws

---

and everywhere, one must do whatever the city and fatherland bid, or else persuade it, *as is just by nature* . . . ?" The Laws, then, tell the citizen, first, that it is just to do as he is told and, second, that it is just by nature either to do as he is told or to persuade.

42. We may note that in the *Apology*, the two things Socrates considers to be impious are (1) the judges' granting justice as a favor when they have sworn an oath to judge according to the laws (*Ap.* 35c2–3) and (2) the accused's attempt to "persuade and force" them "by begging" after they have sworn an oath (*Ap.* 35d2–5).

43. The view that the city does seek instruction from its citizens is advanced by Dyer and Seymour (1885), 139, who say of the phrase *hēi to dikaion pephuke* that it is "an explanation of *peithein*, which implies *didaskein*."

44. We may compare the following two passages: (1) "Neither in a court case nor in war ought I or anyone else *to devise a way to escape death by doing anything at all*" (*Ap.* 38e5–39a1); (2) "And in war and in court and everywhere, one must do whatever the city and fatherland bid, *or else persuade it*" (*Cr.* 51b8–c1). The italicized phrases correspond to each other; it is clear that persuasion in the *Crito* is the counterpart of the *Apology*'s devising a way to escape death by doing anything at all. And we know very well to what the phrase "doing anything at all" refers: the wailing and lamenting and other forms of doing and saying that Socrates regards as unworthy of himself.

45. On Kraut's view (1984), 94, offspring honor their parents either by obeying them or by persuading them as to the nature of justice. But, one may wonder if this is how the Laws think children honor their parents: do the Laws think it appropriate for children to present their parents—especially their angry parents—with a discourse on what is just by nature? It is far more likely that the Laws think children ought either to obey or to appease or placate their angry parents. Indeed, the Laws are quite explicit on this matter: ". . . And one must revere and give way to and fawn upon a fatherland more than a father when it is angry with you . . ." (*Cr.* 51b2–3).

46. On this matter I disagree with Grote (1875), I, 300, who paraphrases the Laws' argument as follows: "The laws allow every citizen full liberty of trying to persuade the assembled public: but the citizen who fails in persuading, must obey the public when they enact a law adverse to his views." Although the Laws do not consider whether a citizen is obligated to obey a law that he believes to be unjust if he has openly opposed it in the Assembly, nevertheless, we know from the *Apology* that Socrates believes it impossible for a man who "fights for the just" (*Ap.* 32a1) to "go up before your multitude to counsel the city" and survive (*Ap.* 31c5–32a3).

do not on this occasion extol the virtues of the democracy in which citizens function regularly as persuaders. The Laws are not idealized and idealistic superlaws;[47] the persuasion they demand is not cerebral but visceral.

The Laws in this part of their speech adopt, as Crito did in his own speech, Socratic talk of justice and piety. But, as what Crito meant by justice bears no resemblance to what Socrates means, so, too, what the Laws mean by justice and piety is worlds apart from what Socrates means. Justice, for the Laws, is submission to them regardless of what they may have done; it is a posture the citizen must adopt with respect to them: "and this is the just," *kai to dikaion houtōs echei (Cr.* 51b7)—that is, being quiet, suffering anything that the city orders when it is angry, and going to war to be wounded or killed at the city's behest.[48] So, too, for piety. Whereas for Socrates it is impious to persuade "and force, *biazoimēn,* you [the judges], by begging" (*Ap.* 35d1–2), for the Laws it is impious *not* to persuade by begging; indeed, they regard the refusal to persuade them in that way as one way (disobedience being the other) of perpetrating violence against them, *biazesthai (Cr.* 51c2).

When, then, the Laws use Socrates' language of justice and piety, they distort it beyond recognition: since justice is for them hierarchical, the meanings they assign to moral terms differ from Socrates' meanings. Nevertheless, the Laws borrow liberally phrases that Socrates uses in the *Apology* and earlier in the *Crito,* changing their sense and turning them against him. First, we may note the Laws' use of the expression "and suffer, keeping quiet," *kai paschein . . . hēsuchian agonta (Cr.* 51b4–5), to indicate how a citizen is to comport himself when the fatherland is angry with him. This identical expression is used earlier in the *Crito* by Socrates to emphasize the importance of avoiding injustice: if the alternative to doing injustice is to be quiet and suffer, *hēsuchian agontas . . . paschein (Cr.* 48d5), then Socrates will be quiet and suffer. Whereas for Socrates, to be quiet and suffer is what a person must do if that is the only way to avoid injustice, for the Laws, to be quiet and suffer is itself what constitutes just conduct.[49]

47. Cf. Kraut (1984), 66, who says of the Laws that they "are ideal observers of the Athenian legal scene." See also Yonezawa (1991), 570–72. Yonezawa argues that "the community of the city" that addresses Socrates in the *Crito (Cr.* 50a8) is different from the actual city of Athens. (See also Colson [1989], 44, who regards *to koinon tēs poleōs,* which he translates "the shared commonality of the state," as "a term pregnant with political connotations.") We may note, first, that "community of the city" is a stock phrase (see, e.g., *Euthyphro* 14b5; Prot. 319d7–e1) and therefore ought not to be invested with too much significance. Second, although Yonezawa contends that this "community of the city" seeks "to produce good members of the state community," there is, in fact, no evidence of this. The Laws and the "community of the city" in the *Crito* argue their case on the grounds that Socrates approves of Athens and of how Athens manages things and demand that Socrates obey specifically the verdicts of the Athenian court, the very court that, as Yonezawa puts it, "looks to its 'private profits' and renders 'emotional judgments'" (573). They do not speak at all of their having produced good citizens.

48. See Anastaplo (1975) (2), 211: "'Justice' is for them [i.e., the Laws] obedience to the law—they acknowledge no bad law." It is interesting that Anastaplo recognizes this to be the Laws' view of justice even though he interprets *ē peithein autēn hēi to dikaion pephuke (Cr.* 51c1) in the standard way, as: "or else persuade it what the just is by nature."

49. The expression "keep quiet" is found as well in the *Apology,* where Socrates declares that he will not keep quiet, *hēsuchian agōn,* as the Athenians would prefer (*Ap.* 37e3), because to do so, *hēsuchian agein,* would be to disobey the god (*Ap.* 37e5–38a1). Socrates also regards keeping quiet as the alternative to putting on "these piteous dramas" in court. The Laws, however, like the judges, prefer these piteous dramas to dignified silence.

Another example of the Laws' turning Socrates' own expressions against him is their use of the expression "and not yield or retreat or leave one's station," *kai ouchi hepeikteon oude anachōrēteon oude leipteon tēn taxin* (*Cr.* 51b7–8). For the Laws, the citizen is forbidden to yield contrary to the command of the city, and the station that he must not abandon is the station at which the city stations him. Yet, in the *Apology*, it is "against the just" that Socrates will not "yield to any single man" even if he must perish as a result (*Ap.* 32a6–7), and the "station" (*tēn taxin*) that Socrates would be most ashamed to leave is the one at which he is placed by the god who orders him "to live philosophizing and examining myself and others" (*Ap.* 28e4–29a1).[50] Indeed, the very word *peithein*, "persuade," a term used repeatedly by Socrates in the *Apology* to signify instruction,[51] is appropriated and distorted now by the Laws for their own ends. For when the Laws complain that Socrates has not "persuaded," they refer not to his having failed to convey the truth about himself to them successfully but to his having failed to show them and the city the proper deference.[52]

The Laws' absolute authoritarianism is certainly incompatible with the Socratic principle that one may never commit injustice. For if one must do whatever one is bid by the city, then, since the city may well issue a command to commit injustice (as it clearly did in the case of the mass trial of the ten generals and in the case of Leon of Salamis in the *Apology*), the citizen may have to commit injustice.

Scholars who believe that the Laws speak for Socrates must, then, find some way of rendering compatible the Socratic principle that one ought never commit injustice with the Laws' rule that one must do "whatever the city and fatherland bid" (*Cr.* 51b9–c1).[53] There are two main strategies employed to this end: (1) to suppose that when the Laws say that the citizen must do "whatever we bid," they mean to limit the citizen's obligation to cases in which he is ordered to *suffer* injustice;[54] and (2) to take the Laws to hold themselves responsible for injustices the citizen commits at their command.[55]

50. Seeing in Crito's case how very differently from Socrates he understands terms like "justice" enables us to appreciate how great is the moral divide between him and Socrates. Similarly, seeing how very different from Socrates' is the sense that the Laws attach to justice, piety, keeping quiet, remaining at the station, and, as we shall soon see, agreement, should enable us to acknowledge that the Laws do not speak for Socrates.

51. Socrates says: "I awaken and persuade and reproach each one of you" (*Ap.* 30e7); "persuading you to care for virtue" (*Ap.* 31b5); "to teach and persuade" (*Ap.* 35c2); "I attempted to persuade each of you not to care for any of his own things until he cares for himself" (*Ap.* 36c5–6); but I am not persuading you of this" (*Ap.* 37a6); "you would be persuaded" (*Ap.* 37b1); "but to persuade you is not easy" (*Ap.* 38a7–8).

52. It is likely that when Socrates says at *Cr.* 49e9–50a1: "And if we go away from here not having persuaded, *mē peisantes*, the city," he is playing upon the ambiguity of the term: he was unsuccessful in "persuading," that is, in teaching, the city that he is innocent, that indeed he is Athens' greatest benefactor, *and* he refused to "persuade" the city in the way that would have been successful, that is, by wailing and lamenting and begging. See Chapter 4, n. 60.

53. This expression or a variant of it appears at *Cr.* 51b3–4, 51e4, and 52a1–2. For Socrates' understanding of the citizen's obligation not to abandon his military post, see the section in Chapter 2 entitled "Authority and Law."

54. Proponents of this view are many. To name just a few: McLaughlin (1976), 191; Wade (1971), 320; DeFilippo (1991), 257; Kraut (1984), 85–87; Allen (1980), 110.

55. See Brickhouse and Smith (1994), 152–53, and Ray (1980), 49.

In support of strategy (1), it has been maintained that (a) the Laws never say that one must *commit* injustice at their behest; all the cases they consider are cases in which they order one to suffer injustice;[56] and (b) since rules often contain exceptions not made explicit by the rules themselves, it is unreasonable to expect of the Laws that they state explicitly that their rule, the rule that obligates the citizen to do whatever the city, the fatherland, and the Laws bid, stops short of requiring that the citizen commit injustice on command.[57] The second strategy draws its support from the parent-child and master-slave analogies: just as when a child obeys a parent and a slave a master, the responsible agent is the parent or master and not the child or slave, so when the citizen obeys the city, the responsible agent is the city.[58]

Let us now consider the first strategy. If we look closely at the text, we see that the Laws' demand for obedience as it is stated is categorical; not only do they specify no exceptions,[59] but they make it quite clear that they tolerate no exceptions (other than the persuasion as entreaty discussed earlier). The distinction between committing injustice and suffering it is completely foreign to the Laws; all they demand is that the citizen do "whatever it [i.e., the city] bids."[60] Moreover, not only is the distinction between committing injustice and suffering injustice foreign to the Laws' idiom, but the very notion of suffering *injustice* is foreign to it as well: the Laws speak of suffering, but never of suffering injustice. As was argued earlier, injustice, from the Laws' point of view, is what citizens commit by their disobedience. Even if the Laws impose suffering on an innocent citizen, there is no injustice committed by them; injustice enters the picture only when the citizen attempts to resist the imposed suffering. The Laws countenance no distinction between suffering that they impose justly and suffering that they impose unjustly.

One could, of course, counter that the Laws do not *say* that one must do whatever they and the city bid, *including committing injustice*, and that their silence in this matter may be interpreted to mean that they would be willing to recognize committing injustice as an exception to their rule.[61] Let us see, then, if we can explain why it might be that the Laws do not explicitly include committing injustice among the things they require citizens to do upon command.

56. See Woozley (1979), 60; Irwin (1986), 404; DeFilippo (1991), 257.

57. Irwin (1986), 401. For a similar view, see Vlastos (1974), 530, and Santas (1979), 45–51. Both Vlastos and Santas argue that the Laws establish a prima facie duty of absolute obedience, whereas Socrates had earlier established a prima facie duty of never doing injustice. When these two duties conflict, Vlastos and Santas argue, one has no alternative but to violate one of them.

58. See Brickhouse and Smith (1994), 153: ". . . the responsible agent of injustice in such cases is the state, and not the citizen acting as the state's 'offspring' or 'slave.'"

59. See Strauss (1983), 62: "They say nothing about any limit to that obedience"; Stephens (1985), 7: "The Laws nowhere add the condition that we are obligated to abide by our agreements and obey our parents provided that they require of us only what is right."

60. DeFilippo (1991), 257, argues that the Laws gloss the word *poiein*, "do," with the word *paschein*, "suffer": what the citizen must *do* is *suffer* in the various ways then enumerated by the Laws. As I argue later in this section, it is perfectly reasonable for the Laws to speak only of suffering as what the citizen must do when told to by the city, even if they demand complete and total obedience. Let us note that in the passage immediately following that cited by DeFilippo, the Laws say twice that the citizen must do "whatever we bid" (*Cr.* 51e3–4 and 52a1–2), yet there is no similar "gloss"; the word *paschein* does not appear at all.

61. Irwin (1986), 404, calls this omission "striking."

We may note, first, that, as was just said, it is not only committing injustice that the Laws do not explicitly include among the things they require citizens to do upon command; they also do not include suffering injustice among the things they require. The Laws speak neither of requiring of a citizen that he commit injustice when so ordered nor of requiring of him that he suffer injustice when so ordered, but only of requiring of him that he suffer when so ordered. The Laws, it seems, simply do not accord importance to the just or unjust content of their commands: the fact of their command makes it just to obey and unjust to disobey.

We may note, second, that the very expectation that the Laws would specify committing injustice as one of the things a citizen must do if they so command him presupposes that the Laws recognize a moral ranking according to which it is worse to commit injustice than to suffer it. Yet, it is probable that the Laws share the view of the many that it is worse to suffer than to commit injustice. They therefore assume that if they require of a citizen that he suffer they have required of him the most they can require: if he will obey a command that puts his own life at risk will he not, a fortiori, obey a command that he endanger not himself but another? If the Laws believe that a citizen wishes most to avoid his own pain and death, why would they think to stipulate that he must be willing not only to suffer and die himself but also to cause others to suffer and die if the Laws so bid? Since it is likely that the Laws expect the citizen to regard committing injustice when the city tells him to as calling for a lesser sacrifice on his part than suffering does, they would see no reason to make explicit the citizen's duty to commit injustice on command.

The third and perhaps most obvious reason for the Laws' silence with respect to committing injustice is that they are addressing Socrates, who is about to refuse to suffer in accordance with their sentence but is not about to disobey a command of theirs to commit injustice. Under these circumstances, what sense would it make for them to say: "even if he is bid to commit injustice"?

The Laws, then, despite their not adding a phrase such as "even if the city orders one to commit injustice," do not qualify in any way the phrase they do use, "whatever it bids." They maintain that the city is endowed with a superiority in relation to the citizen, a superiority recognized by both gods and men of intelligence, as well as by nature, a superiority even greater than that of parents and masters in relation to children and slaves. The chasm that separates the citizen from the city makes reverence in the form of yielding and fawning appropriate. The Laws and the city tell the citizen what to do, and, no matter what the cost to him, the inequality of justice between him and the city makes it just for him to comply. The Laws assign no importance to the possible injustice a citizen might have to commit or suffer as a result of doing their bidding: as they see it, what is just is for the citizen to do their bidding.

Let us consider now the second strategy for reconciling the Laws' categorical demand for obedience with the equally categorical Socratic prohibition on committing injustice. According to this second strategy, if the citizen commits injustice at the Laws' command, the Laws regard themselves as the culpable agent; on this view, the citizen himself has committed no injustice. In evaluating this strategy, we may observe, first, the total absence of textual support for this idea, an idea that is surely significant enough and novel enough to merit explicit mention by the Laws. Second, one would hardly expect the very same Laws that demand of the citizen reverence for the city in the form of yielding and fawning to be offering assurances to the citizen that the city accepts full responsibility for whatever injustices the citizen commits at its command. Having established a strictly hierarchical relationship between the city and the citizen, the Laws stipulate what the citizen owes the city; beyond providing the basic benefits of establishing the structure into which a citizen is born and within which he is nurtured, educated, and lives, the city owes the citizen nothing. Thus far, the sole reason the city gives for the citizen's duty to obey the city's commands is that the city is the boss. Since the command to commit injustice is but one form of command the city can issue, the reason the citizen must obey the city's command in the particular case of committing injustice is the same as it is generally—the superior status of the city with respect to him.[62]

It is important to note that in the *Crito*, the Laws make no distinction between authority and law. For the Laws in the *Crito*, it is immaterial whether it is they or the city or fatherland that bid the citizen to suffer something.[63] From the Laws' point of view, just as what parents and masters say is not "law" but is still binding, so what the city or fatherland bids is binding irrespective of whether it qualifies as "law." The expression "whatever it bids" certainly suggests edicts and decrees at least as much as it does duly constituted laws.[64]

It is hardly surprising that the Laws in the *Crito* are authoritarian, demanding of their subjects unequivocal obedience, requiring of them that they do "whatever we bid." Authoritarianism of this kind is surely typical of ancient legal systems, the rule— not the exception. Indeed, the Laws say precisely what one would expect laws (or orators on behalf of laws) to say in order to ensure their own survival and the survival of the city.[65] They do not, however, say the things one would expect Socrates to say— certainly not any of the things Socrates has always said. The Laws argue for the absolute authority of the city over the citizen; Socrates champions the authority of a man's carefully reasoned principles. The Laws regard the citizen as their slave; Socrates will do nothing unsuitable to a free man.

The Argument from Agreement

We may turn now to the Laws' second ground for the wrongness of Socrates' purported attempt to destroy the city. We may note that the Laws' first ground—the

---

62. We see in the *Apology* how readily citizens commit injustice at their government's command: Socrates alone objected to the mass trial of the ten generals and to bringing in the innocent Leon. Moreover, Socrates notes in the *Apology* the great lengths that most people will go to in court and elsewhere in order to avoid their own personal suffering or death.

63. We may note the Laws' indiscriminate use of the following three expressions: "whatever it bids" (*Cr.* 51b4), "whatever the city and fatherland bid" (*Cr.* 51b9–c1), and "whatever we bid" (*Cr.* 51e3–4 and 52a1–2).

64. There are then no grounds for maintaining that the Laws are speaking only of what a citizen's duty is vis-à-vis duly constituted laws.

65. See Anastaplo (1975b), 208: "The laws say precisely what one would expect to hear from them. Every law expects to be obeyed: it states an imperative; it demands obedience; it knows no alternative. And all laws are in this respect birds of a feather."

hierarchy of citizen and city and its resultant inequality of justice—establishes independent of any other ground the wrongness of Socrates' escape. If the Laws' argument from the inequality of justice between citizen and city is sound, then it cannot be just for Socrates to attempt to destroy the city though it attempts to destroy him: no other argument is needed.[66] Yet, since the Laws had earlier maintained that Socrates *agreed* to abide by all the city's judgments, they have still to prove that point. Hence their second argument, the argument from agreement.[67]

The first argument makes the citizen's duty to obey or persuade nonvoluntary, the result solely of his inferior position vis-à-vis the city. The only element of "agreement" in the first argument is Socrates' presumed acquiescence in the Laws' characterization of him and his forebears as their offspring and slave. The Laws now seek to establish that Socrates is, through his own choice, bound to accept the Laws' judgment.[68]

66. Kraut (1984), 94, n. 4, sees the first argument as requiring a supplement because "the parent-city analogy . . . does not confine legitimate disobedience to those cases in which a citizen is motivated by a desire to avoid acting unjustly. He may also disobey in order to avoid suffering injustice—unless he has made some agreement that disqualifies this objection." On my view, however, the first argument recognizes no legitimate disobedience whatsoever. Irwin (1986), 404, in contrast to Kraut, thinks it is the agreement argument that requires supplementing. For him, it is the Parental Analogy that "shows that Socrates ought to agree to obey the law and that his agreement to obey it is just." On my view, however, what the Parental Analogy seeks to show is not why it is right for the citizen to enter into an agreement to obey the law but rather why it is right for the citizen to obey the law. The Laws, after all, do not say *why* Socrates ought to agree to obey the law; they say simply that he has so agreed. Indeed, the Laws proceed to point out the unusual extent to which Socrates has agreed to be governed by Athens and its laws.

67. Once the Laws have argued that the citizen must do "whatever we bid," whether at the final and most stringent stage of the parent-master argument or in the agreement argument, it follows that the citizen must comply with all the city's judgments, correct or incorrect: the citizen is morally bound not to destroy the law that requires such compliance.

68. Adkins (1960), 263, points out how different the "contract" between the Laws and the citizen is from an ordinary contract "in which there are conditions, foreseeable and specified, in which the contract becomes null and void." Since in this contract nothing the state can do can void the agreement, this agreement establishes a relationship "like the relationship which subsists between a master and a slave." See also Panagiotou (1987), 48–49, who argues that, according to the Laws' first argument, Socrates is born a slave of the city and is while a child a nonvoluntary slave but that, according to their second argument, he becomes a voluntary slave upon reaching the age of maturity: what he agrees to in effect is to be a slave of the city. I think that Panagiotou is partially correct but that he goes wrong at two points. First, contra Panagiotou, Socrates does not speak of the citizen's nonvoluntary slavery as ending when he reaches maturity, at which point he becomes a slave voluntarily. On the contrary, on the basis of the citizen's nonvoluntary slave status, the Laws require that he go to war and submit to court verdicts and, most important, not attempt to destroy the Laws by escape—things done by adults. In the first argument, then, the comparison drawn is not between being a child in Athens and being a child to parents but between being an adult citizen in Athens and being a child to parents. Second, I cannot agree with Panagiotou that what distinguishes the citizen's slave status at the second stage is that he has, as Panagiotou contends, "the right to try to change the very details he is a 'slave' to." The Laws say nothing in their speech about the citizen's attaining upon maturation the right to change the laws by which he is governed. He may stay, say the Laws, or he may leave—having seen the "affairs in the city and us Laws" and "the way that we reach judgments and otherwise manage the city" (Cr. 51e2–3). That the citizen is offered the option of persuading means, as we have seen, that he may seek to curry favor. This option has nothing whatsoever to do with changing the details the citizen is a slave to. It would be odd indeed for the Laws to berate Socrates for not exercising his right to try to change the very details he is a slave to; yet they clearly do berate him for not "persuading."

The great difficulty the Laws face is the absence of any explicit verbal agreement between the citizen—in this case, Socrates—and them. Since they can point to no such explicit agreement, they must rely on tacit agreement, which, in this case, is an agreement that the Laws infer from Socrates' inaction: Socrates, like all citizens, was given the opportunity to leave if the Laws did not satisfy him; he chose not to leave; he thus "agreed *in deed* to do whatever we bid."[69] The Laws' strategy here is very similar to their strategy in the first argument. There the Laws assume that since Socrates has no objection to a certain very small set of laws, he may be taken to regard both himself and his forebears as the city's offspring and slave. Here the Laws assume that since Socrates could have left but did not, he is satisfied with the city and the Laws—in particular with how the Laws reach judgments and otherwise manage the city—and agrees to do whatever they bid. Yet, here, as in the first argument, the Laws assume too much. In the first argument the Laws do not actually know if Socrates regards himself and his forebears as their offspring and slave; they do not know if Socrates agrees that justice is unequal between him and the city; they do not know if Socrates agrees that he cannot justly do to them what they do to him; and they surely do not know that he accepts the notion that he must "persuade" or obey. And in this second argument, the Laws do not know why Socrates has chosen to remain in Athens: they do not know what it is that binds Socrates to his native city; they also do not know if he would consent to their characterization of his staying in Athens as his having "agreed in deed" to do "whatever we bid." Moreover, in the case of each of the arguments, the reader has good reason to suspect that the Laws' assumptions are false. With respect to the first argument, we may note that (1) Socrates is, in his own view, no one's slave,[70] (2) for him, it is the incorrectness of the judgment and not the relative rank of the citizen and city that is the critical issue, and (3) justice, as Socrates understands it, not only does not require that the citizen persuade or obey, but, on the contrary, forbids "persuasion" in the form of obsequious entreaty. With respect to the second argument, we may note, first, that Socrates' reason for rarely leaving Athens may have little to do with either his being generally satisfied

69. The Laws' point cannot be that Socrates' contract, insofar as it is an agreement *in deed*, is more binding than a verbal one. Yet, in commenting on Cr. 52d5, where the Laws repeat the idea that Socrates' contract is a contract in deed but add the phrase "but not in word," *all' ou logōi*, both Adam (1888), 72, and Dyer and Seymour (1885), 142, understand the phrase to signify "not in mere words," thereby suggesting the greater binding force of a contract in deed. Burnet (1924), 206, points out that some editors simply bracket the phrase; he recommends that, since it is "a standing formula," it "not be too closely analysed." The fact is, however, that the phrase suggests not that Socrates did not agree *merely* in word but rather that he did not agree in word at all. We may compare our passage with the passages at Ap. 32a4–5: "not words, but what *you* honor deeds," and at Ap. 32d1: "not in word but in deed." In both these passages the "not in word" comes first and the "but," *alla*, is attached to the deed, thereby suggesting "not *merely* in word but in deed." In our passage, Cr. 52d5, however, the phrase "not in word" comes second and has the "but" attached to *it*, thus signifying "in deed *though not* in word." I suspect that the standing phrase is not "in deed but not in word" but rather "not in word but in deed." Whereas actions in some cases speak louder than words, particularly for the many, a contract "in deed," and certainly one inferred from inaction, cannot equal in force a contract in word.

70. Socrates will do nothing "unsuitable to a free man" and recoils at the prospect of prison because he would be enslaved there to the Eleven. Socrates does not use the word "slave" to characterize even his relationship to the god. As we have seen, to obey the god means to Socrates to practice philosophy and to follow reason for the sake of justice.

with or his having special regard for Athens and her laws: Socrates makes quite clear his *dis*satisfaction with both the one-day trial (*Ap.* 37a7–b1) and the way the judges dispense justice as a favor rather than judge according to the law (compare *Ap.* 35c2–5 with *Ap.* 38d6–e2).[71] Second, it is clear from the *Apology* that Socrates holds "proofs in deed" generally in low esteem, viewing them as "vulgar things, typical of the law courts": these and not *logoi* are what the men of the court honor (*Ap.* 32a4–5). Third, and perhaps most important, Socrates would never have consented to do "whatever we bid."[72] Socrates, as we know from *Cr.* 49e6 and 50a3, as well as from *Rep.* I.331c, believes that agreements are always subject to exception: if one has agreed to do *x* one must do *x* — unless *x* is, on a given occasion, unjust. The agreement that the Laws attribute to Socrates, however, is an agreement to obey without exception whatever the Laws and city bid. If one is dissatisfied with the laws of the city, the Laws say, one may leave, but by staying one agrees to obey absolutely. It may be quite true (1) that the Laws do not coerce one to stay, since one may leave without incurring adverse consequences and (2) that insofar as the Laws do not conceal from the citizen "the way that we reach judgments and otherwise manage the city" (*Cr.* 51e2–3), they do not deceive him into staying, yet, even so, can Socrates' remaining in Athens be reasonably construed as his agreement to obey without exception all judgments and orders of the city? Although the Laws adopt the earlier Socratic language of keeping agreements, their argument from agreement is neither a revival nor a further development of Socrates' principle as stated at *Cr.* 49e6–7. The Laws speak to Socrates using the language of justice and agreements — as Crito earlier talked to Socrates about justice, courage, and goodness — without meaning by these words what Socrates means by them. The agreement of which Socrates spoke at *Cr.* 49e6–7 was verbal and explicit and subject to exception in the event of its being unjust on a particular occasion (the injustice being determined by the agent upon rational reflection); the agreement of which the Laws speak is a tacit one inferred by them from the citizen's inaction and subject to no exceptions; specifically, whereas the Laws do permit the citizen to evaluate Athens and its laws and decide whether to remain or to leave, they do not permit the citizen to determine for himself whether on a particular occasion what the Laws bid is just and hence binding: as long as the citizen stays, he has agreed to do "whatever we bid" without exception. Since Socrates would surely not have agreed "in word," had anyone asked him, to do whatever the Laws and the city bid, we may safely assume that he did not, despite the Laws' contention that he did, agree "in deed" to do whatever they and the city bid.

The Laws do not, of course, pause to check and confirm the correctness of their assumptions. Instead, they proceed to accuse whoever stays in Athens but does not obey them with committing threefold injustice. The threefold injustice is usually understood as consisting of (1) the citizen's disobedience to the Laws who begat him; (2) the citizen's disobedience to the Laws who nurtured him; and (3) the citizen's

---

71. One might argue that the Laws are not responsible for what the judges do. Yet Socrates makes it clear that wailing and lamenting and crying and begging are standard features of the Athenian legal system, features that bring shame on the city. Furthermore, in approving of "fawning" and then of "persuasion," the Laws show themselves to favor just such behavior with respect to an angry fatherland.

72. See the discussion of this issue in Chapter 5.

failure to obey or persuade the Laws—though he has agreed to obey them—if they do something ignobly (mē kalōs),[73] despite their having offered him the options of either persuading or obeying (Cr. 51e4–52a3).[74] I do not think this is the correct way to understand the Laws' charge, or, more precisely, I do not think this is the correct way to understand the third component of the Laws' threefold accusation.

There are two reasons for my doubts about the usual understanding of this passage. The first is that it neglects the phrase that introduces and governs the three injustices. The Laws introduce their charge that "he commits injustice in three ways" (Cr. 51e5) with the phrase: "And when he does not obey," kai ton mē peithomenon (Cr. 51e4). Since the three ways the Laws list are ways in which the citizen who remains commits injustice when he does not obey, it seems improbable that the third way would consist, as on the usual interpretation, of the citizen's failure to obey or persuade.

The second reason is that in their first argument, the argument based upon the parent-child analogy, the Laws also offer the citizen the two options of obeying or persuading. It seems odd, then, that the Laws would now, in summarizing the three injustices of the citizen who does not obey, complain about the citizen's failure to obey or persuade only in relation to his having made an agreement but not in relation to the Laws' having begotten and nurtured him.

I propose, then, that a period be inserted after the phrase kai hoti homologēsas hēmin peisesthai, "although he agreed to obey us" (Cr. 51e6), and that this phrase be understood to contain the whole of the third way in which the disobedient citizen commits injustice. The passage Cr. 51e4–6 would then read as follows: "And when he does not obey, we say that he commits threefold injustice: in that he does not obey us who begat him; in that [he does not obey] us who nurtured him; and in that [he does not obey] although he agreed to obey us." The ou peithetai, "he does not obey," that is explicit in the statement of the first of the three ways in which the citizen fails to obey the Laws is, on this reading, taken to be implicit in the third way, just as it has always been taken to be implicit in the second. When ou peithetai is supplied in the third way—as it is standardly supplied in the second—the construction of the third way matches precisely its construction on the standard reading. In place of "and in that although he agreed to, he neither obeys nor persuades us," kai hoti homologēsas hēmin peisesthai oute peithetai oute peithei hēmas, we have: "and in that although he agreed to, [he does not obey us]," kai hoti homologēsas hēmin peisesthai [ou peithetai]. On this reading each of the three components of the threefold injustice represents a way in which the citizen commits injustice "when he does not obey." Two of the three injustices are related to the alleged filial relation of citizen to city and one to the citizen's presumed agreement with the city.

Now that the Laws have established the threefold injustice of a citizen who does not obey, they go on to reprimand the citizen for not only refusing to obey but for

73. The connotation of the expression "ignobly," mē kalōs, is distinct from that of "unjustly," mē adikōs. Its sense is discussed later in this section.

74. Kraut (1984), 91–92, for example, understands the Laws' charge as follows: "Though he is indebted to Athens for his life and education, and though he voluntarily agreed to obey, he nonetheless plans to violate the city's command without defending his behavior. Thus he does the city a threefold injustice."

refusing as well to take advantage of the generous alternative the Laws provide, the opportunity to "persuade" (Cr. 51e7–52a3):

> He neither obeys nor persuades us if we do something ignobly, although we put forward an alternative to him and do not order him crudely to do whatever we bid, but permit either of two things — either to persuade us or to do it — but he does neither of these.[75]

That Socrates does neither constitutes a separate second offense for which the Laws reproach him: "To these charges [pl.], Socrates, we say . . ." (Cr. 52a3–4). On the proposed reading, Socrates' refusal to pursue either of the two available alternatives — that of obeying and that of persuading — constitutes in effect a second threefold injustice: although he was begotten by the Laws, and although he was nurtured by them, and although he agreed to obey them, he neither obeys nor persuades them.

We may note that, just as in the first argument, the argument that relies upon the parent-child and master-slave analogies, the Laws never say of themselves that they commit injustice against Socrates but only that they "attempt to destroy" him, so, too, in their second argument, the agreement argument, the Laws say of themselves not that they treat Socrates "unjustly," *mē adikōs*, but that they treat him "ignobly," *mē kalōs*. As the Laws use the term "nobly," *kalōs*, it is "nobly" that the city issues laws by which Socrates is born, nurtured, and educated (Cr. 50d4; d7). If the Laws believe they do something "nobly" in making it possible for Socrates to be born, they must surely believe they do something "ignobly" by causing him to die. This is not to say, however, that they think they commit injustice against him. It is Socrates who, according to the Laws, commits by his disobedience "threefold injustice."

Socrates and Crito have now heard two independent arguments for the wrongness of Socrates' attempting through escape to destroy the city, the first grounded in the parent-child and master-slave analogies, the second in the citizen's agreement "in deed" to do as he is bid. Some scholars have noted that, far from supporting each other,[76] these two arguments may actually be incompatible. For, whereas from the perspective of the first argument, the citizen's obligation of submissiveness to the city is thrust upon him, from the perspective of the second, the citizen chooses it.[77] Moreover, could it not reasonably be asked how it is that someone who is the city's child and slave as a result of laws that provide for his birth, nurture, and education is ever in a position to enter freely into an agreement through which he becomes or

---

75. If it seems that, with the change in punctuation that I suggest, this second cause for reprimand — that the citizen neither obeys nor persuades — begins rather abruptly, let us remember that the idea that a citizen must obey or persuade is not a new one but has just been asserted twice in connection with the parent-child analogy (Cr. 51b3–4; 51b9–c1). Moreover, if one silently supplies *ou peithetai* as the understood final words of the preceding sentence, then the *oute peithetai oute peithei hēmas* of the new sentence follows easily. We may note, too, that the structure of the passage Cr. 51e4–52a3 is identical to the structure of the passage Cr. 51b5–c1: in the earlier passage the Laws say first that the citizen must do as told since that is what accords with what justice demands and then go on to say that he must do as told or persuade since this is what justice requires; in the later passage, the Laws berate the citizen first for failing to obey, thereby committing injustice, and then go on to berate him for neither obeying nor persuading.

76. For the view that the two arguments are compatible, see the discussion of Kraut and Irwin, n. 66.

77. See Martin (1970), 26; Young (1974), 22.

continues to be such a slave? Indeed, if there is never a time when one is not the city's slave, when could one operate as a free agent? Do the Laws release the individual from slavery when he reaches the point of maturity so that he can choose at that time between remaining a slave and leaving the city? We know from the first argument that the Laws do not do this, because the subservient relationship of the citizen to the city that is grounded in that argument's parent-child and master-slave analogies persists into adulthood, indeed throughout one's life;[78] it is not exchanged at any point for a subservience grounded solely in agreement.

Given the tension between the Laws' two arguments, and considering that either one, by itself, if sound, would be sufficient to establish the wrongness of escape, we might wonder why the Laws use both. It is perhaps easier to see why they use the agreement argument. They *must* use the agreement argument because they must defend their earlier contention that Socrates has "agreed" to abide by whatever judgments the city reaches in trials (*Cr.* 50c4–6). But why do they use the parent-child analogy when it is at best unnecessary and at worst a hindrance to the aim of establishing Socrates' free agreement to be the city's slave?

In order to understand why the Laws do not proceed directly to the argument from agreement but dwell instead on the seemingly irrelevant parent-child analogy, we must recall that the Laws' goal is really to convince *Crito* that Socrates ought not to escape. Crito, as we well know, does not attach much moral weight to agreements: he is not particularly concerned that Socrates, by escaping, would be violating his agreement to "abide by my penalty," nor, as was argued in Chapter 3, does he hesitate to provide false assurances to the court that Socrates will remain and not escape; moreover, he readily assents to everything Socrates says, whether or not he genuinely agrees with it. What Crito does regard as morally significant are the duties associated with family and with friendship. It represents rather clever strategy, then, for the Laws to digress from their agreement argument long enough to root the case against escape in family relations. Indeed, even when the Laws do discuss agreement as the grounds for the wrongness of Socrates' escape, they argue not for the general rightness of keeping agreements but for the rightness of keeping agreements with them. Just as the Laws insisted earlier not on the general wrongness of returning injustice and bad treatment but on doing so to them, so they insist now not on the general wrongness of breaking agreements but on the specific evil of breaking agreements with them. They establish who they are and in what relation they stand to the citizen before they take up the matter of agreement. Crito is apparently unmoved by universal moral rules; he responds only to the casting of duties in terms of power relations or of ties of family or friendship. It is worth noting that when the Laws summarize the three injustices that disobedience would involve, two of them are related to the parent-child analogy—we begat you and we nurtured you—and only one to agreement. And even as the Laws conclude their speech, they return to the parent image that had long since receded into the background: "Obey us, your nurturers," they say (*Cr.* 54b2).

In order to strengthen their case for Socrates' tacit agreement to do as the Laws bid, the Laws proceed to show that Socrates was extraordinarily satisfied with Athens

---

78. See n. 68.

and with them. They offer as evidence of Socrates' great satisfaction that Socrates hardly ever left the city to visit or learn about other places, that he had children in Athens, and that he expressed at his trial a preference for death over exile. Needless to say, none of these facts about Socrates establishes his satisfaction with Athens and its laws: the reason Socrates rarely left Athens was that he had an important mission to pursue there; he had children in Athens because he lived there; he chose death over exile not because of his great love for Athens and its laws but because to choose exile would have been to say falsely of himself that he merits something bad.[79]

Even more striking, however, than the weakness of the Laws' proofs for Socrates' extreme satisfaction with Athens is how the Laws pass almost imperceptibly from providing these "great proofs" into a vicious and strident denunciation of Socrates. For whereas the third proof—the fact that Socrates chose death over exile—begins ostensibly as a proof of Socrates' contentment with Athens, it ends as a most serious attack on his conduct and character. The Laws introduce their third proof with the word "furthermore," *eti toinun* (*Cr.* 53c3–4), as if they mean merely to continue to support their contention that Socrates was satisfied with them and with Athens. But then they change course: rather than speak of Socrates' love of Athens, the Laws berate Socrates (1) for not having proposed exile as the counterpenalty at his trial so that he could have gone into exile "when the city was willing," as opposed to attempting it now, "when the city is unwilling"; (2) for "pluming" himself on not being vexed, *aganaktōn* (*Cr.* 52c6–7), should he have to die;[80] and (3) for choosing death over exile. The Laws are plainly vexed with Socrates: he is, they say, neither ashamed of "those speeches"—the speeches in which he declares himself unafraid of death and expresses his preference for death over exile[81]—nor properly deferential toward the Laws inasmuch as he seeks now to destroy them; he behaves like the lowliest slave, attempting to escape despite the flagrant violation of his contracts and agreements that escape entails.

The Laws' argument has clearly veered off course. That Socrates chose exile over death attests for them not, as the reader is led to expect, to Socrates' great satisfaction with Athens but rather to the shameless arrogance of his claim to be unafraid of death, to the impudence of his not choosing exile when it was permitted. The Laws show utter and unequivocal disdain for Socrates' choice of death over exile: they regard the speeches in which Socrates declares his preference for death as instances of his "pluming" himself. When the Laws rebuke Socrates for not now being "ashamed of those speeches," they imply that he indeed ought to be ashamed of them, of their insolence and impertinence: how dare a man profess to be beyond the fear of death? In truth, the Laws have good reason to be appalled by Socrates' conduct: a man's assertion that he is not fearful of death is an assertion that the city has ultimately no

79. The weakness of the argument in this passage is underscored by the Laws' reliance on hyperbole: "So vehemently were you choosing us and agreeing to be governed in accordance with us that among other things you also had children in it . . ." (*Cr.* 52c1–3).

80. It is clear from the early part of the *Crito* that Socrates is indeed not vexed, *aganaktein* (*Cr.* 43b10) at death; hence, it is no mere "pluming himself" that he does in the *Apology*. Both Crito earlier (*Cr.* 43c1–3) and the Laws here, however, clearly believe that Socrates ought to be vexed at death.

81. The Laws do not get this point quite right. Socrates says in the *Apology* not that he prefers death to exile but that he prefers death to *proposing* exile.

hold over him; insofar as the city's severest sanction is death, one who does not fear death does not fear the city.[82]

Those who read the Laws' speech sympathetically, believing the views it expresses to be Socrates' views, are particularly susceptible to the following two ways of *mis-construing* the Laws' position in this passage: (1) taking the Laws to approve of Socrates' preference for death over exile and to disapprove, for that reason, of his now failing to act on that preference, and, therefore, (2) interpreting the Laws as rebuking Socrates for feeling no shame with respect to what he is now doing—namely, attempting[83] to save his life through escape—*in the face of* "those speeches."[83] Severing the Laws' views from those of Socrates, however, makes it possible to avoid these two misinterpretations and to see that what the Laws decry is Socrates' haughty in-difference to death, that what offends them is his "pluming" himself in asserting this indifference.[84] Indeed, the Laws are perturbed because, rather than humble himself before the court and suggest exile as his due, Socrates will only consider exile when to choose it is to defy the court. Nor will Socrates assume the deferential posture the Laws demand: he is not even now, now that he is attempting to escape, ashamed of having said that he prefers death to exile; and he does not seem to care that by escaping he is attempting to destroy the Laws. If Socrates escapes, the Laws say, he will be behaving like a runaway slave, violating his contracts and agreements. Although it is certainly odd to speak, as the Laws do here, of runaway slaves' violating their contracts and agreements, nevertheless, since the Laws assign to the citizen the peculiar status of slave not only by birth but by free consent, Socrates' escape be-comes for them simultaneously something a slave does and a violation of contracts and agreements.

The Laws' resentment emerges here, as earlier, as twofold.[85] The very man of whom they say at Cr. 52a3 that "he does neither of these"—neither obeys nor persuades—fails now both to be ashamed of his prideful refusal to propose exile ("when the city

---

82. Socrates is clearly aware in the *Apology* that he appears boastful and that the court will there-fore be angered by his declarations that he is not afraid of death. He expects that there will be distur-bances and cries of protest. See *Ap.* 30b7–c8.

83. Adam (1888), 72, and Burnet (1924), 206, following him, assume that the speeches are per-sonified and then take the expression *out' ekeinous tou logous aischunēi* to mean not "are not ashamed *of* those speeches" but "are not ashamed *before* those speeches." They must make the personification assumption if they wish to read "before these speeches" rather than "of these speeches," because only in the case of people does *aischunein* with the accusative means "to be ashamed before." Yet there are no grounds for this assumption. Unless one is sympathetic to the Laws, one has no reason to doubt that they mean what they say—that Socrates is not ashamed now, as he should be, *of* those speeches. Crito, too, we may recall, was ashamed on behalf of Socrates and on behalf of Socrates' companions in part because of "the way the judicial contest itself took place" (*Ap.* 45e4–5).

84. Let us recall that Socrates' first proposed counterpenalty was that he be given free meals at the Prytaneum since, as he said, he was Athens' greatest benefactor.

85. It is important to note that although the Laws' complaint at this stage of their argument, namely, that Socrates "plumes" himself and breaks his contracts and agreements, looks like a new one, it is, in fact, as we shall see presently, essentially no different from the complaint they have been voicing all along: that Socrates neither persuades nor obeys. This complaint is featured, then, in all three stages of the Laws' justice argument: in the parent-child/master-slave analogy, in the agreement argument, and, now, in the argument from Socrates' extraordinary satisfaction with his city.

was willing") and to defer to the Laws through obeying them now that, as a consequence of his not having proposed exile, the death sentence has been imposed ("the city is unwilling"). Socrates in the *Apology* refuses to propose exile because he regards it as an injustice to himself to imply that he deserves something bad. We now see that the very self-abasing gesture that Socrates avoids at all costs is one of which the Laws, no less than the judges, approve.

In light of the Laws' confirmation of Socrates' suspicion in the *Apology* that had he proposed exile, his proposal would have been accepted, it becomes possible to explain an odd passage that appears earlier in the *Crito*. At *Cr.* 48c4–6, Socrates characterizes the considerations that figure in Crito's decision to arrange for Socrates' escape as "considerations of those who easily kill and, if they could, would bring back to life again, acting mindlessly: namely, the many." What does it mean to say that the many "easily kill and, if they could, would bring back to life again"? We may now venture to say that what Socrates means is that the many—the judges at Socrates' trial—since they attend not to the facts of the case but to what they perceive as Socrates' offensive arrogance, too quickly judge him guilty, thereby placing him in the jaws of death, and, for the same reason, would no less quickly give him back his life were he humbly to propose exile as a counterpenalty. The many, in so behaving, says Socrates, act mindlessly, *oudeni xun nōi* (*Cr.* 48c6). If we look back to the very beginning of the *Apology*, we find Socrates cautioning the judges not to allow themselves to turn against him on account of his peculiar or unfamiliar manner of speech. Rather, he says, they ought to consider this very thing and "apply your mind to this, *toutōi ton noun prosechein*: whether the things I say are just or not" (*Ap.* 18a3–5). For a judge to kill someone and bring him back to life again because he is alternately displeased and pleased by the defendant's manner of speech and his demeanor is for him to act without mind; only when one judges in accordance with the truth of what is said does one "apply one's mind." The Laws, by berating Socrates for not having proposed exile, align themselves with the judges who mindlessly heed a defendant's manner and demeanor rather than the truth of what he says and who would as easily bring him back to life as kill him.

Having come back to the idea of Socrates' contracts and agreements, the Laws next make the point that there was neither compulsion nor deception in Socrates' agreement and that he had seventy years in which to leave Athens if his agreements seemed to him not to be just. Yet, they continue, he did not leave; he did not even choose Sparta and Crete, cities that Socrates on occasion commended for having good laws. Since, the Laws contend, Socrates took fewer journeys away from Athens than other Athenians—including the lame, the blind, and other cripples—Socrates must have been more satisfied with Athens' laws than other Athenians are, for, after all, whom would a city without laws satisfy?

Among the things the Laws say in this final stage of their argument from agreement, there is virtually nothing that serves to advance their cause. They take what were formerly the conditions from which they derived the very existence of a Socratic agreement—that Socrates did not leave Athens though he was free to do so (noncoercion), and that he did not leave despite full disclosure by the city of the way it reaches judgments and otherwise manages its affairs (nondeception)—and treat them now as features of the agreement. It is as if the Laws are saying the following: "Since you remained in Athens even though (1) we permitted you to leave, that is, we did not coerce you, and (2) our ways were open to you to see and evaluate for yourself, that is, we did not deceive you, we infer that you have entered into an agreement with us—in deed. And not only have you entered into an agreement with us but you did so without being coerced and deceived."[86]

Furthermore, the Laws do not say that if Socrates had entered into the agreement under compulsion or deception, his agreements would for that reason be null and void such that he would be released from his obligation to obey. On the contrary, the Laws say what they have been saying all along, that if Socrates was not satisfied with them, he could leave: "Nor were you compelled to take counsel in a short time, but rather you had seventy years *in which you could have gone away* if we were not satisfactory or if the agreements did not appear just to you" (*Cr.* 52e1–5). The Laws, then, categorically forbid disobedience; the only alternative to obedience is departure.[87]

The Laws' expression "or if the agreements did not appear just to you" recalls, but distorts, the qualification *dikaia onta*, "as long as they are just" (*Cr.* 49e6), that Socrates had placed earlier on the requirement to abide by the things one has agreed to. From Socrates' perspective, as we have seen, if one makes an agreement, presumably an explicit verbal agreement, with another, then one ought to keep that agreement unless an occasion arises on which it would be unjust to do so. For the Laws, if Socrates at any point finds the Laws as a whole unsatisfactory such that his implicit agreements to obey all of their judgments and decrees does not appear just to him, he is free to leave the city. According to the Laws, then, the citizen may, if he is dissatisfied in general with the ways of the Laws, decide that his agreements to do "whatever the Laws and the fatherland bid" are unjust and leave the city for that reason. What the Laws do *not* permit when they speak of agreements is the very thing that Socrates would insist upon—the exercise by an individual of his own independent rational judgment with respect to particular acts that the city commands him to do.

Of course, for the Laws to conclude from Socrates' having stayed in Athens for seventy years that he is satisfied with them is for them to repeat an earlier non sequitur: just as it was illegitimate earlier for the Laws to infer from Socrates' having remained in Athens that he had agreed in deed to do whatever the Laws bid (*Cr.* 51e), so it is illegitimate for them to infer now from Socrates' having remained in Athens—no matter how long he remained—that Athens, and particularly Athens' laws, are satisfactory to him or that he considers the agreement that the Laws ascribe to him—namely, the agreement to do "whatever we bid" and to abide by "whatever verdicts the city reaches in trials"—a just one. Moreover, that Socrates remains in Athens

---

86. Burnet (1924), 207, contends that "There was an action for breach of contract . . . in answer to which, as we gather from this passage, it was possible to plead that the contract was void as entered into under duress . . . or in consequence of misrepresentation. . . ." As I argue, however, since Socrates' agreement was purportedly a tacit agreement in deed in which the very agreement is inferred from his having stayed when there was neither compulsion nor deception, any "action" such as the one Burnet describes is irrelevant.

87. Kraut (1984), 30, contends that the Laws imply that one need not honor an unjust procedure—one in which the individual is compelled, tricked, or rushed. In fact, however, the Laws assert only that one may leave, not that one is permitted not to comply with an unjust procedure if one stays.

even though he says on occasion that Sparta and Crete have good laws hardly proves that he thinks Athens has better laws than those cities do: when does Socrates ever say that Athens has good laws?[88] And although it is true that no city without laws can be satisfying, that hardly proves that what binds Socrates to Athens is what he regards as its superior laws.[89]

How much weight ought we to accord to the "great proofs" the Laws offer of Socrates' extraordinary satisfaction with Athens? As we know from the *Apology*, Socrates thinks "great proofs," proofs from deeds as opposed to proofs that are *logoi*, are inadequate.[90] In the *Apology*, there are two instances of "great proofs." The first instance consists of deeds of his own that Socrates recounts to the court in order to show that "I would not yield to any single man against the just because of a fear of death" (*Ap.* 32a6–7). These "proofs," as he says, are "vulgar things, typical of the law courts" (*Ap.* 32a8). The second instance consists of the silence of Socrates' *daimonion* with respect to how Socrates conducted himself at his trial. Socrates infers from the silence of his *daimonion* that death is a good thing for him, yet he feels the need to supplement this presumably great proof with speculations about the character of death. Neither his "great proof" nor his speculations about death, however, do more than provide reasons for thinking "how great a hope there is" that death is good (*Ap.* 40c4–5).

Only in the first of these two instances of "great proofs" in the *Apology* does the actual doer of the deeds interpret them. In the *Apology*'s second case, however, the one in which the *daimonion* is silent, and in the *Crito*'s case of Socrates' not leaving Athens, the interpretation of the deed (or, more precisely, of the nondeed) is undertaken by someone other than its doer. In cases in which a deed or nondeed is inter-

---

88. Kraut (1984), 10, accepts the Laws' argument: "Socrates was greatly satisfied with the Athenian legal system, and preferred it to Sparta and Crete. . . ." Santas (1979), 55, however, thinks, as I do, that the Laws greatly exaggerate Socrates' loyalty to Athens. What is surely most remarkable, however, is that the Laws say nothing about the likely circumstance of Socrates' being especially approving of Athens because of its tolerance of free speech. The Laws speak only in the most general terms of Socrates' satisfaction with Athenian laws. No doubt, from the Laws' perspective, what makes Athens a good city is that it is orderly and law-governed; they do not see why Athens is better than any other orderly, law-governed city. We discussed in Chapter 2 the strong possibility that Athens was in fact no more tolerant of philosophy than were other cities. But even if it were, would the Laws applaud Athens for it; would they not rather be inclined to suppress that feature of the city in their speech?

89. See Strauss (1983), 64. Strauss points out that although it is certainly true that a city without laws cannot please anyone, it does not follow that if Socrates found Athens pleasing, it is because its laws are pleasing: "a city may have other attractions than its laws." Some commentators contend that the Laws' statement means: "For whom would a city satisfy apart from *its* laws?" (See, e.g., Kraut [1984], 177–78; Fowler translates it similarly in the Loeb edition [1914], 185: ". . . for who would be pleased with a city apart from its laws?" Also Grube [1975], and Croiset [1963]. But Grube [1981], 55, translates: ". . . for what city can please without laws?'). Even if the statement's meaning were as Kraut et al. render it, it fails, as Strauss's comment shows, to make a convincing argument: why is it not possible for a person to be satisfied with a city for reasons unrelated to its laws?

90. At *Ap.* 17b2 Socrates says that his accusers who had warned the court that Socrates is a clever speaker "will immediately be refuted by me in deed, *ergōi.*" A refutation "in deed" means that, rather than Socrates' *telling* the court that he is not a clever speaker and then arguing the point, the court will see for itself as he speaks before it. Proofs by way of *erga*, then, like *tekmēria*, are distinguished from proofs by way of *logoi*, which involve rational argument.

preted by someone other than the agent, accuracy is not assured even under the best of conditions, that is, when the interpreter has no vested interest in the interpretation produced; how reliable, then, are interpretations likely to be when the interpreters who propose them have important, even critical, interests at stake?

The Laws' "great proofs," then, by which they seek to demonstrate Socrates' exceptional satisfaction with Athens, are no more successful than their initial argument for his ordinary satisfaction with his city. We must therefore conclude that the Laws' agreement argument fares no better at establishing Socrates' obligation to do whatever the Laws and city bid than does their argument based upon the parent-child and master-slave analogies.

The Laws turn now from their justice arguments to their more practical arguments, making the transition from the former to the latter by way of the notion of Socrates' ridiculousness. If Socrates, a man so thoroughly enamored of his city that he remained there for seventy years, now does not abide by his agreements but instead leaves the city, he will, the Laws say, become ridiculous. In the practical arguments that follow, they warn Socrates of the many other ways in which his ridiculousness will manifest itself should he escape.[91] We turn now to these arguments.

Escape Will Benefit No One

Socrates' escape will make him ridiculous, according to the Laws, because it will not benefit anyone. The Laws consider first the effect of escape on Socrates' friends. By undertaking escape, they say, Socrates will place his companions at risk of being exiled—and hence of being deprived of their city—or of losing their substance.

Next, the Laws address Socrates' own situation. He can choose between two possible types of destination if he escapes: cities with good laws, such as Thebes or Megara, and cities of disorder and lack of restraint, such as Thessaly. If he chooses an orderly city, the Laws contend, he will be regarded as an enemy and as a corrupter of laws. Furthermore, they charge, since a corrupter of laws is likely to be a corrupter of young and senseless human beings, Socrates will confirm the judges in their opinion, so that they will seem to have judged correctly in his case. And if he undertakes "shamelessly" to converse with the decorous men of these lawful cities, how will he converse there about the same things he conversed about in Athens—namely, the worth of virtue and justice and the lawful and the laws, without appearing unseemly?

There are several matters of which we need to take note in this passage. First, the Laws stop just short of committing themselves to the incorrectness of Socrates' verdict. They do not say, as they might have, that *although the judges judged incorrectly*, it will appear, if Socrates escapes, as if they judged correctly; they say only that, if Socrates escapes, the judges will seem to have judged correctly. The fact of the mat-

---

91. The Laws' use of the term *gar*, "for," at *Cr.* 53a8 implies that what is to follow is a further exploration of Socrates' ridiculousness, of which they take note at *Cr.* 53a4. Burnet (1924), 208, confines the specifications of the way in which Socrates will make himself ridiculous to what follows the *gar*: "The particular ways in which he would make himself ridiculous are specified in the next paragraph."

ter is indeed irrelevant to their argument; how Socrates is received depends solely on how things appear.

Second, and not surprisingly, the Laws show that they hold in highest esteem "cities with good laws, *eunomoumenas*, and the most decorous, *kosmiōtatous*, men" (*Cr.* 53c3–4). By "cities that are *eunomoumenas*" the Laws probably mean cities in which law and order reign, cities unlike those of "very much disorder and lack of restraint," *pleistē ataxia kai akolasia* (*Cr.* 53d3–4), which, as they argue, constitute Socrates' only other choice. By "men who are *kosmiōtatous*" the Laws probably mean men who are law abiding: that would explain why the Laws think Socrates would be scorned by such men as a corrupter of laws. The Laws are quite convinced that life would not be worth living for Socrates if he could not be in such cities and in the company of such men. Yet, although Socrates undoubtedly would prefer a city that is orderly to one that is disordered, his single decisive criterion for a good regime would not be its ability to keep its citizens in line but its concern to improve their souls. Furthermore, although Socrates surely values men who are *kosmiōtatoi*, what he values in such men is not so much their orderliness vis-à-vis the city as their internal order, that is, their having souls that are healthy, harmonious, and well balanced.

Third, the Laws do not reflect quite accurately the matters about which Socrates regularly speaks in Athens. Socrates does speak, to be sure, of virtue and justice as being "of the most worth to human beings," but is it true that he speaks in that way of "the lawful and the laws," *ta nomima kai hoi nomoi* (*Cr.* 53c8)? When Socrates specifies in the *Apology* the matters about which he speaks daily, the matters that he considers to be of the greatest worth to human beings, he specifies prudence, truth, justice, virtue, and the best state of the human soul. Socrates does not count the lawful and the laws among his all-consuming preoccupations.[92] Although he does speak on occasion of the lawful, for example, in the *Gorgias*, he intends by it internal lawfulness—not obedience to law. What Socrates never does is make speeches about laws [pl.]; whatever value law has it has in the singular, as the rule by which the healthy soul is governed: "And for the structures, and orderings, *kosmēsesin*, of the soul the name is 'lawful,' *nomimon*, and 'law,' *nomos* [sing.], from which people become lawful, *nomimoi*, and orderly, *kosmioi*; and these are justice and temperance."[93]

Let us turn our attention to Socrates' second alternative. As the Laws see it, if Socrates chooses the second possibility of going to cities with bad and disorderly men, if he flees "the cities with good laws and the most decorous men," life will not be worth living for him. Of course, from the Laws' perspective, nothing can be worse than cities with bad laws, laws that do not instill order and restraint, and with lawless men. But for them to take Socrates' phrase "life is not worth living," a phrase Socrates uses both at the end of the *Apology* and in the second part of the *Crito* to refer, respectively, to the unexamined life and to life with a corrupt soul, and to apply it to life among men who are not "the most decorous" is to do violence to the spirit of

---

92. As we saw in Chapter 2, Socrates does oppose the unlawful when it is also unjust. But he never cites the lawful as one of the causes he champions regularly in his daily discourse in the Athenian agora.

93. *Gorg.* 504d1–3, trans. Irwin (1979).

Socrates' allegiances and concerns.[94] The things that occupy for Socrates the highest position such that without them life is not worth living are justice and philosophy—not the company of law-abiding men.

The Laws assume that if Socrates goes to a lawless city, he will go to Thessaly, where Crito has friends. The Laws argue as follows against the notion that this choice will prove beneficial for Socrates. Since Thessaly is a city in which there is much disorder and lack of restraint, the people there might enjoy hearing about how Socrates ran away in disguise. But surely even in Thessaly someone will mock Socrates for being so greedy of life that at his advanced age he is willing to transgress the greatest laws for the sake of living a bit longer.[95] Perhaps, if Socrates causes no one any distress, no one will mock him in this way, in a way "unworthy of yourself." But in order to avoid provoking such talk, Socrates will have to avoid paining anyone. And the only way for him to do that is to fawn and be a slave. In Thessaly Socrates will then be well fed, but what other benefit will he have, insofar as he will be obliged to fawn and be a slave? And when all Socrates is doing in Thessaly is feasting, how will anyone be able to take seriously Socrates' speeches about justice and the rest of virtue?[96]

The Laws here address Crito's suggestion that Socrates go to Thessaly, where Crito's friends will esteem him and offer him safety and not harm him. The Laws counter Crito's recommendation by pointing out the cost to Socrates of being treated so well in Thessaly: he will have to watch himself lest he offend anyone; in other words, he will have to fawn and be a slave. The Laws show themselves to be quite well aware of how distasteful such a way of life is to Socrates; nevertheless, they seem to expect Socrates to be so concerned about hearing things "unworthy of yourself" that he *will* stoop to the despised life of slavishness and fawning.[97] (The Laws may approve of Socrates' being slavish and fawning in his relation to them, but they still disparage such behavior when it is directed at beings who are his "equals.") Once Socrates' dignity is compromised in this way, the Laws continue, he will make a mockery of his advocacy of justice and the rest of virtue. We may note, parenthetically, that now that the Laws are discussing the lawless city of Thessaly, where Socrates' corruption of the laws of Athens is less likely to be as great a source of distress to its inhabitants as in law-abiding cities, the Laws omit from their list of Socrates' concerns *ta nomima kai hoi nomoi*, the lawful and the laws. No longer of use to their argument, these purportedly vital Socratic issues drop out, and the Laws cite now only the more recognizably Socratic concerns of "justice and the rest of virtue."

94. The phrase is modified, but the sense is clearly the same: At *Ap*. 38a5–6, Socrates' phrase for "worth living" is *biōtos*; similarly at *Cr*. 47e3 and 47e6. At *Cr*. 53c4–5, the Laws' phrase is *axion zēn*.

95. In the *Apology*, the reason Socrates is able to acknowledge that exile is bad is precisely that he is not possessed by so much "love of life," *philopsuchia*, as to delude himself into believing he could practice philosophy unhindered outside Athens (*Ap*. 37c5–d3).

96. We may compare the Laws' prediction that Socrates will feast well in Thessaly if he fawns upon its inhabitants and becomes their slave with his assertion in the *Apology* that as Athens' benefactor—that is, as one who continuously reprimands and annoys it—he merits being fed at the public expense at the Prytaneum (*Ap*. 36d1–37a1).

97. We may compare the Laws' warning in the *Crito* that Socrates will perhaps "hear many things unworthy of yourself" (*Cr*. 53e3) with Socrates' own refusal in the *Apology* to wail and lament and "do and say many other things unworthy of me" (*Ap*. 38d9–e1). Whereas the Laws expect Socrates to be concerned about the unworthy things that will be said about him, Socrates in fact worries about doing and saying things that are unworthy of him.

Far more likely than the scenario the Laws imagine and depict is the one that Socrates presents in the *Apology*. Socrates there sees himself continuing to engage in philosophy, the activity without which life is not worth living, no matter where he goes. Socrates never envisions himself abandoning the practice of philosophy or fawning and being a slave in order to ensure his safety and satiety. If he escapes, his speeches will remain as before—though he is completely aware that a price will be exacted: he will be driven out from city after city.[98]

The Laws turn next to discounting the idea that escape will in some way benefit Socrates' children. If Socrates takes his children to Thessaly, the Laws maintain, they will suffer the disadvantages that come with being foreigners. If, instead, he leaves them behind, their nurture and education will not suffer because—regardless of whether Socrates is dead or in exile—his friends, "if they are of any benefit at all," will take care of them. We may recall that from Socrates' perspective, a person who is of any benefit at all is one who takes account of nothing but justice in deciding a course of action (*Ap*. 28b5–9). For Crito, as we saw in Chapter 3, a friend who is of any benefit at all preserves the life of his friend (*Cr*. 46a1–2). The Laws here assure Crito, indirectly by addressing Socrates, that Socrates' friends will indeed be of benefit as long as they look after Socrates' children by providing them with nurture and education.

The Laws, we may note, deal in this second part of their speech with the concerns that Crito had voiced: concerns about money, reputation, and nurture of children—concerns that Socrates had characterized as concerns of the many. If Socrates does not escape, they argue, Socrates' friends will not have to risk losing money, Socrates' reputation will not suffer, and Socrates' children will not become foreigners and will be properly provided for by Socrates' friends. Insofar as Socrates' friends care for Socrates' children, they need not fear loss of reputation: they will be regarded as having been of benefit to their friend—even though they fail to save his life. Socrates, as we know, does not take seriously any of these considerations; all that matters to him is justice. For as long as he speaks in his own name, there is no discussion of the matters the Laws address in the latter part of their speech.

Having offered their practical arguments, the Laws make one final plea, a plea that is in essence a threat. As they ask Socrates once again to obey them, they revive

---

98. Irwin (1986), 406, contends that the supplementary arguments with which the Laws end their speech make the point that Socrates will not be able to do philosophy elsewhere, thereby leaving open the possibility that if he could do philosophy elsewhere, he would be justified in leaving. In fact, however, the Laws do not argue that Socrates will be unable to practice philosophy. The Laws' contention is that if Socrates speaks of the importance of laws in a lawful place, he will make a fool of himself, since he will have come there with the reputation of being a corrupter of laws, and if he speaks of the importance of justice and the rest of virtue while he seeks to be safe and satisfied by fawning and being a slave in a lawless place, how will anyone still take seriously his commitment to virtue? The Laws do not maintain that Socrates should not escape because there is no place where he will be able to do philosophy; they maintain that Socrates should not escape because there is no place where he will be able to do philosophy without looking like a fool and a hypocrite. See also Young (1974), 24–25, who contends that the Laws, like Socrates, believe that "life without philosophy is not worth living" but that, whereas Socrates derives from this belief that he should not give up philosophy even when so commanded, the Laws derive from this identical belief that Socrates should not flee Athens. Young, I believe, misunderstands the Laws if he thinks they are fans of philosophy; the Laws think that it is lawful cities and decorous men without which life is not worth living (*Cr*. 53c4–5).

the notion that they are his "nurturers." They beseech Socrates not to regard children or living or anything else as more important than justice in order that he be able to tell the rulers in Hades "all these things" (*Cr.* 54b2–5). (I assume that what is meant by "all these things" is that he has not put anything else—not children or living or anything else—above justice.) Since the Laws juxtapose "obey us, your nurturers" and "do not regard . . . anything else as more important than justice," it is certain that the justice of which they speak is the unequal parent-child justice of which they spoke in their first argument, the justice according to which the Laws and the city are to be unequivocally obeyed. Socrates ought to put *that* justice above everything else, the Laws argue, because if he runs away, it will not be better, or more just, or more pious for him or for his family or friends ("those who are your own"—*Cr.* 54b7) *here*, and it will not be better for him when he arrives *there*.

Let us try to flesh out the Laws' warning. It has two components: (1) a warning about how things will be *here*, in the world of the living, for Socrates, his family, and his friends if Socrates escapes and (2) a warning about how things will turn out *there*, in Hades, for Socrates if he escapes.

(1) What will happen *here* as a result of Socrates' choosing life in exile over death is that (a) Socrates and his children and his friends will certainly fare no better: Socrates' friends will risk political and financial loss; Socrates will suffer loss of reputation; and Socrates' children will either (i) do no better—in the event that Socrates leaves them in Athens when he escapes, since the nurture and education they will receive will be the same whether he is in exile or is dead, or (ii) do far worse—in the event that he takes them into exile with him when he escapes, since they will then suffer the unhappy fate of foreigners; (b) Socrates and his friends will not be more just in that they will not have obeyed or properly placated the Laws; and (c) Socrates and his friends will not be more pious since the gods disapprove of irreverent and violent treatment of the fatherland.

(2) What will happen to Socrates *there*, as a result of his choosing life in exile over death, one can only imagine; the Laws do not say. We may note, however, that twice thus far the Laws have mentioned Hades: they advised Socrates that he will do better there if he can say when he arrives that he put justice before children, life, and everything else, and they warned him that he will not do better there if he escapes. When they mention Hades yet again, for a third time in this very brief passage, their words become ominous. The Laws caution Socrates that if he chooses not to die but to go into exile, the Laws here "will be angry with you" and those in Hades "will not receive you favorably." The Laws do not say what such an unfavorable reception entails. But their silence only makes the prospect of it all the more fearful.

The passage in which the Laws issue their most chilling warning reads as follows:

> But now, on the one hand, you will depart having been done injustice, if you depart, not by us Laws but by men; but if, on the other hand, you go away . . . then we will be angry with you while you live, and our brothers, the Laws in Hades, will not receive you favorably there. . . . (*Cr.* 54b8–c7)

As this passage is most frequently understood, the Laws' intention in it is not so much to threaten Socrates with severe consequences should he choose to escape but rather to divest *themselves* of responsibility for the injustice that Socrates will have suffered if he dies: "you will depart having been done injustice . . . not by us Laws but by men."[99] We may recall, however, that the Laws in effect already divested themselves of responsibility by way of the parent-child and master-slave analogies that established the inequality of justice between the city and the Laws, on the one hand, and the citizen, on the other. According to the Laws, nothing the city/master/parent does counts as injustice even if it involves an incorrect or unjust decision; the injustice lies in the citizen's/slave's/child's attempt to do it back. What new point, then, would the Laws be making here?

The Laws do, indeed, make a new point. They contrast, on the one side, the fate that awaits Socrates if he dies now, having been done injustice only by men, with, on the other side, the far worse fate that awaits him at the hand of the Laws and their brothers in Hades if he escapes. Whereas the injustice of men can reach no farther than the grave, the evils that the Laws and their counterparts in Hades inflict can ruin a man both in life and in death. Although the Laws use the term "injustice" only in connection with what men do and not in connection with what they do,[100] what they emphasize here by their *men/de* contrast is the incomparably more severe suffering Socrates will undergo if he "goes away" into exile than if he "departs" to his death. After all, if it is not the Laws but men who will have done Socrates injustice, would that not be so regardless of whether he dies now or flees?

The Laws' message, then, is simply this: as bad as death might seem to Socrates, to live will be far worse. To die will be only to experience what angry men can do; to live will be to experience now what the angry Laws can do and later what their displeased brothers in Hades can do.[101] For the briefest moment, the Laws stand apart from the fatherland to warn Socrates of the special vengeance that is theirs. For it is the Laws — not the fatherland — whose wrath Socrates will incur as a consequence of escape. When the fatherland is angry, *patrida chalepainousan*, the citizen is expected to comply with its orders or fawn upon it (*Cr.* 51b2–3); he is required, in other words,

99. See, for example, A. E. Taylor (1926), 173, n. 1: "This is, in fact, the fundamental distinction on which Socrates founds his whole argument."

100. It is possible that the Laws are taking this opportunity to refute Socrates' initial charge against them. Socrates had said: "The city was doing us injustice," *ēdikei gar hēmas hēpolis* (*Cr.* 50c1). The Laws now say: ". . . you will depart having been injustice not by us Laws, but by men," *ēdikēmenos . . . ouch huph' hēmōn tōn nomōn alla hup' anthrōpōn* (*Cr.* 54b8–c1). We have seen that the Laws regularly echo Socrates' words.

101. Burnet (1924), 211, thinks that the description of Hades in the *Crito* is less reserved than Socrates' description at the end of the *Apology*, insofar as the *Crito*'s description assumes the Orphic doctrine of judgment after death. Burnet accounts for the lowered level of reserve in the *Crito* in terms of the audience: "With Crito there is no need for the reserve which was appropriate before the judges." A more plausible account, however, of the difference between the descriptions of death here and in the *Apology* is that Socrates in the *Apology* is trying to comfort the judges and reassure them that they need not fear for him when he dies, but the Laws are trying to frighten him. We may compare also the account of Hades in the *Gorgias* to the account here. In the *Gorgias* Socrates says that upon arrival in Hades people's souls are laid bare before the judges, revealing any blemishes they have acquired through the commission of injustice. In the *Crito*, however, the judges in Hades receive unfavorably those who have threatened the laws on earth.

to obey or persuade. It is when the citizen does neither, as in the case of Socrates' escape, that the Laws' anger is kindled, *chalepanoumen* (*Cr.* 54c5–7).[102]

If Socrates escapes, the Laws say, he will do injustice and evil in return; he will transgress his contracts and agreements with them and "do bad deeds to those to whom they ought least to be done—yourself and friends and fatherland and us" (*Cr.* 54c4–5). In our discussion in Chapter 4 of Socrates' own reasons for not escaping, we argued that when Socrates uses the phrase "to those to whom these things ought least to be done" (*Cr.* 50a1–2), he refers to those whom Crito (and Greeks generally) would associate with that phrase: oneself and one's friends. The main reason advanced in Chapter 4 in favor of this interpretation of Socrates' phrase was that if Socrates had intended it to refer to someone else, someone new and unfamiliar and as yet un-mentioned, he could not reasonably have expected Crito (or anyone) to understand him. In effect, what the Laws do at the end of the *Crito* is interpret the phrase in precisely the same way as Socrates did earlier—and as Crito and as Greeks generally do—to refer to oneself and one's friends, adding, however, the fatherland and them-selves.[103] This move on the part of the Laws is reminiscent of how they earlier, in their enumeration of the things that Socrates speaks about as being most important in human lives, added *ta nomima kai hoi nomoi*, the lawful and the laws, to justice and virtue. On the present occasion, no less than on the previous one, the Laws' addition distorts the character of the Socratic view. In the present case, by adding themselves and the fatherland, the Laws change the nature of the harm with which Socrates was concerned. Whereas Socrates was concerned lest he treat himself and his friends badly by involving them in injustices that would corrupt their souls, the Laws are concerned lest Socrates treat himself, his friends, his family, and themselves (that is, the Laws and the fatherland) badly by threatening their wealth, their reputa-tion, their safety, and their survival. The superficial resemblance between the Laws'

102. It might be thought that Socrates at the end of the *Apology* threatens his condemners as well, telling them that "vengeance will come upon you right after my death, and much harsher, by Zeus, than the sort you give me by killing me" (*Ap.* 39c4–6). Yet, (1) what Socrates tells his con-demners he tells them as a prediction—not as a threat; (2) what he predicts is that something "will come upon you"—not that he will *take* revenge on them; (3) in fact, he was the one who had pro-tected them all along from younger and less restrained would-be reproachers; (4) the vengeance that he predicts is only that his condemners will be reproached more harshly for not living correctly; (5) it is better for them in the long run, anyway, if they have not chosen of their own accord to live honorably, to be answerable to someone; and (6) the word Socrates chooses for "vengeance," *timōria*, has an interesting range of meaning: besides meaning vengeance, retribution, punishment, and tor-ture, it means help, aid, and succor. The vengeance Socrates predicts, then, is, in fact, but a harshly administered benefit.

103. Adam (1888), 80, asks that we note "the emphatic place of *sauton*: oneself is the last person one should ignore. . . . Socrates' philosophy was egoism." I would contend, on the contrary, that the emphatic place is occupied by "the fatherland and us," the unexpected additions to the Socratic list— which mirrors the ordinary Greek list—of those who constitute "one's own." Furthermore, Socrates is not egoistic if egoism is understood to advocate an individual's according preference to his own inter-ests over the interests of others. Adam cites *Ap.* 37b, where Socrates announces that he will not pro-pose exile because he will not injure himself. But Socrates' point there is that insofar as he is a man who has never injured another, why then would it be right for him to injure himself? This point hardly reflects "egoism"; what it reflects is equal consideration for all human beings in the sense that a just man would injure none of them, himself included.

view and that of Socrates, a resemblance fostered by the Laws' use of the phrase "those to whom they should least be done," conceals what is in fact a very great divergence between them.[104]

In bringing this chapter to a close, let us highlight some of the more striking features of the Laws' speech. First, we may note that the Laws do, at last, admit that Socrates is innocent: the admission is implicit in their assertion that, if Socrates dies now, an injustice will have been done to him—by men (Cr. 54b8–c1). Throughout their discourse, the Laws maintain that Socrates' refusal to submit to his punishment is unjust; since it makes no difference if the verdict was correct or not, the matter never even comes up. From the Laws' perspective, justice simply is the unqualified submission of the citizen to the city and the Laws: a citizen must obey all verdicts because he is the city's child and slave, and because he has agreed to do "whatever we bid." Once the Laws are satisfied that they have made their case, however, they are prepared to acknowledge what it was never their purpose to deny: Socrates' innocence.

Second, let us observe the tone the Laws adopt in addressing Socrates—the sarcasm and bitter scorn and mockery evident in their argument. There are at least four clear instances of the Laws' use of a shockingly disrespectful tone in their speech, apart from the generally badgering and reproachful and accusing manner that pervades it: (1) ". . . you who in truth care for virtue" (Cr. 51a6–7);[105] (2) "Are you so wise . . . ?" (Cr. 51a7);[106] (3) "But you were then pluming yourself" (Cr. 52c6); and (4) "And what else will you be doing but feasting in Thessaly?" (Cr. 53e5–6).[107] Even in the face of evidence as unequivocal as this, scholars who regard the Laws' speech

104. The Laws, as we have seen, frequently use Socrates' own expressions in their speech, without meaning by them what Socrates meant. We may compare (1) the Laws' term "persuade" (Cr. 51b3, 51c1, 51e5–6, 52a2) with Socrates' at Cr. 50a1; (2) the Laws' expression ". . . and keep quiet" (Cr. 51b5) with Socrates' similar expression at Cr. 48d5; (3) the Laws' expression ". . . nor leave your station" (Cr. 51b8) with Socrates' at Ap. 29a1; (4) the Laws' expression "and in war and in court and everywhere . . ." (Cr. 51b8–9) with Socrates' at Ap. 38e5–6; (5) the Laws' expression ". . . when the city is unwilling" (Cr. 52c5) with Socrates' at Cr. 48e3; (6) the Laws' expression ". . . or if the agreements did not appear just to you" (Cr. 52c4–5) with Socrates' at Cr. 49e6; (7) the Laws' expression ". . . will life be worth living for you?" (Cr. 53c4–5) with Socrates' at Ap. 38a5–6; (8) the Laws' expression ". . . are of any benefit at all" (Cr. 54a9–b1) with Socrates' at Ap. 28b7; (9) the Laws' expression ". . . do not regard children or living or anything else as more important than justice" (Cr. 54b3–4) with Socrates' at Cr. 48d3–5; (10) the Laws' expression ". . . better or more just or more pious" (Cr. 54b6–7) with Socrates' at Ap. 32d2–3, Ap. 35c8–d1, Cr. 47c9–10, Cr. 48a9–10; (11) the Laws' expression ". . . so shamefully doing injustice in return and doing evil in return" (Cr. 54c2–3) with Socrates' at Cr. 49b10–d9; (12) the Laws' expression ". . . transgressing . . . agreements and contracts with us" (Cr. 54c3–4) with Socrates' at Cr. 49e6–7, 50a2–3; and (13) the Laws' expression ". . . doing evil deeds to those to whom they ought least to be done" (Cr. 54c4–5) with Socrates' at Cr. 50a1–2.

105. Burnet (1924), 202; Adam (1888), 66; and Tyler (1862), 176, all note this instance.

106. Adam (1888), 67, notes this instance. Cf. Ap. 25d8–10, where Socrates says to Meletus: "What then, Meletus? Are you so much wiser at your age than I am at mine, that you have become cognizant that the bad always do something bad. . . ?" We may note that the phrase "Or are you so wise that you have been unaware. . . ?" (Cr. 51a7) governs the rest of the Laws' argument based upon the parent-child and master-slave analogies, from Cr. 51a8 to 51c4. For that entire stretch the Laws taunt Socrates.

107. Adam (1888), 78, and Tyler (1862), 179, note the sarcasm here.

as Socratic are still able to see in it "familiar intimacy and indeed tenderness toward Socrates."[108]

Third, we may note how prominent in the Laws' argument are laws, law abidingness, cities with good laws, and law-abiding citizens—as opposed to justice, virtue, and the best state of the soul. The Laws think that an individual could not remain in a city for any reason other than satisfaction with its laws; that a corrupter of law is easily a corrupter of youth; that it is the company of decorous men that makes life worth living; that Socrates' speeches in the Athenian agora were about justice, virtue, *the lawful and the laws*; that those who ought least to have bad things done to them are oneself, one's friends, the fatherland, *and the Laws themselves*. The Laws' greatest concern is lest Socrates' escape destroy them; their existence is of paramount importance in their eyes: they do not see how the city can continue to exist if Socrates and private citizens generally weaken the effectiveness of the city's judgments; they therefore contend that they are to be obeyed and revered absolutely.

Whereas there is nothing surprising in the Laws' placing emphasis on their own survival and their own centrality[109]—indeed, the Laws say precisely what one would expect laws to say on their own behalf if they could talk—there is something very odd about identifying the Laws' views as Socratic. For Socrates, the Laws can only become worthy through their promotion of what is really important, namely, the excellence of the souls of the citizens in their charge; they do not merit esteem on account of ensuring their own perpetuation.[110] Socrates remains in Athens to advance the cause of justice and philosophy, not because he is most satisfied with Athenian law. What is important to him is to keep souls—not the Laws—from "corruption."[111] For Socrates it is philosophical examination—not dwelling among the most fervently law-abiding men—that makes life worth living. Socrates' speeches are about justice and virtue, about prudence and truth and the best state of the human soul; Socrates fights for the just—not for the legal. When Socrates says that one ought least to do bad things to "one's own," the bad things are injustices that corrupt the human being's more valuable part, the soul; he is not worried about citizenship, money, children, reputation, or the perpetuation of the existence of the fatherland and the Laws. The single thing that Socrates cares most about—improving the moral state of the citizens of Athens—is conspicuously absent from the speech of the Laws.[112]

---

108. Allen (1980), 82.

109. See Anastaplo (1975) (2), 209: "Indeed, the laws can even be said to be intent only on looking out for themselves."

110. As we know from *Rep.* I, rulers ought to rule not for the sake of promoting their own advantage but for the sake of promoting the advantage of the citizens, that is, increasing the virtue in the citizens' souls.

111. Compare the Laws: ". . . nor do you heed us Laws, insofar as you are attempting to corrupt us, "*epicheirōn diaphtheirai* (Cr. 52c9) with Socrates: "But is life worth living for us with that thing corrupted, *met' ekeinou . . . diephtharmenou*, which the unjust maims and the just profits?" (Cr. 47e6–7).

112. This is not to say that laws do not in fact help preserve citizens' souls from injustice through threat of sanctions. It is to say that if the Laws do preserve citizens' souls from injustice, they do so inadvertently as they aim at their own survival and the survival of the city. To judge from the Laws' speech, ensuring the health of souls is the farthest thing from their minds. Even the nurture and education they mention are not related by them to instilling moral virtue in the soul.

Fourth, let us summarize the many ways in which the Laws' views diverge from what we would have expected of them had they been Socrates' mouthpiece rather than, as I have argued, his opponents. They characterize the citizen as a slave to the city; they regard justice as something determined by hierarchical relations; they view agreements as binding without exception; they demand that the citizen do "whatever we bid"; they approve of "persuasion" by means of fawning; they deride Socrates' speeches at his trial; they believe that law abidingness—not virtue and philosophy— is what makes life worth living (for Socrates!); they defend the importance of their sheer survival—not the importance of their promoting the welfare of the citizens they govern. The Laws' concern with life itself—their own—rather than with living well, that is, nobly and justly, ought to be sufficient in itself to preclude the assimilation of the Laws' way of thinking to Socrates'.[113]

Finally, let us characterize the Laws.[114] The Laws are oratorical bullies. Their declamations, their exaggerations, their disrespect for Socrates, and their ominous threats make them unfit for the pedestal upon which many of the scholars who regard the Laws as Socrates' spokesmen seek to place them. The Laws jump from unfounded premises to wild conclusions;[115] they fail to consider alternative explanations for phenomena they cite; and they are consumed with the single ideal of law. Their speech, analyzed without a predisposition to regard it as Socratic, is unworthy of admiration. The Laws, just like people, must strive for something loftier than their own perpetuation if they are to merit respect and not just inspire fear.

113. We learn from the *Gorgias* (517b–c; 518e–519a) that Socrates thinks the great orators have done much to keep their city alive and strong and rich but have done nothing to improve it, that is, to care for the souls of its citizens. It is not unexpected, then, that the orators of the *Crito*, namely, the Laws, defend eloquently the law that establishes as valid all the city's judgments: such a law keeps the city powerful and perpetuates it.

114. Anastaplo (1975b), 314, n. 8, notes that "Socrates brings 'on stage' not Justice (a single being) but the Laws (a multitude)." The implication of this remark is, I believe, twofold: (1) that the Laws' arguments are of the sort to be expected from any many—that is, they are conventional as opposed to wise—and (2) that they speak for their own interests and not for the interests of justice.

115. See Vlastos (1974), 519, who notes that "time and again we see the diction running to hyperbole and the thought blown about by gusts of feeling." For this reason Anastaplo (1975b), 208, says: "The laws are, in a sense, unscrupulous."

7

The Corybantic Cure

Dear friends . . . Seirênês weaving a haunting song
over the sea we are to shun.

Homer, *Odyssey* xii, ll. 519–59,
trans. Fitzgerald (1963), 214

In the space of just a very short stretch of text, from *Cr.* 54d2 to the dialogue's end at
Cr. 54e2, Socrates reacts to the Laws' speech. In these few lines of text Socrates does
precisely what he does in the lines introducing the speech: he puts distance between
himself and the Laws. As in the earlier section where Socrates hints that what the
Laws are about to say represents not what Socrates but what an orator would say,
here, too, Socrates hints, subtly but in several ways, that although he acts *as* the Laws
recommend, their reasons are not his reasons. Socrates' hints may be discerned in
(1) his comparison of the way in which he hears the Laws' speech to the way in which
the Corybantes hear the flutes; (2) his advising Crito as to the futility of speaking
now; and (3) his exhortation that he and Crito abandon Crito's proposed course and
go instead in the way the god leads.

The Corybantic Metaphor

What does Socrates mean by comparing his experience of "hearing" the speech of
the Laws to the Corybantic experience of "hearing" the flutes? In order to answer
this question we must consider generally the nature of the Corybantic experience
and specifically how Plato conceives of it in his works.

Corybantes were worshippers of Bacchus. Their wild and enthusiastic rites featured deafening flute and drum music and furious dancing.[1] Euripides describes the
Corybantic ritual as follows in *The Bacchae*:

1. See Kitchel (1898), 161; also Burnet (1924), 211, and Dodds (1964), 79.

In your caves the triple-
Crested corybantes
Made the rounded timbrel
Tight with hide and beat its
Tense ecstatic jangle
Into the sweetened airs
Breathed by Phrygian-flutes.
They gave it in the hand of
Mother Rhea to drum-beat
Shouting bacchants raving.[2]

People who were afflicted with various nervous and hysterical conditions engaged in the Corybantic rite. They would dance in a frenzy to deafening flute and drum music, would become excited to the pitch of exhaustion, and would then fall into a sleep "from which they awoke purged and cured."[3] Even after the flutes stopped playing, those who participated in these rites remained in their Corybantic frenzy, no longer hearing the music but instead imagining that they were still hearing it.[4]

Plato makes reference to the Corybantes in the *Symposium* (215d–e), the *Euthydemus* (277d), the *Ion* (534a; 536c), and the *Laws* (VII.790dff.).[5] In the *Symposium*, Alcibiades says with reference to Socrates: "For the moment I hear him speak I am smitten with a kind of sacred rage, worse than any Corybant, and my heart jumps into my mouth, and the tears start into my eyes. . . ."[6] The *Euthydemus* mentions the dancing and playing of musical instruments that precede Corybantic initiation. In the *Ion* (534a), the Corybantes are depicted as not being in their senses when they compose their lovely lyric poems: "But when they launch into melody and rhythm, they are frantic and possessed, like Bacchic dancers who draw honey and milk from rivers when they are possessed but cannot when they are in their right minds."[7]

In the *Laws* the Athenian Stranger compares the way in which mothers soothe and lull their sleepless children to sleep to the remedies administered to those afflicted with the Corybantic symptoms of phobia and anxiety: in both cases, what is required is motion and sound rather than silence. A mother's rocking and crooning put the baby to sleep; the Corybantes are lifted out of their disturbed condition and brought back to their senses by dance and music.

The Corybantic condition, then, is one bordering on mania, involving psychic disturbance and disorder. The externally imposed disorder of wild and loud music and dancing is designed to vanquish the inner disorder of fear and hysteria. The therapy provided for disturbed souls by the Corybantic flutes, then, takes the form of an exaggerated version of the very malady it is meant to cure.

2. *Bacchae*, ll. 124–29, trans. Roche (1974), 83.
3. Burnet (1924), 211.
4. Burnet (1924), 211–212; Kitchel (1898), 161.
5. There is also a reference at *Phaedrus* 228b7, where one who shares in another's frenzied enthusiasm is called *ton sunkorubantionta*.
6. Trans. Joyce (1961).
7. Trans. Bloom (1987).

What does it mean for Socrates to compare the effect of the Laws' speech to the effect of Corybantic flutes? The comparison suggests, first, that the Laws' speech might provide some sort of cure. And it suggests, second, that there might be someone in need of that cure.

If we ask who it is in the *Crito* who is agitated and restless and in need of calming, the answer is Crito. In the dialogue's opening scene, Crito marvels at how pleasantly Socrates sleeps (*Cr.* 43b5), lamenting that he himself is "in such great sleeplessness and pain" (*Cr.* 43b4). For Crito, Socrates' impending death is a great calamity (*Cr.* 43c2), but he notes that Socrates, unlike Crito and Socrates' other companions, is not in the least vexed in his present circumstances. If the Laws' speech is intended, like the Corybantic flutes, to effect the restoration of repose and restfulness to a troubled soul, the troubled soul must be Crito's.[8]

Crito is indeed hushed by the speech of the Laws. He offers no protest, no argument; rather than plead with Socrates to heed him rather than them, he confesses finally: "But, Socrates, I have nothing to say" (*Cr.* 54d8). Crito is reduced to docility; perhaps he is at last at peace with Socrates' decision. The Crito who is described at the beginning of the dialogue as unable to sleep, as suffering from *agrupnia* (*Cr.* 43b4), who can only watch—and marvel at—his friend who sleeps so pleasantly in his cell is, at last, calmed and soothed. As we have seen, the Corybantic frenzy, like the mother's rocking of her fretful infant, has finally a soporific effect. If the Laws' speech brings Crito repose, the Laws will have effected their cure.

The way in which a cure of this kind works is by overcoming or vanquishing through external noise and motion the disturbed person's internal agitation and turmoil.[9] The Laws' speech is, in fact, an amplified version of Crito's.[10] If Crito's speech is a symptom of his disorder, of the vexation and agitation in his soul, then the Laws cure him, quiet him, calm him, by their louder and more strident speech. They restore him to his senses, and he no longer urges Socrates to escape.

But what effect do the frenzied rites of the Corybantes have on someone serene and at peace? How does someone without fear, anxiety, or psychic disorder or disturbance of any kind respond to the deafening music and furious dancing characteristic of the Corybantic cure? For someone who is not ill, Corybantic music is no doubt painfully overwhelming, excruciatingly loud, deafeningly so. The calm, unvexed, psychically stable Socrates is affected in just this way by the Laws' speech. The noise, *ēchē*,[11] of the Laws' arguments, he says, "booms" within him, making him unable to hear the other arguments, Crito's.[12] Whereas as a result of the Laws' speech Crito is left with nothing to say, Socrates is rendered unable to hear.[13]

8. We know, anyway, that the Laws' speech is directed to Crito, because it is he—not Socrates—who is intent upon Socrates' escape.

9. In the *Laws*, the Athenian Stranger speaks of the shaking motion bringing about the cessation of the grievous, *chalepēs*, palpitation of the heart (*Laws* 791a); in the *Crito*, Crito speaks of the news that is to him and to Socrates' other friends grievous, *chalepēn* (*Cr.* 43c7). The news is not, as Crito notes, grievous to Socrates.

10. The relationship between the Laws' speech and Crito's is discussed in Chapter 8, in the section entitled "Engaging Crito."

11. Often rendered "echo," *ēchē* in fact means sound or noise; *ēchō* is the word for echo.

12. In context, "the others," *tōn allōn*, that Socrates is rendered unable to hear, can only be Crito's. The Laws' intent—certainly in the latter part of their speech—is to counter each of Crito's arguments.

The Laws' speech, then, like the Corybantic flutes to which it is compared, has the peculiar effect of calming those who are agitated and disturbing those who are calm. Yet philosophy, too, is described in Plato as having Corybantic effects. The effect upon Alcibiades of Socrates' philosophical speech (as quoted earlier, *Symp.* 215d–e) is indeed remarkably similar to the effect that the Laws' speech has on Socrates. Alcibiades experiences "corybantically," in a frenzy, Socrates' plain speech, regardless, as he says, of whether he hears it directly from Socrates himself or as repeated by someone else. Why would philosophy, soberly communicated, give rise to a frenetic reaction? In the case of Alcibiades, we may attribute his crazed reaction to his sick soul: those whose lives are not governed by reason often find quite maddening people whose lives are so governed, people who are models of temperance and sobriety. Alcibiades recognizes the depraved condition of his life, but, as he confesses, he flees Socrates' philosophical words lest they change him, lest they, as we might say, effect a Corybantic "cure."

Alcibiades further assumes that everyone who comes into contact with Socrates reacts to philosophy as he does, that everyone — including Socrates himself — is "staggered," "bewitched," feels "in the heart or soul" as if "bitten by something more poisonous than a snake," by "this philosophical frenzy, this sacred rage" (*Symp.* 215d; 218a–b). But Alcibiades' assessment of philosophy's effect on everyone is hardly accurate; it is yet another symptom of Alcibiades' depravity. Although Socrates may on occasion be lost in thought (*Symp.* 175b; 220c), philosophy does not make him vexed or agitated.[14] And, at least as Plato's dialogues attest, his more philosophical companions welcome philosophical discussion and are sorry when it must end: they do

---

And they just ended their speech by entreating Socrates not to let Crito persuade him to do as he says rather than as the Laws say (*Cr.* 54c8–d1). Therefore, when Socrates remarks that the noise of the Laws' arguments makes him unable to hear the others, what he is saying is that the volume of that noise makes it impossible for him even to hear the other side, Crito's side, let alone be persuaded by it. Socrates, then, cannot hear Crito's arguments for escape. Miller (1996), 121, proposes that "the others" refers to "a *third* set of *logoi*, neither Crito's nor the Laws'" (emphasis in original) but Socrates' own. I argue in the last section of this chapter that when Socrates finally recommends that he and Crito act in accordance with the way in which "the god is leading," he is advocating that they follow the philosophical arguments he advanced earlier. The booming of the Laws' speech has not, then, closed off Socrates' access to his own arguments, perhaps because, insofar as they are his own, he has no need to "hear" them. (See also Anastaplo [1975b], 208, for the view that the arguments that Socrates can no longer hear are the ones that represent "the voice of reason.")

13. Plato tells us in the *Ion* (536c2–6) that those carried away by the Corybantic frenzy "perceive sharply only that song which belongs to the god by whom they are possessed and have plenty of figures and phrases for that song but pay no heed to others. . . ." On the basis of this passage one might suppose that Socrates, who, as a result of the Laws' speeches in the *Crito* is "unable to hear the others," qualifies as a classic Corybant. Yet, Socrates is not really like the *Ion's* possessed. His loyalty is indeed exclusive, restricted to the god of philosophy. Socrates has no allegiance, however, to the booming noise of the Laws' speeches. All this noise does is render him unable to hear the others.

14. It is true that Socrates in the *Phaedrus* passage cited earlier (*Phaedrus* 228b7, see n. 5) calls himself a "fellow-corybanter" and even describes himself as "sick," *nōson* (*Phaedrus* 228b6), with desire to hear speeches, and as a "lover," *erastēs*, (*Phaedrus* 228c2), of speeches, *tōn logōn*. Yet Socrates depicts himself in this way because this is how he imagines Phaedrus sees him. It is Phaedrus, however, who is in fact the mad lover of speeches; it is he who is the genuine "corybanter" with respect to discourses. For it is Phaedrus who loves passionately — and indiscriminately — all speeches. Socrates,

not experience what Alcibiades describes. It is quite specifically the unphilosophical and more corrupt interlocutors who have strong, even violent, reactions to Socrates and his plain conversation.[15]

Meno is a case in point. In the early part of the *Meno* (*Meno* 79e–80d), Meno complains that Socrates has worked witchcraft, has put him under a spell. He cautions Socrates against practicing his sorcery outside Athens. Meno accuses Socrates of having a "numbing" effect upon those with whom he comes into contact. He maintains that Socrates induces *aporia*, perplexity. Yet, let us observe, in order for elenchus to have its "numbing" effect, its victim must believe, falsely, in his own expertise or wisdom. Socrates, insofar as he is aware of his own ignorance, is not "numbed" by the elenchus; instead, it is out of his own perpetual numbness, his own unrelenting perplexity, that he "numbs" others, that he infects them, as it were, with his own *aporia*. The effect that Socrates produces is precisely as Meno describes it at *Meno* 79e7–80a2: "Socrates, even before I met you they told me you are a perplexed man yourself, and reduce others to perplexity"; but the "others" who are *reduced to* perplexity when encountering Socrates are those who fancy themselves wise. Philosophy, then, numbs the unphilosophical who start out with a misplaced confidence in their untested beliefs; since, however, the philosophical start out perplexed, not assuming they know what they do not know, philosophy leaves them as they were.

If philosophical argument has no "Corybantic" effect upon those who are philosophically oriented and healthy in soul, if, in particular, philosophical argument has no such effect on Socrates, what, may we suppose, is Socrates' assessment of the worth of the Laws' speech insofar as he describes its effect upon him as "Corybantic"? What can he mean by his talk of their noise booming within him, a noise so loud that it drowns out competing arguments? It seems most unlikely that Socrates would use the Corybantic simile or depict the Laws' arguments as noise booming within him if what he wished to convey about them was their intellectual rigor and perspicuity: philosophical argument does not "boom." Socrates had introduced the speech of the Laws by characterizing it as what "someone, especially an orator" (*Cr.* 50b6–7) would

---

as becomes clear as the dialogue continues, is not a lover of speeches generally but a lover of learning, a *philomathēs* (*Phaedrus* 230d3), a lover of reason, a *philologos* (*Phaedrus* 236e5), and, finally, a lover of "collections and divisions" that is, of dialectical reasoning (*Phaedrus* 266b3). Socrates only playfully pretends to be smitten as Phaedrus really is by Lysias's discourse on the relative merits of the lover and nonlover, calling himself a "fellow-bacchanter," *sumbakcheuōn* (*Phaedrus* 234d5). Lysias's rhetorical speech actually impresses him not at all. Furthermore, whatever emotional impact we might have expected Lysias's rhetorical display to have upon Socrates, however fleetingly, is absent, no doubt because of the absence of the orator himself: the effects of oratorical speech are lessened—for all but true devotees—when the speech is heard secondhand. In the *Phaedrus* it is not discourse that drives the philosopher mad but (at least apparently) the vision of the Forms themselves and, in the case of the Form of the Beautiful, the vision of even its earthly manifestations.

15. Witness such characters as Euthyphro, Meno, Anytus, Polus, Callicles, Thrasymachus. It is interesting that Alcibiades says of himself that orators and oratorical speech do not affect him as Socrates does; oratorical speech does not turn his "whole soul upside down" and make him feel as if he were "the lowest of the low" (*Symp.* 215e). That is because oratory, as the *Gorgias* tells us, flatters; Socratic speech at least on occasion makes the unphilosophical and immoral experience shame.

say. Perhaps, then, it is as rhetoric that the Laws' speech has "Corybantic" effects, its noise soothing the disturbed and vexing the serene.

Let us look at some instances of "booming" and related notions in the *Protagoras*, where sophists and orators abound. The *Protagoras* describes Prodicus, ironically the very sophist known for drawing fine distinctions, as having a deep voice "that made such a booming noise, *bombos*, in the room that the words themselves were indistinct" (316a1–2). Later on in the *Protagoras*, Socrates says the following of public speakers: "Ask them anything about what they have said, no matter how small a point, and just as bronze, once struck, goes on sounding, *ēchei*, for a long time until you take hold of it, so these orators, *rhētores*, spin out an answer a mile long to any little question" (*Prot.* 329a4–b1). At *Prot.* 315b1, Protagoras is said to draw students from every city through which he passes, "charming them with a voice like Orpheus—and they follow spellbound." And, as Socrates describes his own reaction to Protagoras's great speech, he "stayed gazing at him, quite spellbound, for a long time" (*Prot.* 328d4–5). Similarly, when Protagoras poses his question about Simonides' poem, Socrates says: "At first, what with his argument and the applause of the others, my eyes went dim and I felt giddy, as if I had been hit by a good boxer" (*Prot.* 339e1–3).[16] According to the *Protagoras*, then, sophists "boom"; orators keep on sounding once "struck." Sophists charm; they produce a spellbinding effect; they knock one out. We may compare with these passages in the *Protagoras* the beginning of the *Apology*, where Socrates says that the persuasive speaking of his accusers made him "nearly forget myself" (*Ap.* 17a2–3). None of the oratorical displays that Socrates describes does more than incapacitate and disarm the audience; it is not philosophical or logical acuity that they evidence: they persuade by virtue of the sheer length of the discourse, the quality of the voice, the charisma of the speaker, the deftness with which he speaks. For Socrates, people interested in truth would do better to talk with each other. Indeed, the same holds even for people interested in entertainment. As Socrates remarks at *Prot.* 347c–e, it is vulgar people who require voices other than their own for entertainment; more refined people need no extraneous voices, including flutes (!), but only their own voices in conversation.[17]

Despite the great likelihood that the Corybantic comparison is an unflattering one, one that suggests that the Laws' speech was just so much frenetic, deafening sound and far indeed from the well-reasoned argument that would convince a thinking man like Socrates, the widely held conviction that the Laws speak for Socrates causes many to take this comparison—and some even the idea of "booming"—as a commendation of it. Adam, for example, says with respect to the speech's booming: "Socrates might have said much the same of his *daimonion semeion*: compare *Apol.* 40A–B. I think Plato meant to suggest that the pleading of the Laws coincided with the voice of the divine sign."[18] Or Tyler:

---

16. Translations of the *Protagoras* passages in this paragraph are by C. C. W. Taylor (1991).

17. It is, of course, quite possible that what Socrates means by the kind of "entertainment" in which all that is needed is the participants' own voices in conversation is indeed philosophical exchange.

18. Adam (1888), 80.

In the case of Socrates, it is the voice of the Laws, in other words, the voice of the God, that rings in his ear and possesses his soul. The passage is one of singular beauty. The Laws stand before him personified, embodied, clothed with more than human authority. They reason with him. They expostulate with him on the folly and wickedness of the course which his friends are pressing upon him. They draw nearer and nearer to him, and speak in more earnest and commanding tones, till at length he can see and hear nothing else. . . ."[19]

But Corybantes do not argue: they are loud and wild. All Socrates' references in the *Protagoras* to booming, to going on and on, to working a spell, to knocking one out, mock sophists and orators and suggest, if anything, that for all their dramatic effect there is little of substance in *what* these men say. That Socrates associates the Laws' speech with Corybantic flutes and booming noise signals his *dissatisfaction* with the Laws' performance—not his approval of it. It is not, after all, to human reason that Corybantic flutes play.

Why Crito Would "Speak in Vain"

By far the most common explanation offered for Socrates' warning Crito at the end of the dialogue that it would be futile for him to speak now is that Socrates is so completely convinced by the Laws' arguments that Crito's speaking against them would be useless. Kraut, for example, says: "When the Laws come to the end of their speech, Socrates endorses their argument without reservation," and ". . . the harmony between Socrates and the Laws is emphasized once again at the end of the dialogue."[20] Even those who think Socrates' reference to the Corybantes signals his less than wholehearted endorsement of the Laws' speech have difficulty dismissing the evidence of what seems to be a clear Socratic assertion that what the Laws say represents the way things seem to him now. Calvert fairly squirms as he says: "What we do have for sure is that Socrates expresses no apparent disagreement with the Laws' speech, and adds that he believes Crito will not be able to find fault with it. This *could* mean that Socrates is endorsing what the Laws say, but it could equally indicate something more like passive acquiescence" (emphasis in original).[21]

Despite Socrates' agreement with the Laws' conclusion, his use of the Corybantic metaphor, coupled with his remark that the noise of the Laws' *logoi* "booms" within him, virtually precludes the possibility that he finds persuasive the reasons the Laws advance in support of their conclusion. Moreover, if Socrates considers the arguments contained in the Laws' speech to be well reasoned, if he judges their *logos* to be *beltistos* and therefore the one to be obeyed, why does he not say so? If the Laws' *logoi* have anything to recommend them besides their loudness, surely Socrates would praise them for it. But he does not.

19. Tyler (1862), 180.
20. Kraut (1984), 40.
21. Calvert (1987), 22.

If it is not Socrates' assessment of the Laws' speech as singularly meritorious that causes him to warn Crito of the futility of attempting to speak against it, what, then, *is* the cause of Socrates' warning? Why does he say to Crito in this passage: ". . . if you speak against them, you will speak in vain" (*Cr.* 54d6)? Why does Socrates, who encourages Crito before the Laws' speech to speak up and challenge his views (*Cr.* 48d8e1; 49e1–2), now discourage him?[22]

Indeed, one would be hard pressed to find another passage in Plato in which Socrates discourages further discussion.[23] He is always eager to continue, to see if anything might be said in opposition to what has emerged thus far, and especially to be refuted if he is wrong: "And if you refute me, I shan't be upset with you as you were with me; instead you'll go on record as my greatest benefactor" (*Gorg.* 506c1–3).[24] Even when Socrates regards his view as having been clamped down by "iron and adamantine arguments," even when he regards as ridiculous anyone who has ever attempted to speak otherwise than he has spoken, he leaves open the possibility of his having been wrong, such that further discussion is always in order.[25] It is difficult to understand, then, why Socrates, no matter how strongly he holds his current views and no matter why he holds his views so strongly, is not willing to see whether Crito has anything to urge against them that might cause him to change his mind.

The answer to this puzzle lies in the effects on Socrates of the *noise* of the Laws' speech. It is not that Socrates no longer *wishes* to converse with Crito; it is that, owing to the deafening loudness of the Laws' speech as it booms within him, he is unable to do so: he cannot, as he says, "hear" opposing arguments. The Laws' rhetoric, it would seem, drowns out its competition. As it works its Corybantic spell on Socrates, his intellect is temporarily impaired, and it become almost useless for Crito to attempt to overcome the disabling effects on his friend of the Laws' blaring sound. We must not think, then, that the Laws' speech has so strengthened and solidified Socrates' views that he has, as a result, become intractable—indeed, it is not even the case that he is no longer open to philosophical exchange. We may observe that, despite the din, Socrates, being Socrates, stops short of shutting the door completely on Crito's response; he says, after all, in the very next sentence: "Nevertheless, if you suppose

---

22. Let us note that Socrates' warning suggests not that there is something about Crito that would make a response on his part futile at this time but that there is something about Socrates that would make it useless for Crito to speak now.

23. See Hyland (1968), 46.

24. Trans. Zeyl (1987).

25. *Gorg.* 508e6–509a7. It has been argued (see Brickhouse and Smith [1994], 38–39), that Socrates does know what the truth is here but does not know why what is true is true. It does not seem quite correct, however, to understand "how these things are," *hopōs echei* (*Gorg.* 509a5), to mean "how [i.e., why] these things are the way they are." The expression means "how these things stand" just as *houtōs echein* (*Gorg.* 509b1), answering *hopōs echei*, means "they stand thus." What Socrates is saying, then, is that even though he does not know how these things stand he sets them down as standing as he sees them, since those who argue otherwise inevitably appear ridiculous. Cf. *Gorg.* 461a7: *tauta oun hopēi pote echei,* "and so how exactly these things stand." Furthermore, as Socrates continues his argument, he regards what he has set down (*tithēmi*—509a7) as being only provisionally true. He says not "since this is so" but "if this is so," *ei de houtōs echei* (*Gorg.* 509b1). In my view, Socrates holds that if one does not know why something is so—in both technical and moral matters—one does not, for that very reason, know that it is so.

that you will accomplish anything, speak" (*Cr.* 54d7). But it will not now be as easy as it usually is for Socrates to listen and to think.

Let us consider the passage, *Cr.* 54d5–6, in which Socrates apprises Crito of the futility of offering objections to the Laws' arguments. I quote the passage in Greek and then offer my rendering of it.[26]

alla isthi, hosa ge ta nun emoi dokounta, ean legeis para tauta, matēn ereis.

But know that (*alla isthi*), so far as (*hosa*), at any rate (*ge*), the things now seeming to me (*ta nun emoi dokounta*) [go], if you speak against them (*ean legeis para tauta*), you will speak in vain (*matēn ereis*).

In context, "the things now *seeming* to me," *ta nun emoi dokounta,* can only refer to the Laws' speeches, since they are what Socrates has just said he *seems* to hear, *dokō akouein* (*Cr.* 54d2–3), as the Corybantes seem to hear, *dokousin akouein* (*Cr.* 54d3–4), the flutes. By having already used forms of the same verb, *dokeō,* Socrates has clearly designated which things are the things now seeming to him.[27] Just as no flautists are actually playing the flutes the Corybantes seem to hear, so no Laws are actually delivering the speeches Socrates seems to hear. The Corybantes imagine the sound of flutes; Socrates imagines the speeches of the Laws. The things that now "seem" to Socrates are the imagined—and merely imaginary—speeches of the Laws.[28]

The *alla* with which this passage begins is not strongly adversative. It clears away the minor distraction of the *tōn allōn* of the previous clause, "the others" that Socrates is unable to hear because of the booming noise of the Laws' speeches, and introduces a reaffirmation of the dominance in his consciousness of the Laws' speeches. Appearing with the imperative *isthi,* "know," repeated from the beginning of the previous sentence ("know well, *eu isthi,* that these things I seem to hear" [*Cr.* 54d2]) and thus returning the reader to the matter of the Laws' speeches, *alla* signals the transition from the description in the previous sentence of a particular state of affairs (the booming of the Laws' speeches within Socrates) to a statement in this sentence

26. I wish to acknowledge, with gratitude, my debt to Professor Hayden Pelliccia, who graciously permitted me to draw upon his considerable expertise in Greek as I worked out this translation.

27. Although *ta nun emoi dokounta* could refer to any things that are seeming to Socrates now, it is clear from the context that the things that are seeming to him now are the Laws' speeches. Given so plain a referent for *ta nun emoi dokounta* in the text, why must one cast about for some other sense to assign to it? Some scholars have rendered this phrase "my current opinions/beliefs" on the model of *Rep.* VI.506e2–3: *tou ge dokountos emoi ta nun,* "to what is, at any rate, my present opinion." See, for instance Grube's translation (1981), 56: "As far as my present beliefs go, if you speak in opposition to them, you will speak in vain." Also Treddenick (1961), 39: "I warn you that, as my opinion stands at present, it will be useless to urge a different view." And Allen (1984), 129: "Be assured that if you speak against the things I now think true, you will speak in vain." Let us note, however, that the *alla* with which our sentence begins is not strong enough to introduce something entirely new—that is, to effect a shift from the booming of the Laws' speeches that are the subject of the previous sentence to Socrates' current opinions that are, on the view of these scholars, the subject of this one.

28. Cf. *Rep.* VI.505d6–8: ". . . while in the case of the just and honorable many would prefer the semblances, *ta dokounta,* without the reality in action, possession, or opinion, yet when it comes to the good nobody is content with the possession of the semblances but all seek the reality" (trans. Shorey [1961]).

of what is to be done in light of it (Crito must recognize the futility of any attempt on his part to speak against those speeches).[29]

The *hosa* here is like the *hosa* in the phrase *hosa ge tanthrōpeia* at Cr. 46e3.[30] There Socrates remarks that "so far as the human things go," Crito is not about to die and will, for that reason, not be led astray by the present calamity. Here Socrates' point is that, so far as the Laws' speeches go—that is, considering how they boom and deafen—if Crito speaks against them, he will speak in vain.

The force of the *ge* I take to be that were it not for the booming noise that Socrates is experiencing, he would surely have encouraged Crito to talk with him;[31] unfortunately, however, the momentary effects of rhetoric are such as to render discussion pointless. The *tauta* refers to *ta nun emoi dokounta*, which, in turn, refers to the Laws' speeches.[32] The *para* is understood to mean "in opposition to," as it does, for example, at Cr. 49d1 and 52d2.[33]

To summarize. Socrates has just said of the Laws' *logoi* that their noise booms within him, with the result that he cannot "hear" the other *logoi*, Crito's. In light of this situation—that is, because of the deafening effect upon Socrates of the Laws' *logoi*—Socrates must warn Crito of the futility of his attempting to challenge them. But, Socrates concludes, if Crito still believes he can accomplish something by speaking, he may speak.

The Way the God Is Leading

After the Laws' speech, Crito has nothing to say. Earlier, after his exchange with Socrates, Crito had said that he does not understand and so has no answer to Socrates'

---

29. See Denniston (1954), 13–14. Denniston's discussion of this use of *alla* is found in Section II, subsection 4. Denniston points out that *alla* followed by an imperative signals "a transition from arguments for action to a statement of the action required . . . *alla*, in this sense, usually occurs near the end of a speech, as a clinching and final appeal . . ." (14). Parallel instances in the *Crito* may be found at Cr. 45a3; 44b5–6; 46a7–8.

30. See Burnet (1924), 191, who renders *hosa ge tanthrōpeia* as "humanly speaking."

31. Some scholars have attached the *ge* to *nun*, so that Socrates is seen to be expressing in this passage what Adam (1888), 80, calls his characteristic "diffidence"; he is seen not as insisting upon the rightness of his view but as stating only how things seem to him now. See, e.g., Dyer and Seymour (1885), 147, and Kitchel (1898), 161, who regard this passage as "softening," for Crito's sake, Socrates' assertion of his point of view. I wonder, however, why, if Socrates is showing diffidence, he apprises Crito so strongly of the hopelessness of his opposition. Dyer and Seymour, Kitchel, and Adam also call attention to the tenderness in the mode of address with which Socrates begins this section: *ō phile hetaire Kritōn*, "my dear comrade, Crito" (Cr. 54d2).

32. Since *tauta* is generally taken to refer back to *ta nun emoi dokounta*, the sense it is given usually follows the sense given to *ta nun emoi dokounta*. Thus, for Grube, Treddenick, and Allen (see n. 27), *tauta*, like *ta nun emoi dokounta*, refers to "my current opinions." For Fowler in the Loeb edition (1914), 191, however, even though *ta nun emoi dokounta* refers to what Socrates "now believes," *tauta*, rendered "these words," refers, apparently, to the Laws' speeches. It is not clear how the Wests (1984), 114, take either term: "Know that insofar as these things seem so to me now, if you speak against them, you will speak in vain."

33. Unlike *pros tauta* as found at Cr. 51c3 and 52d6, which permits the response to the things said, *tauta*, to be in either agreement or disagreement with them, *para tauta* implies that the response will disagree with the things said.

question (*Cr.* 50a4–5). But he does not say that he does not understand the Laws. He does understand them and for that very reason has nothing to say.

Socrates tells Crito to let it go—that is, to abandon his escape plan—and to act in this way, namely, as the Laws propose, but to do so "since in this way the god is leading." Socrates does not say "since in this way the Laws are leading" or "since in this way the arguments of the Laws are leading"; he says "since in this way the god is leading." How are we to understand Socrates' recommendation to Crito that they abandon the escape idea "since in this way the god is leading"?

One possibility is to identify the Laws' speech with the command of the god. Thus, we find Tyler, for example, saying of the Laws' speech: ". . . it is the voice of the god."[34] And Adam: "The very pleading of the Laws is but the voice of the divine sign made articulate."[35] But is it reasonable to think that Socrates would regard what the Laws say as the directive of "the god" or of the "divine sign"?

Allen suggests that, whereas in the *Apology* (30d) Socrates places obedience to the god above obedience to Athens, "in the *Crito*, obedience to lawful authority is itself a matter of holiness and divine apportionment (51b)." Allen is here recalling the Laws' statement that the fatherland is more holy, *agiōteron*, than mother and father and all other forebears "and more highly esteemed among gods . . ." (*Cr.* 51b1).[36] Yet, that Socrates speaks at the dialogue's close not of "gods" but rather of "the god" suggests that he wishes to dissociate the god whose lead *he* wishes to follow from the gods in whose name the Laws demand the citizen's absolute obedience.[37]

Indeed, the appeal to "the god" in the dialogue's last line is rather jarring.[38] And Socrates does nothing to tie "the god" to the speech of the Laws. It seems, then, that his advice to Crito is that they give up on the plan to escape *not* because of what the Laws have said but because "the god" is leading "in this way." The Laws and the god lead, as it happens, in the same way, but *Socrates'* reason for choosing to go that way is that that is the way "the god" leads.

What does it mean to Socrates to act in accordance with the way "the god" is leading? As was argued at length in Chapter 2, "the god" for Socrates is the initiator of his philosophical mission, and to obey "the god" is simply to do what seems best to one after one engages in serious reasoned argument.[39] Since what Socrates' god demands is the practice of philosophy in pursuit of justice, what it means to Socrates not to escape "since in this way the god is leading" is that it is because his own principled reasoning leads to this conclusion that he ought not to escape.

---

34. Tyler (1862), 180.

35. Adam (1888), xvi; also, 80.

36. It should not surprise us that the Laws would say of the fatherland that it is very holy and most highly esteemed by gods. But would Socrates say that?

37. Burnet (1924), 212, says with respect to "God leads the way": "Here there can be no question of any particular gods. The words are definitely monotheistic." What Burnet is noticing, I think, is the striking shift from "gods" at *Cr.* 51b1 to "the god" here.

38. Although Socrates himself had spoken earlier, at *Cr.* 43d7–8, of "the gods" [pl.], it is clear that he intended there the conventional gods who would determine when the ship will come in. It is surely not these gods to whom he refers here by "the god" [sing.].

39. See, esp., *Ap.* 28e4–6, 29d3–5; also 33c4–5 and 37e5–38a1. As was argued in Chapter 2, "the god," associated initially with the god at Delphi, namely, Apollo, is quietly divested of all association with a traditional god.

Just as in the *Apology* Socrates will obey the god—practice philosophy—rather than obey the men of Athens whom he honors and loves (*Ap.* 29d2), the judges, so here will he follow his own philosophical reasoning with respect to what is just rather than be guided by the rhetorical declamations that constitute the speech of the Laws. As he says early on in the *Crito*, he obeys nothing but "the *logos* that seems best to me upon reasoning" (*Cr.* 46b5–6).

Is there any possibility that the speech of the Laws *is* the *logos* that seems best to Socrates upon reasoning? None whatsoever. Socrates is completely loyal to his old *logoi*. This loyalty is a theme that runs through the entire middle part of the dialogue: the old principles, those to which he and Crito have always agreed, must not be cast aside now, no matter what the cost.[40] And, as was argued in Chapter 4, Socrates has his own reasons for not escaping, reasons based entirely upon these old, familiar principles. The newfangled *logoi* of the Laws are noise, the kind of noise rhetoricians make for the sake of ensuring the city's survival and perpetuation. It is not noise, however, that persuades Socrates but, rather, his own reasoned arguments.[41]

Socrates is pious, but not in the way the Laws understand piety. He is pious because he practices philosophy for the sake of justice. To do philosophy for the promotion of the just is, for Socrates, the essence of piety; it is to act in the way in which the god leads. Socrates may not know what death has in store—that, as he says at the close of the *Apology*, is known to no one but the god (*Ap.* 42a4–5)[42]—but he is confident that by refusing to escape he follows the god's lead: he acts upon his own best reasoning, taking nothing into consideration but justice alone.[43]

40. Socrates never says about the Laws' *logoi* what he says about his own—that they are old *logoi*, *logoi* to which he and Crito have always agreed and that he believes in now as he always has.

41. See Anastaplo (1975b), 210: "The fact remains that Socrates does not flee. We confront, then, the question not of the reasons Crito and the typical reader are given, but of the reasons Socrates has for acting as he does." And Hyland (1968), 47: "Socrates had decided on independent grounds, of which most students can name several, not to escape." Also Strauss (1983), 66: "Socrates did stay in prison, he chose to stay, he had a *logos* telling him to stay. But is this *logos* identical with the *logos* by which he persuades Kriton? We have indicated why this is not likely. There are then two different *logoi* leading to the same conclusion. The *logos* which convinces Socrates would not convince Kriton and vice-versa."

42. Or, "to no one *unless* to the god," reading *plēn ei* instead of *plēn ē*.

43. Socrates is willing, as we recall, to obey his true superior, whether god or man; but it is clear, now that he names "the god" as the one he will follow, that he does not see the Laws as his superiors. And, of course, for Socrates, to obey the god is to obey one's own reason.

8

A Fool Satisfied

Answer a fool according to his folly.
Proverbs 26:5

What is Socrates' purpose in inventing the Laws' speech? Why does he endow his moral opponents with such stunning rhetorical skill? In order to understand Socrates' motivation for creating the Laws and their speech, let us consider the position in which Socrates finds himself just before bringing the Laws into the conversation. As we saw in Chapters 3 and 4, (1) Crito proves himself to be thoroughly unphilosophical, and (2) Socrates' argument against escape utterly fails to persuade him. Faced with these two facts, Socrates must assess his options and determine how to proceed.[1] Since there is surely no value in Socrates' prolonging the charade of philosophical exchange,[2] and since Socrates has no intention of escaping, there are two things he can now do: (1) he can simply assert his refusal to escape, or (2) he can try to persuade Crito in some nonphilosophical way of the rightness of his decision not to escape.

Neither of these alternatives is morally unproblematic, however, for neither is free of coercion. If Socrates chooses the first alternative, Crito will, of course, be prevented

---

1. Socrates knows it will not be easy to deal with Crito. As he says immediately following Crito's presentation of his case for escape: "Dear Crito, your eagerness is worth much if some correctness be with it. If not, the greater it is the harder it is to deal with" (Cr. 46b1–3).

2. See, for example, E. West (1989), 76: "Socrates is severely limited in what he can expect by the concerns and character of his respondent"; also Anastaplo (1975b), 211: "Since Crito cannot answer [Socrates' question at Cr. 49c9–50a3]—since he cannot think through this particular problem—Socrates must handle him in another way: he must bring in the general arguments of the laws"; "Socrates had been prepared to explore with Crito the demands of justice—but Crito was not equipped to cooperate."

from carrying out his escape plan, but he will not have abandoned his plan voluntarily and he will have learned nothing. If Socrates chooses the second, then, insofar as his method of persuasion operates outside the bounds of reasoned argument, he will replace what we earlier called "teaching-persuasion" with what we called "coercion-persuasion": rhetorical appeals designed to arouse passion are inherently coercive; they inhibit the ability to think.

Of these two imperfect alternatives, it is the latter that is the more attractive to Socrates. Socrates is, after all, explicitly committed to acting "after persuading you, not while you are unwilling" (Cr. 48e3–5), and, of the two available alternatives, only alternative (2) persuades at all. There can be no doubt that Socrates' preference is to persuade Crito through philosophical argument, but, when it proves impossible to sway Crito by such means, he adopts the means of rhetorical persuasion. Although coercive, rhetorical persuasion does not quite preclude thought: there are those who are able to resist even an especially skillful rhetorical appeal. Socrates can be sure, however, that Crito will not resist the appeal of the Laws. The Laws will succeed where Socrates has failed precisely because they do not require of Crito, as Socrates does, that he exert himself either to think more deeply and rigorously or to overhaul his moral outlook.[3]

That Socrates invents the speech of the Laws represents his recognition that he must, if he is to persuade Crito, sacrifice the ideal mode of discourse, that is, philosophical conversation or "teaching-persuasion," for a poor substitute, coercive speech-making.[4] But Socrates' resorting to rhetoric is a matter of more than just a change in form of discourse, a change from philosophical argument to "philosophical rhetoric";[5] it is a matter also of a change in content.[6] Socrates does not now rhetoricize on behalf of the same things for which he had previously argued philosophically, namely,

---

3. As we shall see, the Laws, unlike Socrates, will not trouble Crito with such considerations as potential harm to the soul and the insignificance of the opinion of the many, or with the objectionableness of such practices as bribery and paying gratitude.

4. It is clear both from Gorg. 517b–c and from the Statesman (292–293) that a genuine statesman — that is, one who possesses the political technē — may use compulsion as well as persuasion for the sake of improving the citizens. In the Gorgias, coercive measures such as just punishment are regarded as a benefit to those upon whom they are conferred because they presumably improve the soul (Gorg. 476a–479d). And Socrates regards as the work of a good citizen "forcing change in appetites, not indulging them, persuading and forcing them towards what will make the citizens better" (Gorg. 517b5–c2). That Socrates resorts to a coercive kind of persuasion in the Crito despite his lacking the political technē may attest to how strong his desire is to try to improve Crito's soul: Socrates' usual noncoercive methods were unsuccessful; Socrates is about to die; Crito is greatly in need of improvement. And although the rhetorical speech of the Laws is coercive, nevertheless, since it is not irresistibly so, Socrates may believe that the particular demands of the present situation warrant — even mandate — its use. We may recall in this connection Socrates' belief, discussed in Chapter 4, that he, though no expert, is one of those men whom he designates as "prudent," phronimoi, and "most decent," epieikestatoi. As such, he believes his opinions merit the honor and serious attention of other men.

5. The phrase "philosophical rhetoric" is applied to the speech of the Laws by Allen (1980), 82, and (1984), 107; also by E. West (1989), 77.

6. It is surely possible for Socrates to cast in a nonphilosophical mode the same points he makes philosophically in order to make them more persuasive. See, for example, Socrates' employment of the myth at the end of the Gorgias. But here Socrates uses the Laws to make a nonphilosophical appeal in defense of points other than those he had made philosophically.

the importance of preserving the soul from injustice, the unimportance of the opinions of the many, the wrongness of returning injustice and *kakourgein* to anyone, the morally problematic character of stealth, bribery, flattery, and of breaking one's explicit and just verbal agreement. Instead, he has the Laws articulate the "many things" that someone, especially an orator, would have to say on behalf of the law that orders that all judgments, correct or incorrect, reached in trials be authoritative. The Laws aim not at producing impassioned devotion to justice and the health of the soul; they stir the passion of patriotism. The Laws' speech promotes the non-socratic "ideal" of citizens' succumbing slavishly to all edicts and verdicts of the fatherland, whether right or wrong.

Socrates' use of a means of last resort to defend ideas with which he is at odds reflects his assessment of what is needed to produce a "willing" Crito. The speech of the Laws is tailor-made for Crito. It addresses concerns specific to him, concerns that from a philosophical point of view are of no importance and to which no philosophical response could be given. It speaks to Crito in terms he can understand and to which he can be sympathetic. Moreover, though it offers a new conception of justice, the new conception it offers—unlike Socrates' conception—is concrete enough and familiar enough for Crito to grasp and accept.

We may note that not only do the Laws win Crito over by respecting his concerns and limitations, but they do so as well by shielding him from censure. Despite the fact that escape is Crito's idea, the Laws direct their ire and rebuke solely at Socrates.[7] As we saw in Chapter 5, although the Laws are imagined to come and stand before "us," they *accuse* Socrates: "Tell me, *Socrates*, what do you have in mind to do?" (*Cr.* 50a8–9). Indeed, only at the very end of their speech do the Laws implicate Crito in the escape plot: "But let not Crito persuade you to do what he says rather than what we say" (*Cr.* 54c8–d1). Throughout their speech, the Laws scold only Socrates: they reproach him for not doing what he is required to do given (1) his relationship to the Laws, (2) his agreements with the Laws and the city, and (3) his presumed extraordinary satisfaction with them. Never do the Laws lecture Crito about his responsibilities or reprimand him for failing to fulfill them.

In addition to addressing Crito's concerns and protecting him from reproach, the Laws' arguments, as we saw in Chapter 7, calm Crito and soothe him. The speech that is for the serene Socrates a deafening noise booming within him is for the vexed Crito the frenzy that quells his agitation.[8] And the Laws' speech actually provides Crito with something he most desperately craves—the means for saving his own reputation.[9] If Crito is persuaded and can persuade others that, as the Laws contend,

7. Socrates was not protective of Crito in this way prior to the speech of the Laws. Socrates regarded Crito as the instigator of the escape and as a full participant in it. See *Cr.* 46c2–3; 48c2; 48c6–48d5; 49e9–50a3.

8. Young (1974), 8, regards as the primary purpose of the Laws' speech the offering of comfort to a grieving Crito. Yet, although Crito is certainly saddened by Socrates' impending death, he is, as we have seen in Chapter 3, also conce. ned about the loss of his reputation. Indeed, the Laws' speech calms Crito's anxieties so that he can accept Socrates' decision with greater equanimity, but it also addresses his worries about his reputation.

9. Crito, of course, would have preferred to save his reputation by having Socrates escape. As Crito makes quite clear at the beginning of his argument, "the many will not be persuaded that you yourself were not willing to go away from here although we were eager for it" (*Cr.* 44c3–5).

Socrates' escape is in fact worse than his death for all concerned—and especially for Socrates—Crito can still be perceived as Socrates' good friend despite not having rescued him. When Crito's detractors accuse him of caring more for money than for his friend, Crito can now defend his good name with an arsenal of new arguments furnished by the Laws.[10] Thanks to the Laws, Crito can now point out that he would hardly be doing Socrates a good turn by helping him escape if Socrates has no place to go where he can live as he likes and yet be free of ridicule, if his children will be cared for no better if he lives than if he dies, if Socrates will so anger the Laws by escaping that life both before and after death will be made most unpleasant for him. And Crito can assure his detractors as well that he and Socrates' other friends can actually be of benefit to Socrates by caring for his children once he is gone.

Despite the variety of ways in which the Laws show consideration for Crito, however, the fact remains that for much of their speech, they speak harshly, leveling criticisms that are most severe. Nevertheless, it is not to be inferred from their harshness and from the severity of their reprimands (1) that their speech does not aim at flattery, or (2) that it must therefore be an instance of "philosophical rhetoric," the "true rhetoric" described in the Gorgias (at 503a–b), the rhetoric that aims at justice and the improvement of souls.[11] For although the Laws are harsh and their reprimands severe, they are harsh only to Socrates, never to Crito, and they reprimand only Socrates, never Crito. Whereas it is certainly true that the Laws do not gratify Socrates, it is not at Socrates' but at Crito's gratification that they aim. The Laws do not challenge, mock, and insult Crito; what they do is challenge, mock, and insult Socrates. And they do gratify Crito—by addressing his concerns, shielding him from criticism, calming and soothing him, and providing him with the means for saving his reputation.

Although the Laws' rhetoric aims, then, not at truth but at flattery, and although it can therefore not be regarded as "philosophical" or "true" rhetoric, nevertheless it may be presumed to have as its goal, in some measure, the improvement of Crito's soul. Since Socrates' consistent and overriding motivation in dealing with others is to benefit them by improving their souls, and since, as we have seen, Crito is included

10. See Strauss (1983), 66: "Kriton is concerned above all with what the people of Athens will say if he has not helped Socrates to escape from prison: what Socrates tells Kriton, Kriton can and will tell the people." I am not certain that I interpret Strauss correctly here. I understand him to be saying that Socrates provides Crito with a justification—one the Athenians will believe—for his not having helped his friend to escape, namely, that escape would harm in tangible ways both Socrates himself and his friends and would not significantly benefit his children. Anastaplo (1975b), 210, however, says almost the same thing as Strauss but, it seems, with a very different meaning. Anastaplo says: "Socrates knows what the report would be that Crito . . . would convey to his fellows. . . . For Crito had been concerned that he might be criticized, by the very people who had condemned Socrates, for not having used his wealth to help his friend escape." What Anastaplo means by his statement is not that Socrates provides Crito with a justification to present to the Athenians for his decision not to help Socrates escape but that Socrates provides Crito with an explanation of why he was unsuccessful despite his best efforts: that Socrates refuses to break the law "even in circumstances when they themselves would break it." Perhaps, then, this is Strauss's meaning as well.

11. See Gorg. 517a5, 522c1–4. According to Allen (1980), 82, the Laws' speech is "aimed at persuasion based on truth and indifferent to gratification, not at flattery based on gratification and indifferent to truth. The Laws in the Crito speak as physicians of the soul." Also (1984), 107: "Yet the speech of the Laws is hardly flattery: it leads Socrates to his death. And the Gorgias also envisages a philosophical rhetoric aimed at excellence of soul, indifferent to whether it gives pleasure or pain to the hearers. . . ."

among those whom Socrates believes he ought least to treat badly, it would be most incongruous if Socrates had no intention of improving Crito's soul. Now that Crito has shown himself utterly impervious to the improvement that living philosophically provides, and since there can be no doubt that in Socrates' judgment "philosophical" rhetoric, rhetoric that confronts men directly with truths they prefer not to hear, is unlikely to prove more appealing to Crito than foul-tasting medicine to a child, Socrates has recourse to the only method likely to work: nonphilosophical rhetoric. At the same time that the Laws' rhetoric caters to Crito and avoids offending him, it aims, as we shall see, at improving Crito's soul — a little.

The contention, then, of this chapter is that despite Socrates' preference for joint inquiry over rhetorical persuasion, and despite his having no regard for the case against escape that the Laws propound, Socrates invents the Laws and their speech both because he wants Crito to go along with his decision and because he wishes to benefit him. We now consider in turn the ways in which the Laws' speech is specifically designed to engage Crito and to benefit him. We conclude by taking note of how Plato attempts to strengthen the resistance of the careful reader to the rhetorical force of the speech of the Laws.

Engaging Crito

Crito and the Laws have much in common. Crito wants Socrates to obey him; the Laws want Socrates to obey them. Crito makes an emotional appeal in which he cites practical considerations and even considerations of "justice" in order to secure Socrates' obedience; so do the Laws. Both Crito and the Laws are authoritarian;[12] if the Laws are more so, it is only because they have the power to back up their demand for absolute obedience.

Crito and the Laws understand each other. The things that matter to both are life, money, reputation, friends, family, and power. For both, "justice" derives its meaning from these. For Crito, as we recall from Chapter 3, justice is refraining from doing anything that would help enemies or harm family and friends; justice is relational. For the Laws, justice requires absolute obedience to them and to the city on the assumption that the city as fatherland ought not to be harmed by its citizen-children; for the Laws, too, then, justice is relational. And since justice is relational for both Crito and the Laws, neither can share the Socratic view that it is never right to do injustice or bad things in return; Crito and the Laws share instead the view of the many, a view that distinguishes between what may be done to enemies and what may be done to friends or family. The advantage of Crito's and the Laws' sharing this view is that it enables them to take "common counsel," something that Socrates and Crito are not able to do — indeed, something that Socrates and the Laws are not able to do.[13]

---

12. West (1989), 79: "... the impersonated voice of the laws does not reveal Socrates' own political theory but mirrors back to Crito his own authoritarian attitudes."

13. Socrates points out that those who are unable to take counsel together will necessarily "have contempt for each other when they see each other's counsels" (Cr. 49d4-5). The Laws show their contempt for Socrates; may we not safely assume that Socrates has contempt for the Laws as well?

The Laws adopt in addressing Socrates the same mode of discourse that Crito uses. Crito delivers a speech; so do the Laws. Neither engages Socrates in conversation: once they get going in earnest, they do not stop.[14] As orators, both Crito and the Laws have an audience—not an interlocutor. What is essential to the Socratic question-and-answer method but completely alien to rhetoric is the possibility of revision, of taking something back, of changing the premises, of challenging the logical structure of the argument as it proceeds. Both Crito and the Laws mount an attack; their goal is not to encourage but to quash opposition.

The Laws' tone and manner resemble Crito's as well. We have already discussed at length the ways in which Crito (Chapter 3) and the Laws (Chapters 5 and 6) mock and threaten Socrates and preach to him about justice and virtue. They use against him the virtue terms he most treasures: as Crito says to Socrates, "You seem to me to be attempting a thing that is not even just" (Cr. 45c5–6), so the Laws say, "The things you are attempting to do to us are not just" (Cr. 51c7–8). Indeed, the most shockingly sarcastic and disrespectful remark that Crito makes in his speech to Socrates is echoed by the Laws: just as Crito says, "particularly if one has claimed to care for virtue through his whole life" (Cr. 45d7–8), the Laws say, "you who in truth care for virtue" (Cr. 51a6–7). Both imply that Socrates' current course (for Crito, Socrates' refusal to escape; for the Laws, Socrates' intention to escape) shows that Socrates does not really care, and, indeed, has not really cared, for virtue after all.

Both Crito and the Laws invoke the guilt-inducing expression *to son meros*, "as far as it lies in you."[15] Crito, in berating Socrates for abandoning his children, says that "as far as it lies in you" (Cr. 45d2), Socrates' children will do what they do by chance; the Laws, in rebuking Socrates for attempting to escape, demand to know what Socrates thinks he is doing "if not destroying the laws and the whole city, as far as it lies in you" (Cr. 50b1–2).[16] By using the phrase *to son meros*, Crito and the Laws are able to imply that Socrates will have done wrong (1) regardless of his intent, (2) regardless of whether the anticipated consequences will or are even likely to result, and (3) regardless of whether Socrates will have been solely responsible for them if they do. In the case of Socrates and his children, Socrates surely does not wish to abandon his children to the whims of fortune; Socrates has every reason to believe that his friends will assume the responsibility of caring for his children in the event of his death; and, if Socrates' friends fail to care for Socrates' children, they will surely bear part of the responsibility for Socrates' children's being victims of chance. None of these factors, however, alters the fact that *as far as it lies in Socrates*, his children will be subject to chance. Similarly, in the case of Socrates and the Laws and the city, despite Socrates' having no intention to destroy the city, despite the extreme unlikelihood that Socrates' escape will have any real effect on the survival and stabil-

---

14. See Chapter 5, n. 33.

15. This expression also makes the charge of both Crito and the Laws appear less wildly implausible. That both use it suggests that they sense the outrageousness of their charges without it.

16. Also at Cr. 54c8: The Laws say that their brothers, the Laws in Hades, will not receive Socrates favorably, knowing that he attempted to destroy the Laws in Athens, "as far as it lay in you," *to son meros*. The Laws use a similar expression at Cr. 51a5, *kath' hoson dunasthai*, "to the extent that you can."

ity of the Laws and the city, and despite the fact that even if there were a serious threat to the existence of the city it would arise as a result not of just Socrates' lawbreaking and the lawbreaking he inspires but as a result of there being many other lawbreakers otherwise inspired,[17] the Laws can still maintain that Socrates, *to son meros*, is attempting to destroy them and the city.

Both Crito and the Laws denounce Socrates for the way in which he conducts himself at his trial, a mode of conduct of which Socrates himself most heartily approves (*Ap.* 38e3–5). It seems clear that both Crito and the Laws believe Socrates should have humbled himself before the judges and done what was necessary in order to have his life spared. Crito is ashamed for Socrates with respect to "the way the judicial contest itself took place" (*Cr.* 45e4–5), specifically because Socrates fails to avoid death. And the Laws denounce Socrates for having "plumed" himself on not being afraid of death and on preferring death to exile; they think he should now be "ashamed" of those speeches (*Cr.* 52c8).

Both Crito and the Laws encourage and expect Socrates to be concerned about how things will appear in the eyes of others. Crito implores Socrates to be concerned enough about reputation to protect him from the fate of having people believe that he values money above friends. He is distressed, and counts on Socrates to share his distress, about how ridiculous, *katagelōs* (*Cr.* 45e5), the handling of the whole matter by Socrates and his friends will appear if Socrates ends up dead. The Laws warn Socrates that if he chooses to escape, men in lawful cities "will look askance" at him, and he will "confirm the judges in their opinion, so that they will seem to have judged the lawsuit correctly" (*Cr.* 53b7–c1); "the affair of Socrates," they say, "will appear unseemly" (*Cr.* 53c8–d1). They also taunt him, twice, about how ridiculous he will seem: at *Cr.* 53a7, where the Laws say that Socrates will become ridiculous, *kategelastos*, if he goes out of the city despite his demonstrated lifelong great satisfaction with it—especially since no good will come of it for himself, for his friends, or for his family; and then again at *Cr.* 53d4, where the Laws conjure up the image of a ridiculous, *hōs geloiōs*, Socrates running away from prison in disguise.

Crito and the Laws both have a high regard for power. Crito thinks that Socrates ought to concern himself about the opinion of the many because the many have the power to take life (*Cr.* 44d1–5; 48a10–b2). The Laws think Socrates ought to obey them because they and their brothers, the Laws in Hades, have more power to harm him, or power to do him greater harm, than do the men who could do no more than execute him, that is, the judges who sentenced him to death (*Cr.* 54b8–c8).

It is instructive to note how different is the Laws' depiction of Hades in the *Crito* from Socrates' depiction of it in the *Apology*.[18] First, in the *Apology*, Hades is a place

---

17. Indeed, the Laws implicitly recognize this fact when they suggest that a city cannot continue to exist in which judgments "are rendered ineffective and are corrupted by private *men*"—men, plural. They could not plausibly have replaced "by private men" with "by a private man." Moreover, that the Laws say "by private men" suggests that it is not specifically Socrates whom they regard as a threat to their continued existence on account of his celebrity; they perceive as a threat disobedience by private men generally.

18. See Chapter 6, n. 101. To be sure, neither the *Apology* nor the *Crito* gives or means to give a full description of Hades. For that very reason, however, it is most significant which aspects of Hades each dialogue selects.

where, it is to be hoped, "inconceivable happiness" — at least as Socrates understands it — will be found. In the *Crito*, by contrast, Hades is a place where a fate worse than death awaits anyone who has angered the Laws on earth. Second, the *Crito* replaces the *Apology*'s "judges in truth" (*Ap.* 41a2), judges who will surely vindicate the innocent Socrates, with "our brothers, the Laws in Hades" who stand ready to condemn Socrates for his affront to their earthly siblings. What these differences suggest is that, whereas in the *Apology* Socrates wants to relieve the worries of his human "judges" about what he might face in Hades, the Laws in the *Crito* want to cause Crito worry about what awaits Socrates. And what is most likely to frighten Crito? Not some abstract justice as determined by "judges in truth," but the kind of justice in which kin look out for kin and brother avenges brother.

Since Crito and the Laws think alike, the Laws do not belittle Crito's concerns but rather take them seriously enough to refute each of them. Crito tells Socrates not to worry about the loss of money or worse that Crito and Socrates' other companions might incur as a result of Socrates' agreeing to escape; the Laws tell Socrates that that *is* something to worry about. Crito tells Socrates that he can go to Thessaly and be unharmed and respected there: no one there, he says "will cause you pain," *hōste se mēdena lupein* (*Cr.* 45c4); the Laws tell Socrates that the only way he will escape harm even in this land of disorder and lack of restraint, where the story of his escape might be a source of some amusement, is if he causes no one any pain, *an mētina lupēis* (*Cr.* 53e2), and fawns upon and becomes everyone's slave (*Cr.* 53e4). Crito expresses dismay with regard to Socrates' abandoning his children to chance; the Laws reassure Socrates that his children need not fare badly: if Socrates' friends are of any benefit at all, they will surely take care of his children whether he is dead or in exile.[19]

The points, then, that Crito makes in his speech to Socrates are not dismissed by the Laws — as they are by Socrates — as just so much misplaced zeal but are rather attended to and addressed. Indeed, even though the Laws urge Socrates not to regard children or living or anything else as more important than justice (*Cr.* 54b3–4), they clearly recognize children and living and other things as important. Unlike Socrates, who thinks no consideration counts for anything in comparison with justice (*Cr.* 48d3–5; also *Ap.* 28b5–9) — and indeed regards all other considerations as those of the many (*Cr.* 48c2–6) — the Laws think other considerations do count and count enough to merit a serious response. If the Laws do not think other considerations count more than justice, it is because they understand justice to mean deference to them.[20]

By answering point for point each of Crito's objections to Socrates' remaining in prison, the Laws give him reasons that make it possible for him to agree that Socrates

---

19. We note the irony that in the *Apology* (41e) Socrates entrusts the care of his children not to his friends but to his enemies — to those who voted to condemn him.

20. It might be thought that when the Laws implore Socrates not to regard even living as more important than justice, they are teaching Crito that virtue is more important than life itself. But, as we saw in Chapter 6, the Laws' notion of justice is obedience to them, and the reason they advise Socrates to put justice ahead of life itself is that the consequences of his disobedience to them will be even worse for him than death. The implication is that angry Laws, both here and in Hades, can hurt a man more than angry men can.

ought not to escape, reasons that he can understand and that work within the parameters of his moral outlook.

In effect, what the Laws do in their speech is extend Crito's conception of justice so that it can easily encompass obedience to the Laws and the city. Since, for Crito, the height of injustice involves harming "one's own"—that is, oneself, one's family, and one's friends—all the Laws need to do is have Crito admit the city into the class of things that qualify as "one's own." The Laws accomplish this end by speaking of the city as a "fatherland" and by promoting the image of the city as parents, parents of even higher standing than biological parents, parents to whom is owed the unqualified obedience that a slave owes a master. Once they cast the city as fatherland, the Laws can explicitly name the city and themselves among those who ought least to be treated badly: "yourself and friends and fatherland and us" (Cr. 54c5). Once the Laws fix the notion of city as superparent in Crito's mind, Crito's acquiescence in their conception of what justice requires follows readily.[21]

The Laws devote a large part of their speech to the parent analogy, although what they are supposed to be proving is that Socrates by escaping would be violating an *agreement*, the agreement to obey all verdicts just or unjust. Comparing themselves and the city to parents, the Laws deliver a rather protracted sermon on the injustices of doing violence to them and to the city, of attempting to destroy them and the city even in return, of failing to yield to and fawn upon the fatherland, of shirking the duty to obey the fatherland no matter what it bids at whatever cost. As we noted in Chapter 6, all the benefits the Laws cite as grounds for the citizen's obedience are benefits associated with the parental role: birth, nurture, and education. Of the three ways in which, according to the Laws, a disobedient citizen does injustice, two are related to the parent analogy: not obeying "us who begat him" and not obeying "us who nurtured him" (Cr. 51e5–6). Indeed, despite the lengthy agreement argument they present, the Laws return finally to family matters: "Obey us, your nurturers," they advise at Cr. 54b2, once again reminding Socrates of their parental relationship to him, and they invoke at Cr. 54c6–8 their brothers, the Laws in Hades, who, they say, will not take kindly to Socrates' attempt to destroy the Laws of Athens.

The Laws' analogy between city and parent is not a typically Socratic one.[22] The Laws use it because loyalty to family is a notion to which Crito's moral sense resonates.[23] Similarly, the Laws characterize a citizen's disobedience to the verdict of

21. Dover (1974), 218–19: "On the assumption that devotion to one's parents is virtuous, patriotism can be justified by treatment of one's own land as a parent." It is likely that Crito can accept the notion of complete obedience, whether to parent, master, or city, far better than he could a more nuanced notion of obedience that calls upon him to draw fine distinctions. Crito understands loyalty, and loyalty is especially resistant to degrees. Insofar as Socrates hopes to secure Crito's law abidingness not only in the matter at hand but in the future as well, it is best that Socrates speak in absolute terms.

22. West (1989), 77, calls the parent analogy "an *uncharacteristic* figure of speech" (emphasis in original) and also "this un-Socratic analogy."

23. According to Congleton (1974), 440, Socrates personifies the Laws "in deference to Crito's inability to deal with abstractions." There may well be some truth to this view, but the more important reason, I think, for the personification of the Laws is that, once personified, they can easily be depicted as parents. Perhaps another reason for the personification of the Laws is to make it possible for the reader to distinguish their voice from Socrates'.

the city as his committing violence against it and attempting to destroy it because, for Crito, there can be no worse crime than that of committing violence against parents or attempting to destroy them. The Laws again exploit Crito's strong sense of filial obligation when they maintain that disobedience to the city would constitute an unholy act, since the gods accord even greater venerability to the city than to parents and ancestors.[24]

Most significant is that the Laws' speech makes no reference to any of the considerations to which Socrates alluded, considerations to which Crito already showed himself to be indifferent. The Laws make no mention of the stealth involved in escape, or of the bribery or paying of gratitude, or of causing harm to the *souls* of those whom one ought least to expose to such harm—oneself and one's companions. Nor do they call attention to the specific verbal agreement to "abide by my penalty" that Socrates would be violating. All of these considerations, as we know, failed to impress Crito when Socrates proposed them.

When the Laws speak of the source of obligation, they speak of parents, masters, and gods, all of whom are located squarely within Crito's moral universe. Although the Laws do also speak of Socrates' tacit and long-standing contracts and agreements with them, they do not discuss these contracts and agreements until they have established themselves as the agents responsible for his birth, nurture, and education. Moreover, the Laws link Socrates' contracts and agreements to his satisfaction with Athens, a city which, according to them, he prefers to all others. The Laws do not speak of the importance of any general obligation to keep one's promises or even of Socrates' duty to honor his express verbal agreement to abide by his penalty. Agreements such as Socrates', when conceived independently of any special relationship obtaining between the parties, are unlikely to strike Crito as giving rise to moral obligation.

Benefiting Crito

When the Laws first make their appearance in the dialogue, Crito and Socrates are at an impasse. Crito has tried, but to no avail, to persuade Socrates to escape; Socrates has fared no better in his attempt to persuade Crito that escape would be wrong. Crito at this point surely still wants to help Socrates, but he has no options; there is nothing more he can do. He has exhausted his resources, offering every kind of argument he can think of. But all the arguments Crito can think of are conventional ones: even his arguments about what is just, noble, and brave are conventional. What Crito cannot do is speak Socrates' language, the language of philosophy, the language of justice and the soul, as Socrates speaks it. It is at this point that an asymmetry emerges between philosopher and nonphilosopher: no matter how much Crito wishes to help Socrates, he cannot, because he cannot speak Socrates' language; Socrates, however, if he must, *can* speak Crito's. Although Socrates avoids countering Crito's conventional arguments with conventional arguments *of his own*, he does create the Laws

24. West (1989), 77, contends that the Laws use the unsocratic parent analogy in order to "restore Crito's characteristic sense of piety and respect."

so that someone can meet Crito on his own ground.[25] In order to help his friend, Socrates abandons his usual mode of discourse, his philosophical idiom, and calls upon the Laws to speak to Crito.

In this section we shall see what Socrates hopes to achieve with respect to improving Crito's soul and how very low he must set his sights. Let us begin by considering the nature of the challenge facing Socrates. Crito, as we have seen, has proved himself to be utterly unphilosophical. Moreover, Crito does not regard himself as bound, certainly when a friend's life is at stake, by ordinary moral rules—not even by such basic rules as adhering to a just agreement—or by law. This is not to say that Crito is a bad man or worse than most; he surely means well. Yet Crito is indifferent to the claims of principle and law.

Since Socrates knows by now that he cannot make Crito responsive to the claims of principle, he seeks instead to make him responsive to the claims of law. Socrates' method of dealing with his friend thus involves what Congleton aptly calls "individualism and gradualism":[26] Socrates gradually effects in Crito a change for the better— he makes Crito responsive to the claims of law—by recognizing and working within the parameters of Crito's own individual conception of what is right and what is important. Unfortunately, however, the change thus effected is necessarily minimal.

One change that constitutes a benefit to Crito is the expansion of Crito's conception of "one's own" beyond oneself and one's human family and friends to include a "father" who is the city and the Laws. It is, however, not quite accurate to conceive of Crito's improvement as consisting in his being, as Congleton puts it, "shaken . . . from his tendency to the favoritism of helping friends and harming enemies, and introduced to the notion of law."[27] For since the "notion of law" to which Crito is introduced is tied to the notion of city as fatherland, it is tied as well to Crito's tendency to the favoritism of helping "one's own." Socrates does not expect Crito to appreciate the importance of law *as opposed to* furthering the interests of "one's own"; for that reason Socrates assimilates lawfulness to the promotion of the interests of "one's own"—newly expanded. Socrates does not eradicate Crito's notion of favoritism in the sense of helping friends and harming enemies; he merely extends the favoritism to include the Laws and the fatherland.

The Laws, as we noted in Chapter 6, speak as readily of the citizen's obligation to do whatever the city and fatherland bid as they do of the citizen's obligation to do whatever the Laws bid. The Laws, then, do not restrict the citizen's obligation to what is required by duly constituted law but extend it to all orders, edicts, and verdicts of the city as fatherland. According to the Laws' speech, the fatherland does not derive its authority from the laws but rather *all* commands derive their authority from the fatherland, an entity to be revered and yielded to more than any human parent or ancestor. Crito is thus not asked to ascend from a notion of "one's own" to an appreciation of law as law but to make the less demanding transition from a narrow notion of "one's own" to a broader one that encompasses the fatherland. Crito is taught not

---

25. White (1996), 114, sees the Laws' speech as "a way . . . of meeting Crito on his own terms. . . . This speech actually mirrors the speech it is responding to."

26. Congleton (1974), 438.

27. Congleton (1974), 438.

the importance of the rule of law but the necessity of obeying all laws, edicts, and verdicts issued by the city as fatherland. Whatever change there is in Crito's views, then, it is a change that requires no fundamental shift of perspective.

A second benefit to Crito may arise out of the emphasis the Laws place on the notion of "abiding." Crito does not care much about the principles that Socrates has endorsed throughout his life and to which he, too, has allegedly assented. Although Socrates repeatedly emphasizes the importance of adhering in all circumstances, no matter how dire, to the old principles—unless, of course, someone presents arguments sufficiently powerful to dislodge them—Crito believes that when one faces death, all that matters is outflanking it. But the Laws seek to bind Socrates, even in the face of death, to the counsel he has taken for seventy years, the seventy years in which he could have left Athens if he were not satisfied: "But will you in fact not abide now by what you have agreed to?" (*Cr.* 53a5–6). The Laws replace Socrates' emphasis on abiding by principles (*Cr.* 49e2, 49e4, 50a2), his recognition that principles themselves abide (*Cr.* 48b5, b7, b9, b10), and his commitment to abiding by his penalty (*Ap.* 39b6) with their own insistence that Socrates abide by his long-standing tacit agreements and contracts with them. It is surely good that the Laws expose Crito to the idea of adhering to a lifelong commitment even in the face of death; he is, after all, a man who believes that the imminence of death changes everything. Yet the Laws, as we have seen, do not go so far as to encourage abiding by agreements generally; they expect Socrates to be faithful to his agreement with them because they begat, nurtured, and educated him and because he is presumably exceedingly pleased with them.

How does Crito benefit from the Laws' attempt to change his views if the Laws do not require of him that he adopt a new moral outlook but permit him to retain his old one, if they ask only that they and the city be admitted to the realm of his moral concerns, if they demand only that those whom one ought least to treat badly include now not just oneself and one's friends but the "fatherland and us" (*Cr.* 54c5), if they require abiding specifically by agreements made with them and the city?

However minimal the changes may be that the Laws can effect in Crito's views, these changes have the potential to improve Crito's soul. For a man like Crito, a man both unphilosophical and with a tendency to corruption, obedience to the law— even when indistinguishable from obedience to "whatever the city and fatherland bid"—is preferable to self-determination. As Anastaplo says, "someone such as Crito cannot be depended on to make the proper judgment. Rather, he is better off . . . if he is persuaded he should act as prescribed by law. For men are far more apt than not to break the law for the wrong reasons. . . ."[28] Since in all probability a man like Crito—a man who subscribes unreflectively to a morality aimed at promoting the interests of one's family and friends—will commit injustices less frequently if he obeys the law than if he does not, then insofar as the speech of the Laws succeeds in making Crito law abiding,[29] it stands to improve the condition of his soul.[30]

28. Anastaplo (1975b), 209–10.

29. Hyland (1968), 47, speaks of "the therapeutic purpose of restoring Crito to his status as obedient citizen," but in fact Socrates must teach Crito to be an "obedient citizen."

30. The Laws' speech is not required in order to prevent Crito from committing the impending wrongful act of aiding Socrates in his escape: as long as Socrates refuses to escape, Crito will be effectively prevented from aiding him. Similarly, the Laws' speech is not required in order to prevent the

Although Socrates' intention in creating the speech of the Laws is to benefit Crito by improving his soul, the Laws themselves speak of no such thing. If the Laws are to be effective, they must speak to Crito in Crito's terms, hence in nonsocratic terms. Care for the soul is a Socratic idea, an idea that Crito has not quite assimilated despite his lifelong association with Socrates. Speaking in Crito's terms requires, therefore, that no reference be made to the soul. Ironically, it is only because the Laws display no interest in improving souls that Socrates can use them successfully to improve Crito's soul.[31]

Crito is indeed persuaded. The next time we encounter him, in the *Phaedo*, he is attending to the arrangements connected with Socrates' death. But even though Crito has reconciled himself to Socrates' death, we see in the *Phaedo* that he has not changed: he still hopes to delay the moment of Socrates' death, reminding Socrates that others in his predicament eat, drink, and enjoy sexual relations before facing their execution (*Phaedo* 116e1–6). Yet, by the time of the *Phaedo*, Socrates knows Crito quite well. He therefore knows that he has done all he can: "I have made an argument for some time and at some length. . . . I seem to have spoken in vain to him" (*Phaedo* 115d2–5).[32] Socrates makes no further attempt to engage Crito in joint inquiry; in place of discussion, he provides reassurances about his future and explanations of his current choices. Crito offers no opposition. All that is left for Socrates to say is: "Obey, and do not do otherwise" (*Phaedo* 117a3).

Protecting the Reader

The speech of the Laws must accomplish two tasks simultaneously: it must produce a "willing" Crito by persuading him that the city can rightfully demand unqualified obedience, but it must shield the careful reader from being similarly persuaded. We have considered thus far how the speech of the Laws persuades Crito; let us look now at the safeguards that Plato puts into place in order to help the reader avoid the same fate.

That the Laws do not speak for Socrates may be inferred, as we have seen, from the introduction to the speech of the Laws, discussed in Chapter 5, and from Socrates' reaction to the speech, discussed in Chapter 7. Plato lets the reader know in several

---

destruction of the city: insofar as Socrates has no intention of escaping, Crito will not be able to implement the escape plan that would purportedly threaten the survival of the city. Of course, the city is in no real danger of disintegration no matter what either Socrates or Crito does. Although the Laws insinuate that Socrates' escape is nothing short of an attempt to destroy the city since a city cannot survive if private citizens disobey its verdicts, their insinuation is, as Socrates says, just the sort of thing an orator would say on behalf of the law establishing the bindingness of all verdicts.

31. The rhetoric Socrates employs is, then, standard rhetorical fare containing no "philosophical" elements. The rhetoric itself is not the "good" rhetoric, the "philosophical" rhetoric, the rhetoric that speaks the truth and is indifferent to pleasure and pain, that is imagined in the *Gorgias* (see Allen [1984], 108; also see Chapter 5, n. 13, and this chapter, n. 11). Any "higher" purpose the speech has, any concern for Crito's true welfare, that is, for the welfare of his soul, is external to the speech itself.

32. Translations in this section from the *Phaedo* are by Gallop (1975).

ways before the speech that Socrates and the Laws do not see eye to eye on anything but the conclusion they reach: (1) by the change in tone and in method of argument—indeed, by the change in speaker; (2) through Socrates' characterization of the Laws' speech as consisting of the "many things" an *orator* might say in defense of the legitimacy of all verdicts whether correct or incorrect; and (3) by the adversarial relationship between Socrates and the Laws. And after the speech as well, Plato provides a number of indications that Socrates remains unconvinced of the soundness of the Laws' arguments: he has Socrates (1) make reference to the Corybantic rites; (2) characterize the Laws' arguments as noise that booms within him, drowning out competing arguments; and (3) recommend that he and Crito follow *the god*.

But the reader is given many more reasons to believe that the Laws' arguments are not Socratic. The very features of the Laws' speech that make it appeal to Crito are features that would make it repugnant to Socrates: that it is unabashedly authoritarian; that it resorts to threats; that it is concerned with appearances; that it speaks of the city as fatherland and of the relation of citizen to city as one of child to parent; that it confines its talk of agreement to agreement with the Laws and the fatherland; that it addresses seriously all of Crito's considerations, considerations that Socrates regards as considerations of "the many"; that it steers clear of all "Socratic" ideas, in particular, the idea that one ought to care first and foremost for one's soul, avoiding injustice—including such injustices as stealth, bribery, flattery, and the breaking of explicit verbal promises—at all costs.

It is surely no easy task to construct an argument both strong enough to persuade Crito and weak enough to fail to persuade the reader. In order for Crito to be convinced by the Laws' argument, the argument cannot be wholly implausible; indeed, Crito must be made to believe that Socrates himself is persuaded by it. The speech Plato composes is in fact at first glance neither absurd nor obviously flawed. And the Laws' apparent appropriation and application of such Socratic notions as non-retaliation, upholding of agreements, and not harming those one ought least to harm lend to their speech a distinctly "Socratic" cast. But if the Laws' argument is to raise grave doubts in the minds of the dialogue's readers, it must be at the same time discernibly flawed and detectably unsocratic—and it is. Its flaws, however, are subtle, involving for the most part, as is the case generally in well-crafted oratorical displays, overstatement, exaggeration, and insufficiently supported conclusions—not outright nonsense.[33] And its unsocratic character is obscured by the superficial resemblance between the Laws' distortions of Socratic notions and the Socratic notions they distort. Thus, it takes some effort on the reader's part to recognize the fallacies in the Laws' argument and to appreciate its deviance from Socratic thinking. If some readers of the *Crito* are insensitive to the flaws in the argument of the Laws or to its unsocratic character, it is perhaps because they find it difficult to imagine that Plato might allow Socrates to appear to be promoting an argument he does not genuinely

33. See Grote (1875), I, 305–306: "The discourse which we read in the Kriton is one of his [Plato's] best specimens [of rhetoric]: appealing to pre-established and widespread emotions, veneration for parents, love of country, respect for covenants—to justify the resolution of Sokrates in the actual case: working up these sentiments into fervour, but neglecting all difficulties, limits, and counter-considerations."

endorse—especially when the argument supports a course of action that he clearly does endorse.[34]

Nevertheless, this is precisely what Plato does in the *Crito*. And in so doing, Plato shows his readers the possibility of a kind of philosopher who does more than follow a set of premises to their logical conclusion. Not that Socrates does not do that as well: in the middle part of the *Crito*, as we have seen, Socrates sets forth his views and the reasons from which they follow. Yet the last part of the dialogue reveals Socrates as a philosopher so responsive to the needs of a particular person at a particular time[35] that he abandons his methods—even his truths—for the sake of his friend, that is, for the sake of his friend's soul. The sacrifice Socrates makes for his friend is surely, then, as great as the one Crito is willing to make for him.

Plato may have other aims as well in designing the speech of the Laws, aims unrelated to portraying Socrates as a philosopher sensitive to Crito's specific needs. It has been suggested by some, for example, that Plato uses the speech of the Laws to burnish Socrates' image, to reverse the negative impression of him with which the Athenians were left as a result of the *Apology*.[36] Others have added that Plato seeks to enhance Socrates' reputation in order to enhance, by extension, the reputation of philosophers generally: insofar as Socrates is popularly regarded as representative of philosophers, it is likely that what the Athenian public comes to believe about him it will come to believe about all philosophers.[37] Yet a third explanation of why Plato composes the Laws' speech might be that Plato genuinely believes that it is best for those who are unphilosophical to obey the laws no questions asked. According to this last view, the argument contained in the speech of the Laws is directed not only at Crito but at all readers who are not inclined to develop and adhere to their own carefully reasoned moral principles.[38]

Whereas these suggestions offer reasonable accounts of Plato's intentions in incorporating the speech of the Laws into the *Crito*, one may wonder if they do justice to the structure of the dialogue as a whole. For the *Crito* contains not only the speech of the Laws but Socratic elenchus as well: it contains, that is, two responses to Crito's argument for escape—a philosophical response that fails to persuade Crito, followed by a rhetorical one that succeeds in persuading him. The dialogue's movement from philosophy to rhetoric suggests that Plato's overriding interest in the *Crito* is to show his readers, first, a philosopher for whom philosophy is interactive and responsive, but, second, a philosopher who is also a friend.

---

34. Perhaps, too, Plato underestimated the lengths to which his readers would go and the ingenuity and subtlety they would muster in order to render the Laws' speech compatible with Socratic moral notions.

35. See White (1996), 125: ". . . its idea is not to make arguments good for all time, in all contexts and languages, but to carry on a conversation that is appropriate to this relation, with this person . . . and this language. . . .This is true at once of Socrates' conversation with Crito and of Plato's with us, his readers."

36. See Grote (1875), I, 302–303.

37. See Anastaplo (1975b), 210.

38. Anastaplo (1975b), 212: "Plato's readers are left with the salutary suggestion that until they really know what they are doing, until they are equipped and disciplined enough to think through the reasons for appropriate disobedience in particular situations, they will do well to abide by the laws. . . ."

9

Restoring the Radical Socrates

> I please myself with imagining a State at last . . .
> which even would not think it inconsistent with its
> own repose if a few were to live aloof from it, not
> meddling with it, nor embraced by it, who fulfill
> all the duties of neighbors and fellow-men.
> Thoreau (1989), 39–40

The dissociation of Socrates and his views from the views expressed by the Laws in their speech makes possible the full restoration to the Socrates of the *Crito* the radical independence of mind that characterizes the Socrates of the *Apology*. We have seen in Chapter 4 how perfectly consonant are the *Apology* and the *Crito*—that is, up until *Cr.* 50a6, where the Laws are introduced into the discussion. Indeed, throughout the *Crito*, even after *Cr.* 50a6, whenever Socrates speaks in his own name, whether before the Laws' speech, in protest against the Laws' initial outburst against him (at *Cr.* 50a8–c9), or after the speech concludes, what he says is completely in accord with the positions espoused and embodied by the Socrates of the *Apology*. As Socrates in the *Apology* is committed to the life of philosophy, so Socrates in the *Crito* will obey nothing but the *logos* that seems best to him upon reasoning.

Many scholars have been willing, for the sake of bringing Socrates and the Laws closer together, to domesticate both. Thus, they contend, on the one hand, that Socrates will do whatever the laws and city bid short of committing injustice and, on the other, that the laws and city demand of a citizen that he do whatever they bid short of committing injustice.[1] Yet both Socrates and the Laws take stands more radical

---

1. Those scholars who interpret the Laws' ostensible demand for absolute obedience as a demand for obedience to everything that the city commands except committing injustice typically justify their interpretation by reading the Laws' speech in light of Socrates' principle that injustice ought never to be committed: if Socrates believes that injustice ought never to be committed, and if the Laws speak for Socrates, then the Laws and the city cannot require of the citizen that he obey them when they demand the commission of injustice. As Gómez-Lobo (1994), 66, puts it: "Moreover, such obedience

than these: Socrates, for his part, will not commit injustice even when the law so bids, but he will not suffer injustice either just because the law so orders him;[2] the Laws, for their part, demand of the citizen complete accession to the will of the city or fatherland: from their perspective, the citizen's only alternatives to obedience are to "persuade"—that is, to entreat and fawn—or to leave.

Only on the assumption that the positions of Socrates and the Laws are irreconcilably divergent is it immediately evident why there must be an abrupt change of speaker at *Cr.* 50a6: views sharply opposed to one another are best expressed in different voices. How can the Socrates who in an earlier part of the *Crito* champions the cause of obeying the dictates of one's own reason turn around and passionately argue the case for the citizen's duty to obey absolutely the city and its laws? Socrates must assign the articulation and defense of this duty to the laws themselves and so invents personified versions of the laws to do their speaking for them.

On the far more widely held assumption that there is no new and distinct point of view corresponding to the new voice of the Laws, however, it is difficult to explain why a new speaker is needed. Indeed, most interpreters of the *Crito* simply offer no account for why Socrates stops speaking in his own voice. Two exceptions to this rule are Adam and Kraut. According to Adam, ". . . Plato wishes to save Socrates from the charge of selfishness and lack of feeling when his friends were so deeply moved, and hence the fatal argument comes not from his mouth but from the Laws."[3] Yet is it true that Plato withholds delivery of a "fatal argument" from Socrates? Does he not, on the contrary, in fact assign to Socrates an argument at once more fatal and less sympathetic to Crito's point of view than the argument he assigns to the Laws? As we saw in Chapter 8, the argument of the Laws succeeds precisely because it is far more considerate of Crito than Socrates' argument is. Whereas Socrates dismisses Crito's concerns as considerations "of the many" who act "mindlessly," thereby showing his contempt for them, the Laws take seriously and respond to each of Crito's concerns; whereas Socrates allows nothing to be taken into account but the justness or unjustness of escape, the Laws make their case in terms that Crito can understand, showing him how much worse it will be for everyone concerned if Socrates escapes now rather than dies. The Laws are gentler to Crito and more accepting of him than Socrates is when he engages Crito in philosophical exchange: whereas Socrates de-

---

[i.e., to legal injunctions that require unjust action] is implicitly ruled out by the explicit proviso that an agreement (and, *a fortiori*, Socrates' agreement with Athens) will be binding only if it is just. No agreement that demands an unjust deed can be itself just. . . . The speech of the laws, then, should not be read as an exhortation to blindly obey positive law." Let us note, however, that interpreting the Laws' demand in light of Socrates' principle assumes in advance that the Laws and Socrates share a common moral perspective. It is precisely this assumption that I challenge in this book. The Laws' words, read apart from this assumption, can only be taken to require absolute obedience.

For a view that domesticates only Socrates' view, see Brickhouse and Smith (1994), 151–53. For Brickhouse and Smith, the Laws do demand absolute obedience, and Socrates willingly accedes to that demand.

2. That is why Socrates is able to stand up to the Laws when they charge him with attempting to destroy them and the city and say to them: "For the city was doing us injustice and did not pass judgment correctly" (*Cr.* 50c1–2).

3. Adam (1888), 61.

nounces both himself and his friends, the Laws protect Crito by denouncing only Socrates; moreover, the Laws demand much less of Crito than Socrates does with respect to his changing his moral outlook. If Plato's intention were to make Socrates appear less selfish and unfeeling, he surely would have allowed *him* to speak the words of the Laws. The only reason he assigns these words to the Laws is that these words represent not Socrates' perspective but that of the city.

Kraut advances the idea that Plato puts the argument against escape into the mouth of the Laws so that he "can represent the dialogue's political philosophy as the theory a city ought to propound to its citizens, and not merely as a theory Socrates proposes to Crito." According to Kraut, Plato's assigning this argument to the Laws rather than to Socrates does not imply that "their philosophy is in some way unsocratic."[4] Yet, why could Socrates not have presented in his own name a theory of what all cities ought to propound to their citizens? Furthermore, we may note that the Laws particularize their "theory," directing much of it specifically to Socrates, speaking of what Socrates has agreed to and how satisfied Socrates has been with Athens and its laws; they even allude to the particular disadvantages that will accrue to Socrates qua champion of virtue should he seek refuge in another city. Had Plato's purpose been to universalize the theory that the Laws propound to Socrates, he surely would have had them present their case in more consistently general and impersonal terms. Moreover, the adversarial tone that Plato has the Laws adopt in addressing Socrates is hardly one that he would have all cities adopt in addressing their citizens. That tone, as was argued in Chapter 8, is a tone adapted to the unique situation of the *Crito*: the Laws mimic the abusive rhetoric employed by Crito in addressing Socrates—and at the same time deflect it away from Crito—in order to make Crito receptive to their point of view.

Contra Kraut, the Laws do indeed espouse a point of view that is unsocratic. They disagree with Socrates on the most basic questions: Does a man owe his first allegiance to his city or to his *logos*?; Does a citizen agree in advance to submit to all pronouncements of his city right or wrong?; Is it ever just to return evil for evil? The Laws and Socrates so differ in their fundamental moral outlooks that they can no more take counsel together than Crito and Socrates can. The only difference is that the Laws and Socrates, unlike Crito and Socrates, share on this occasion the same conclusion.

The differences between the Laws and Socrates far outnumber this single convergence of conclusions. Socrates wants to reason; the Laws wish to issue fiats that will be obeyed. Socrates believes people are bound to principles at which they arrive through their own rational reflection; the Laws contend that citizens are bound to agreements inferred from their inaction—that is, to their "agreement in deed" to do whatever the fatherland and the Laws bid. Socrates is committed to the furtherance of justice and philosophy; the Laws would have him safeguard the interests of Athens and her laws. It is not possible to bridge the gap between what Socrates requires of a man and what the Laws require. Nor is it possible for a man to divide his allegiance in a way that would satisfy both Socrates and the Laws. One can obey but a single master. If reasoned argument alone must be obeyed, then "whatever we bid"

4. Kraut (1984), 41.

must not be—and vice versa. If one's loyalty is to the *logos*, then one's loyalty cannot be to Athens—and vice versa. If one is bound to those principles to which one has agreed as a result of one's own active involvement in philosophic investigation, then one is not bound to a tacit agreement inferred by another merely from one's inaction—and vice versa.

What the Laws regard as inviolable and absolute, Socrates regards as subject to qualification; what Socrates regards as binding without exception, the Laws regard as inconsequential. For the Laws, the citizen's agreement to do "whatever we bid" admits of no exceptions for as long as (1) the citizen remains in the city, and (2) he chooses not to "persuade" or is unsuccessful in his attempt to "persuade"; indeed, according to the Laws, the citizen, just by virtue of having been born in Athens, is bound for as long as he remains there to revere, yield to, and fawn upon his fatherland more than upon his own parents. Yet, as far as the Laws are concerned, the citizen has no duty to exercise his own independent judgment and to conduct himself accordingly—quite the contrary.[5] For Socrates, by contrast, the citizen (in the absence of a moral expert) is bound absolutely and without qualification to do what is just according to his own carefully considered judgment; the Laws' and the city's demands on him are subject always to review by the citizen's own moral reasoning and cannot override the results of such "private" cogitations. For the Laws, it is agreements with them that bind absolutely; for Socrates, agreements—irrespective of who the parties to the agreement are—bind only when just.

By the time Crito implores Socrates in the *Crito* not to escape, Socrates, as we know, has already reached the conclusion that the right thing for him to do is to remain in prison and be executed.[6] Yet, if Socrates has already determined that he ought not to escape, we may safely assume that his determination is grounded in reasons, old reasons, that is, in those principles that were established by him and his companions on prior occasions and that reflect a moral perspective that has remained constant throughout his life "and still does now" (*Cr.* 49e1). He makes it clear that neither does he need new reasons nor are new reasons likely to influence him. Yet what the Laws provide *is* new reasons! Rather than encourage Socrates to cling steadfastly to his tried and true beliefs in the face even of death, the Laws advance new *logoi*, *logoi* about duties to obey the city and fatherland, *logoi* that, if accepted, would displace and supersede the old Socratic ones.[7]

---

5. It is instructive that even when the Laws contend that Socrates was more satisfied than other Athenians with Athens and its laws, they make no reference to Athens' greater tolerance of free speech. From the Laws' point of view, what is good about a city is its being one with good laws, that is, with laws that ensure order and restraint. The Laws can attach only negative value to open dissent and the airing of original or idiosyncratic ideas: nonconformity threatens order.

6. At *Cr.* 44b5–6 Crito says, "But, daimonic Socrates, *even now* obey me and save yourself," implying that Socrates had previously rebuffed Crito's attempts to convince him to escape. And at *Cr.* 48e1–3, Socrates says, "And if not, blessed man, then stop telling me the same arguments again and again." Crito had apparently tried unsuccessfully in the past to persuade Socrates to escape; Socrates, however, will not escape unless Crito has some better *logos* to offer than the one that has thus far led Socrates to decide against escape.

7. As Anastaplo (1975b), 315, n. 15, notes, Socrates does not say about the arguments advanced by the Laws that they have "been established by him and his companions on other occasions."

But the Laws' new *logoi* do not stand a chance of influencing Socrates. Socrates, in the *Crito* as in the *Apology*, is radically independent, answering in the final analysis to no one but himself—that is, to his reason. His god is a god who demands of him nothing less. Socrates has not agreed in advance to do whatever his city bids; neither by virtue of having been born, nurtured, and educated through the agency of the Laws nor by virtue of having remained in Athens voluntarily is he duty-bound to exchange the authority of his rational faculty for that of the city and its laws. We know that he disobeys the authority of his government in the *Apology* when its command is unjust in his judgment; is it any wonder, then, that he is surprised to hear the Laws contend in the *Crito* that he has agreed to abide by *all* judgments that the city renders (*Cr.* 50c4–7)? Socrates will, of course, abide by those verdicts he believes to be just; he will even abide by a verdict he believes to be unjust when this is what justice demands on a particular occasion.

Socrates is hardly one to "revere, yield to, and fawn upon" his fatherland as the Laws require. Let us remember how Socrates conceives of his relationship to his fatherland. As Socrates sees himself, he is a gadfly. His job is to vex and disturb his complacent and drowsy city. Rather than revere, yield, and fawn, Socrates, as he puts it, "awakens, persuades, and reproaches" (*Ap.* 30e7). Interestingly, not only in this passage but quite frequently in the *Apology*, Socrates describes the activity in which he engages as "persuasion" (see *Ap.* 30a8, 31b5, 35c2, 36c5); if, however, the city recognizes "persuasion" as an acceptable alternative to obedience, why does it execute him? It executes him, of course, because the kind of persuasion that Socrates practices is not the kind of which the city approves: whereas for Socrates persuasion is paired with awakening and reproaching, for the city persuasion is aligned with obedience as another way of showing deference and submissiveness. Indeed, the very kind of persuasion that constitutes Socrates' all-consuming occupation precludes the kind of persuasion that the Laws prescribe: if Socrates is to persuade the Athenians to care about justice and virtue and having their souls in the best state possible, and if he is to persuade them to put these goals above life itself, he cannot for the sake of saving his life be willing "to say the sorts of things to you that you would have been most pleased to hear" (*Ap.* 38d6–7); whatever appeal he makes to the city and its officials must be made strictly on grounds of justice.

If Socrates will not submit to the Laws and will not endorse such submission, it is in part because submission benefits neither the one who submits nor the one who is submitted to. Unlike both Crito and the Laws, Socrates never demands to be obeyed.[8] He prefers that people obey the best *logos*, not that they do "whatever I bid." Although Socrates, like the Laws, sees himself in the role of a father—he approaches the Athenians, as he says, "as a father or older brother might do" (*Ap.* 31b4–5)—there is a vast and telling difference between the kind of father to which Socrates compares himself, on the one hand, and the kind of father to which the Laws compare themselves, on the other. For when Socrates compares himself to a father, he compares himself at the same time to an older brother; he sees himself not as an authoritarian

8. See my discussion of the exception to this rule in the *Phaedo* in the section in Chapter 3 entitled "The Unphilosophical Crito."

figure but as an intellectually and morally more mature adviser and guide. By contrast, when the Laws compare themselves to a father, they compare themselves at the same time to a master: they are to be obeyed without question and no one may rightfully return to them the bad things they do. Socrates is a father who encourages reciprocity: if he corrects others, he likes nothing better than to be corrected in return; and though he refutes others, he believes that were others to refute him they would confer upon him the greatest benefaction. From Socrates' perspective, then, the city of Athens, by looking to its citizens not for constructive criticism but for reverence, obedience, and fawning, denies itself what is in its own best interest.[9] Let us recall in this connection Socrates' last request of his condemners: he beseeches those who have been punished and pained and reproached by him to reciprocate by punishing and paining and reproaching his children—"if they seem to you to care for money or anything else before virtue" (Ap. 41e3–5). The benefit that Socrates spends a lifetime so selflessly bestowing upon his city he seeks finally, at the end of his life, to have bestowed in return upon his children.[10]

The Laws' understanding of benefit and harm is the conventional one. Consequently, the Laws react to perceived harm or offense or to the threat of such harm or offense in the most vulgar fashion. We may compare Socrates' reaction to having been falsely accused, unjustly condemned, and cruelly sentenced to die to the Laws' reaction to Socrates' alleged attempt to destroy us "as far as it lay in you" (Cr. 54c8). At the end of the Apology, Socrates says the following with respect to his condemners and accusers: ". . . and I at any rate am not at all angry, ou panu chalepainō, at those who voted to condemn me and at my accusers" (Ap. 41d6–e1). At the end of the Crito, by contrast, the Laws warn Socrates that "if you go away . . . then we will be angry with you, hēmeis te soi chalepanoumen, while you live, and our brothers, the Laws in Hades, will not receive you favorably there . . ." (Cr. 54c2–7). Whereas Socrates is able to assess his situation dispassionately and to assign blame where it is deserved without succumbing to anger,[11] the Laws are not: if they are crossed, they warn Socrates, he will incur both their wrath and the wrath of their brothers. Indeed, the fatherland, too, is susceptible to anger (patrida chalepainousan—Cr. 51b3). The great irony here, of course, is that Socrates, a mere human being, does not give way to passion even in the face of gross injustice and death; yet the fatherland and the

9. As Socrates says to his condemners in the Apology: "For if you suppose that by killing human beings you will prevent someone from reproaching you for not living correctly, you do not think nobly. For that kind of release is not at all possible or noble; rather, the kind that is both noblest and easiest is not to restrain others, but to equip oneself to be the best possible" (Ap. 39d3–8).

10. We may note how differently from Socrates Crito and the Laws would have Socrates' children treated: Crito and the Laws would have Socrates' children provided with conventional goods, including conventional education, rather than have them subjected to the unpleasant chastisements whose end is the well-being of the soul. For further discussion of Socrates' relationship to his children, see Chapter 3, n. 15.

11. It is interesting that Socrates' prison guard who is to administer the hemlock says in the Phaedo (116c7–8) that he knows Socrates will be angry, chalepaineis, not with him but with those truly responsible. Yet Socrates, as we know from the Apology, is angry with no one at all; he exceeds even the guard's high expectations. Perhaps this is another instance in which Socrates' way "does not seem human" (Ap. 31b1).

Laws, though not people at all, become immediately incensed and vengeful with arguably far less provocation.[12]

The Laws, then, as they are portrayed in the *Crito*, are unworthy to set a moral example. Their overriding concern with self-preservation and their apparent indifference to virtue certainly disqualify them as moral experts. Yet, if for Socrates justice is best served by a moral expert who can provide the proper guidance, how is justice to be served when no such expert is available? Is not law or governmental authority at least second best? The *Crito* teaches us that there is something better and more to be trusted than law and authority—namely, the *logos* that seems best to one upon rational reflection. It is thus one's own reasoned principles that are second best. Law and authority are only third best:[13] they protect the many from injustices to which they would be prone if left to their own devices.[14] The kind of ethic that Crito embraces, however—the ethic of promoting the interests of one's own, an ethic that divides the world into friends and foes and in which the law and the city play a very minor role, if any—is less admirable than an ethic of law and authority: for the most part, a man who practices the favoritism of protecting and promoting his own is capable of far greater and more frequent injustices than one who is fundamentally law abiding. Crito's morality is not, to be sure, the worst there is, nor is it outright immorality. There is a morality worse than Crito's—the "morality" that makes a virtue out of vice; that glorifies the "natural justice" of the jungle; that condones, indeed, commends, the willful exploiting by the self-styled stronger of the so-called weaker.[15] And there is also the sheer immorality that does not even seek to parade as morality, the immorality associated with the tyrant whose vast power enables him to disregard openly everyone's interests but his own. Since, however, Crito is, if not at the lowest moral level, nevertheless at a level no higher than the fourth, Socrates enlists the Laws to make the case for the third level, for law and authority—after he

12. Socrates recognizes that although no serious harm, that is, harm to the soul, will befall him, his condemners and accusers did intend to harm him, and for that they merit blame. The Laws, as we noted in Chapter 8, need not think that Socrates actually means to harm them, or that Socrates will in fact succeed in harming them, or that if they are harmed that Socrates is alone or even mainly responsible, in order for them to blame him for attempting their destruction to *son meros*, "as far as it lies in you."

13. Strauss (1983), 58, considers the possibility that if "no expert regarding the just, noble and good things is available, if the best that one can find among human beings is knowledge of one's ignorance regarding the most important things," one must, or at least may, "in that case obey the opinion of non-experts, a kind of opinion of non-experts, the most authoritative kind, *i.e.*, the laws of the city." Strauss does not appear to recognize that for Socrates the opinions reached through reasoning by human beings who are aware that they are ignorant of the most important things have a greater claim to obedience by these very human beings than do the opinions of the laws of the their city.

14. In this way, laws accomplish even unintentionally what Socrates pursues intentionally—the improvement of souls. As Strauss (1983), 66, notes: ". . . Socrates did not think that there could be an unqualified duty to obey the laws. But this did not prevent him from thinking, nay, it enabled him to think that the demand for such obedience is a wise rule of thumb as distinguished from an unqualifiedly valid law."

15. Callicles and Thrasymachus are proponents of the superiority of what is conventionally termed "injustice."

has tried, and failed, to raise Crito to the second level, *his* level, the level of reasoned argument.[16]

That Socrates' decision in the *Crito* to remain in prison and not escape reflects directly and solely his own rational deliberations about what is most just is confirmed in the *Phaedo*, where Socrates uses this decision to illustrate the difference between a cause, *aitia*, and that without which a cause would not be a cause.[17] The true cause of his being now in prison rather than in exile, Socrates says, is that now that the Athenians for their part have thought it better to condemn him, he for his part

> thought it better to sit here, and more just to remain and submit to whatever penalty they will order. Since, by the Dog, as it seems to me, long ago these sinews and bones would have been in either Megara or Boeotia, carried there by an opinion of what is best, if I did not think it more just and nobler to submit to whichever punishment was ordered by the city than to flee and run away. (*Phaedo* 98e3–99a4)[18]

Socrates makes it clear in this passage that the Athenians do as they think best and he does as he thinks best. Had he thought it better—more just and more noble—to escape, he would have escaped, carried to Boeotia or Megara by his view of what is best. The reason he stays in Athens is not because he is so commanded but because, having been so commanded, he himself determines that his Athenian prison cell is the best place to station his sinews and bones. Just as in the *Apology* Socrates qualifies his approval of one's remaining where one is stationed by a ruler by adding the phrase "holding that it is best" (*Ap.* 28d7), so in the *Phaedo*, though he remains in prison when the Athenians put him there, he does so because "I thought it better . . . and more just . . . and nobler" to do so.

Socrates remains in prison because he has determined that to do so is best. He has concluded that his other option, escape, would involve him in committing injustices, and for Socrates it is always better to suffer than to commit injustice. Yet Socrates does not remain in prison because he obeys whatever he is bid by the city and its laws. He does not even remain in prison because he obeys whatever he is bid by the city and its laws short of committing injustice. For Socrates it is not the case that a citizen's relationship to his city and its laws or any purported "agreement" between them obligates him to suffer injustice; there is only one thing that obligates a man to suffer injustice, and that is the duty not to commit it. Socrates, an innocent man in his own eyes, does not feel bound to languish in prison awaiting death for

---

16. Calvert (1987), 29–33, contends that Socrates commends obedience to law because he lacks moral knowledge, because he is no moral expert. But Socrates says explicitly that he obeys the *logos* that "seems best" to him. And he tells Crito that they must obey as well the result of their joint inquiry (*Cr.* 46d4–7). It is not, then, because Socrates is no moral expert that he has the Laws advocate, for Crito's benefit, obedience to their authority: he himself does not submit to their authority. It is only because Crito cannot engage successfully in philosophical inquiry that obedience to law and authority represents an improvement *for him*.

17. Among other things, Socrates' citing Megara and Boeotia (=Thebes) in the *Phaedo* as the places to which he would have gone had he chosen to escape is a clear reference to the *Crito*, where the Laws suggest these cities as likely destinations for him.

18. Trans. Gallop (1975).

the sake of obedience to the city; he is quite explicit that in judging whether or not he ought to submit to the death penalty, he need take into account only one consideration: "whether we will do just things by paying money and gratitude to those who will lead me out of here, or whether in truth we will do injustice by doing all these things . . ." (*Cr.* 48c8–d3).

Socrates in the *Crito* is no more a man committed first and foremost to law and order than is Socrates in the *Apology*. It is the Laws for whom law-governed cities and law-abiding men make life worth living. But for Socrates, it is the examined life, the life of philosophy, that is the only life worth living, the life that promotes justice and thereby the well-being of the soul. Because the Laws do not speak for Socrates, what they say in the *Crito* need not and ought not to be reconciled with the views of Socrates in the *Apology* and in the early parts of the *Crito*. Moreover, the flaws in the Laws' case against escape need not and ought not to be covered over, excused, or regarded as great subtleties.[19] While the Laws defend oratorically the absolute authority of the city, Socrates remains

> an isolated and eccentric individual, a dissenter, not only departing altogether from the characters and purposes general among his fellow-citizens, but also certain to incur dangerous antipathy, in so far as he publicly proclaimed what he was.[20]

19. See, e.g., Kraut (1984), 7, who contends that ". . . when we take their argument apart and examine it line by line, we can see how ingenious and well-constructed it is. They state their points carefully and anticipate objections. Putting together a series of sensible principles they arrive at a powerful conclusion. The *Crito* deserves a higher reputation than it currently enjoys as a sophisticated piece of reasoning."

20. This is Grote's characterization of the Socrates in the *Apology* and *Gorgias*. See Grote (1875), I, 303. But because Grote assumes that the Laws' speech is Socrates' as well, he thinks that this characterization of Socrates does not apply to the Socrates of the *Crito*. Once the Laws' views are divorced from those of Socrates in the *Crito*, Grote's characterization becomes as appropriate for the Socrates of the *Crito* as it is for the Socrates of the *Apology* and *Gorgias*.

Bibliography

Adam, J., ed. 1888. *Plato: Crito*. Cambridge: Cambridge University Press.

Adkins, A. W. H. 1960. *Merit and Responsibility*. Oxford: Oxford University Press.

Allen, R. E. 1972. "Law and Justice in Plato's *Crito*." *Journal of Philosophy* 69: 562–66.

———. 1980. *Socrates and Legal Obligation*. Minneapolis: University of Minnesota Press.

———. trans. 1984. *The Dialogues of Plato*. Vol. 1. New Haven: Yale University Press.

Anastaplo, George. 1975a. "Human Being and Citizen: A Beginning to the Study of Plato's *Apology of Socrates*." In *Human Being and Citizen: Essays on Virtue, Freedom and the Common Good*. Chicago: Swallow Press, 8–29, 233–46.

———. 1975b. "Citizen and Human Being: Thoreau, Socrates, and Civil Disobedience." In *Human Being and Citizen: Essays on Virtue, Freedom and the Common Good*. Chicago: Swallow Press, 203–13, 313–16.

Arendt, Hannah. 1958. *The Human Condition*. Chicago: University of Chicago Press.

Aristotle. 1934. *Nicomachean Ethics*, rev. ed., trans. H. Rackham. Loeb ed. Cambridge, Mass.: Harvard University Press.

Bloom, Allan, trans. 1986. *The Republic of Plato*. New York: Basic Books.

———, trans. 1987. *Ion*. In *The Roots of Political Philosophy: Ten Forgotten Socratic Dialogues*, ed. Thomas L. Pangle. Ithaca, N.Y.: Cornell University Press.

Bolotin, David. 1979. *Plato's Dialogue on Friendship: An Interpretation of the 'Lysis,' with a New Translation*. Ithaca, N.Y.: Cornell University Press.

Bonner, Robert J., and Gertrude Smith. 1930, 1938. *The Administration of Justice from Homer to Aristotle*. 2 vols. Chicago: University of Chicago Press.

Bostock, David. 1990. "The Interpretation of Plato's *Crito*." *Phronesis* 35: 1–20.

Brandwood, Leonard. 1976. *A Word Index to Plato*. Leeds: W. S. Maney and Son.

Brickhouse, Thomas C., and Nicholas D. Smith. 1989. *Socrates on Trial*. Oxford: Oxford University Press.

———. 1994. *Plato's Socrates.* Oxford: Oxford University Press.

Brown, Hunter. 1992. "The Structure of Plato's *Crito.*" *Apeiron* 25: 67–82.

Burnet, John, ed. 1990–1907. *Platonis Opera.* 5 vols. Oxford: Clarendon Press.

———, ed. 1911. *Plato's Phaedo.* Oxford: Clarendon Press.

———, ed. 1924. *Plato's Euthyphro, Apology of Socrates, and Crito.* Oxford: Clarendon Press.

Calef, Scott W. 1992. "Why Is Annihilation a Great Gain for Socrates?: The Argument at *Apology* 40c3–e2." *Ancient Philosophy* 12: 285–97.

Calvert, Brian. 1987. "Plato's Crito and Richard Kraut." In *Justice, Law and Method in Plato and Aristotle,* ed. Spiro Panagiotou. Edmonton, Alberta: Academic Printing and Publishing, 17–33.

Church, F. J., trans. 1986. *Crito.* In *The Dialogues of Plato.* New York: Bantam.

Colson, Darrel. 1985. "On Appealing to Athenian Law to Justify Socrates' Disobedience." *Apeiron* 19: 133–51.

———. 1989. "*Crito* 51A–C: To What Does Socrates Owe Obedience?" *Phronesis* (34): 27–55.

Congleton, Ann. 1974. "Two Kind of Lawlessness: Plato's *Crito.*" *Political Theory* 2: 432–46.

Croiset, Maurice, trans. 1963. *Platon: Œuvres complètes.* Vol. I. Paris: Société d'Édition "Les Belles Lettres."

DeFilippo, Joseph G. 1991. "Justice and Obedience in the *Crito.*" *Ancient Philosophy* 11: 249–63.

Denniston, J. D. 1954. *The Greek Particles.* 2d ed. Oxford: Clarendon Press.

Dodds, E. R., ed. 1959. *Plato: Gorgias.* Oxford: Oxford University Press.

———. 1964. *The Greeks and the Irrational.* Berkeley: University of California Press.

Dover, K. J. 1974. *Greek Popular Morality in the Time of Plato and Aristotle.* Oxford: Blackwell.

———. 1975. "The Freedom of the Intellectual in Greek Society." *Talanta* 7: 24–54.

Dyer, Louis, ed. 1885. *Plato: Apology of Socrates and Crito,* rev. Thomas Day Seymour. Waltham, Mass.: Blaisdell.

Ferrari, G. R. F. 1987. *Listening to the Cicadas: A Study of Plato's 'Phaedrus.'* Cambridge: Cambridge University Press.

Fitzgerald, Robert, trans. 1963. *The Odyssey.* Garden City, N.Y.: Doubleday.

Fowler, H. N., trans. 1914. *Crito.* In *Plato.* Loeb ed. Cambridge, Mass.: Harvard University Press.

Fox, Marvin. 1956. "The Trials of Socrates: An Interpretation of the First Tetralogy." *Archiv für Philosophie* 6: 226–61.

Friedländer, Paul. 1958, 1964/65, 1969. *Plato.* Trans. H. Meyerhoff. 3 vols. Princeton: Princeton University Press.

Gallop, David, trans. 1975. *Plato: Phaedo.* Oxford: Clarendon Press.

Goebel, Ed., ed. 1893. *Platons Apologie des Sokrates und Kriton.* 2d ed. Paderburn: Ferdinand Shoningh.

Gómez-Lobo, Alfonso. 1994. *The Foundations of Socratic Ethics.* Indianapolis: Hackett.

Grote, George. 1875. *Plato and the Other Companions of Sokrates.* 2d ed. 3 vols. London: John Murray.

Grube, G. M. A., trans. 1975. *The Trial and Death of Socrates.* Indianapolis, Hackett.

———, trans. 1981. *Plato: Five Dialogues: Euthyphro, Apology, Crito, Meno, Phaedo,* rev. Richard Hogan and Donald J. Zeyl. Indianapolis: Hackett.

Hyland, Drew A. 1968. "Why Plato Wrote Dialogues." *Philosophy and Rhetoric* 1: 38–50.

Irwin, Terence. 1977. *Plato's Moral Theory: The Early and Middle Dialogues.* Oxford: Clarendon Press.

——, trans.1979. *Plato: Gorgias*. Oxford: Oxford University Press.

——. 1986. "Socratic Inquiry and Politics." *Ethics*: 400–415.

James, Gene G. 1973. "Socrates on Civil Disobedience and Rebellion." *Southern Journal of Philosophy* 11: 119–27.

Jowett, B., trans. 1953. *The Dialogues of Plato*. 4th ed. Oxford: Oxford University Press.

Joyce, Michael, trans. 1961. *Symposium*. In *The Collected Dialogues of Plato*, ed. Edith Hamilton and Huntington Cairns. Princeton: Princeton University Press.

Kahn, Charles. 1989. "Problems in the Argument of Plato's *Crito*." *Apeiron* 22 (4): 29–43.

Kitchel, C. L., ed. 1898. *Plato's Apology of Socrates and Crito*. New York: American Book Co.

Kral, Iosephus, ed. 1885. *Platonis Apologia et Crito*. Lipsiae: G. Freytag.

Kraut, Richard. 1984. *Socrates and the State*. Princeton: Princeton University Press.

Liddell, H. G., R. Scott, and H. S. J. Jones. 1966. *A Greek-English Lexicon*. 9th ed. Oxford: Clarendon Press.

Lipsius, Justus Hermann. 1915. *Das attische Recht und Rechtsverfahren*. Leipzig: O. R. Reisland.

Lofberg, John O. 1979. *Sycophancy in Athens*, and Irving Barkan. 1979. *Capital Punishment in Ancient Athens*. New York: Arno Press.

——. 1928. "The Trial of Socrates." *Classical Journal* 23: 601–609.

Lyotard, Jean-François. 1983. *Le Différend*. Paris: Les Éditions de Minuit.

MacDowell, Douglas M. 1978. *The Law in Classical Athens*. Ithaca, N.Y.: Cornell University Press.

McLaughlin, Robert J. 1976. "Socrates on Political Disobedience: A Reply to Gary Young." *Phronesis* 21: 185–97.

McPherran, Mark. 1986. "Socrates and the Duty to Philosophize." *Southern Journal of Philosophy* 24: 541–60.

——. 1991. "Socratic Reason and Socratic Revelation." *Journal of the History of Philosophy* 29: 345–73.

Martin, Rex. 1970. "Socrates and Disobedience to the Law." *Review of Metaphysics* 24: 21–38.

Merton, Thomas, ed. 1964. *Gandhi on Non-Violence*. New York: New Directions.

Mill, John Stuart. 1979. *Utilitarianism*. Indianapolis: Hackett.

Miller, Mitchell. 1996. "'The Arguments I Seem to Hear': Argument and Irony in the Crito." *Phronesis* 41: 121–37.

Morrow, Glenn R. 1960. *Plato's Cretan City: A Historical Interpretation of the 'Laws.'* Princeton: Princeton University Press.

Mulgan, R. G. 1972. "Socrates and Authority." *Greece and Rome*, 2d ser., 19: 208–12.

Nehamas, Alexander, and Paul Woodruff, trans. 1995. *Plato: Phaedrus*. Indianapolis: Hackett.

Nietzsche, Friedrich. 1967. *On the Genealogy of Morals*, trans. Walter Kaufmann and R. J. Hollingdale. New York: Random House.

Nussbaum, Martha. 1985. "Comment on Edmunds." In *Proceedings of the Boston Area Colloquium in Ancient Philosophy*, ed. John Cleary. Vol. 1. Lanham, Md.: University Press of America, 231–40.

Panagiotou, Spiro. 1987. "Justified Disobedience in the *Crito*?" In *Justice, Law and Method in Plato and Aristotle*, ed. S. Panagiotou. Edmonton, Alberta: Academic Printing and Publishing, 35–50.

Pangle, Thomas A., trans.1980. *The Laws of Plato*. Chicago: University of Chicago Press.

Ray, A. Chadwick. 1980. "The Tacit Agreement in the *Crito*." *International Studies in Philosophy* 12: 47–54.

Reeve, C. D. C. 1989. *Socrates in the 'Apology.'* Indianapolis: Hackett.

Roche, Paul, trans. 1974. *Three Plays of Euripides: Alcestis, Media, The Bacchae*. New York: W. W. Norton.

Rouse, W. H. D., trans. 1961. *Euthydemus*. In *The Collected Dialogues of Plato*, ed. Edith Hamilton and Huntington Cairns. Princeton: Princeton University Press.

Santas, Gerasimos Xenophon. 1979. *Socrates: Philosophy in Plato's Early Dialogues*. Boston: Routledge and Kegan Paul.

Seymour, T. D. 1902. "Note on Plato's *Phaedo*, 115D." *Classical Review* 16: 202.

Shorey, Paul, trans. 1961. *Republic*. In *The Collected Dialogues of Plato*, ed. Edith Hamilton and Huntington Cairns. Princeton: Princeton University Press.

Smyth, Herbert Weir. 1956. *Greek Grammar*, rev. Gordon M. Messing. Cambridge, Mass.: Harvard University Press.

Stephens, James. 1985. "Socrates on the Rule of Law." *History of Philosophy Quarterly* 2: 3–10.

Strauss, Leo. 1952. "Persecution and the Art of Writing." In *Persecution and the Art of Writing*. Chicago: University of Chicago Press, 22–37.

———. 1983. "On Plato's *Apology of Socrates* and *Crito*." In *Studies in Platonic Political Philosophy*, ed. Thomas L. Pangle. Chicago: University of Chicago Press, 38–66.

Taylor, A. E. 1926. *Plato: The Man and His Work*. New York: Humanities Press.

Taylor, C. C. W., trans. 1991. *Plato: Protagoras*. Oxford: Clarendon Press.

Thoreau, Henry David. 1989. *On the Duty of Civil Disobedience*. Chicago: Charles H. Kerr.

Treddenick, Hugh, trans. 1961. *Crito*. In *The Collected Dialogues of Plato*, ed. Edith Hamilton and Huntington Cairns. Princeton: Princeton University Press.

Tyler, W. S., ed. 1862. *Plato's Apology and Crito*, rev. ed. New York: D. Appleton,

Vlastos, G. 1974. "Socrates on Political Obedience and Disobedience." *Yale Review* 63: 517–34.

———. 1991. *Socrates: Ironist and Moral Philosopher*. Ithaca, N.Y.: Cornell University Press.

Wade, Francis, S. J. 1971. "In Defense of Socrates." *Review of Metaphysics* 25: 311–25.

West, Elinor J. M. 1989. "Socrates in the *Crito*: Patriot or Friend?" In *Essays in Ancient Greek Philosophy III: Plato*, ed. John Anton and Anthony Preus. Albany: State University of New York Press, 71–83.

West, Thomas G., and Grace Starry West, trans. 1984. *Plato and Aristophanes: Four Texts on Socrates*. Ithaca, N.Y.: Cornell University Press.

White, James Boyd. 1996. "Plato's *Crito*: The Authority of Law and Philosophy." In *The Greeks and Us: Essays in Honor of Arthur W. H. Adkins*, ed. Robert B. Louden and Paul Schollmeier. Chicago: University of Chicago Press, 97–133.

Woozley, A. D. 1971. "Socrates on Disobeying the Law." In *The Philosophy of Socrates*, ed. Gregory Vlastos. Garden City, N.Y.: Doubleday, 299–318.

———. 1979. *Law and Obedience: The Arguments of Plato's 'Crito.'* Chapel Hill: University of North Carolina Press.

Xenophon. 1923. *Memorabilia*, trans. E. C. Marchant. Loeb ed. Vol. 4. Cambridge, Mass.: Harvard University Press.

Yonezawa, Shigeru. 1991. "Socrates' Two Concepts of the Polis." *History of Political Thought* 12: 566–76.

Young, Gary. 1974. "Socrates and Obedience." *Phronesis* 19: 1–29.

Zeyl, Donald J., trans. 1987. *Plato: Gorgias*. Indianapolis: Hackett.

Index

compared to parents, 107, 144
relation to citizens, 15n.21, 102, 103–
107, 108, 129, 148, 156, 159, 162,
163, 164
and Socrates, 99, 132, 165
wrongs against, 102, 103, 107, 128, 130,
132, 154
fawning, 103–104, 105, 111–112, 115n.71,
126, 133, 154, 162, 164, 165, 166
fine, 34n.68, 35, 39, 75
Fitzgerald, Robert, 134
flattery, 72, 148, 149, 159
Forms, 37n.75, 137n.14
Fowler, H. N., 58n.3, 123n.89, 143n.32
Fox, Marvin, 53n.47
free speech, 123n.88, 164n.5
freedom, 25–26, 34, 76, 101n.15, 121–122
Friedländer, Paul, 76n.59
friends (see also Socrates, friends of;
Socrates, Crito, friend of S.), 53, 126
Achilles seeks to avenge, 8, 9
helping and harming, 4, 45n.17, 49–50,
51, 53–54, 66–67, 72, 78, 127, 150,
156, 157
reputation of preferring money to, 40,
44, 149, 152

Gallop, David, 46n.20, 158n.32, 168n.18
Gandhi, M. K., 59n.5
generals, the ten, 10n.7, 13–15, 87n.12,
109, 112n.62
Glaucon, 64n.25
god(s) (see also god, the), 16, 28, 28n.55,
40n.3, 59n.7, 155
and city or fatherland, 15–16, 107, 111,
128, 144, 155
concerned for good men, 31–32, 33n.65
and the god, 16, 144
and Socrates, 7, 15–16, 20, 37n.75
as superiors, 11n.9, 34n.69, 59n.7
god, the (see also god(s); Socrates, divine
mission of; Socrates, the god of)
and daimonion, 17, 18
and justice, reason, and philosophy, 4n.4,
10–13, 16, 23, 26–27, 28–29, 34n.69,
37, 60, 109, 114n.70, 144, 145
obedience to, 10–11, 12, 12n.12, 13,
13n.14, 16, 23, 23n.46, 26–27,
34n.69, 37, 60, 104n.32, 108n.48,
114n.70, 144, 145, 165

Goebel, Ed., 106n.39, 106n.41
Gómez-Lobo, Alfonso, 161n.1
good man, 9, 30–31, 31–32, 33n.65
government, 5–6, 5n.8, 10n.7, 10n.8,
75n.55, 104, 165
gratitude, 65–67, 72, 73, 76–77, 80, 85, 94,
99, 101, 102n.18, 147n.3, 155
Grote, George, 14n.19, 61n.8, 84n.1,
86n.8, 107n.46, 159n.33, 160n.36,
169n.20
Grube, G. M. A., 25n.47, 123n.89,
142n.27, 143n.32

Hades, 32, 36–37, 45n.18, 97, 128–129,
151n.15, 152–153, 154, 166
happiness, 8, 36
Hesiod, 36
Homer, 36, 134
honor, 24, 27, 31n.59, 59n.6
household, 101–102, 107
Hyland, Drew A., 5, 141n.23, 145n.41,
157n.29

Ibycus, 20
illegality, 14–15
impiety, 11, 14, 15–16, 28–29, 102, 107,
108, 155
imprisonment, 30, 33–35, 35n.70, 37, 75,
76n.56
imprudence, 63–64
individual(s), 6, 6n.9, 8–12, 24, 118, 163
inferior, 99, 100, 101–102
injustice (see also citizen(s), injustice; city,
and injustice; city, and justice; justice;
Laws, the, and justice; Laws, the,
obedience to, and (in)justice;
Socrates, injustice)
and citizen, 5–6, 109–110, 110–112,
115–117, 161, 168–169
and city, 88, 89, 91, 95, 98, 99, 109,
129n.100, 154, 161, 162n.2
commanded, 5–6, 9, 10n.8, 37, 89, 95,
109–112, 162
and death, 31, 32–33, 37, 43, 75–76, 82,
104, 129
and doing bad things, 11n.9, 31, 67–69,
68, 68n.36, 69–71, 150, 159
of escape, 64–71, 72, 79–81, 130
of exile, 33–35, 37, 65, 76, 121
and law, 13–15, 90–91, 96, 162